The Best of Tom Slemen 1

Tom Slemen

Copyright © 2012 Tom Slemen

All rights reserved.

ISBN:-10: 147828417X
ISBN-13: 978-1478284178

DEDICATION

For Alastair Machray, Jane Haase and Emma Johnson

CONTENTS

1	A Marriage Made in Hell	1
2	Somewhere Only We Know	6
3	Golgon	25
4	Terror on the M62	42
5	The Story of Springheeled Jack	46
6	A Picture of Evil	54
7	The Black Elves of Bloody Acre	59
8	The Old Swan Vampire	67
9	Of Unsound Mind	73
10	Ship of the Seven Murders	83
11	Reaper at the Roadside	88
12	Manilu the Lodge Lane Vampire	94
13	Witches Stay Away from my Door!	104
14	Mr Bill	115
15	The St Luke's Abduction	124
16	The Devil in the Cavern	130

17	A Sinister Shadow Falls	135
18	Bloody Mary	142
19	The Winsford Vampire	146
20	The Wind from Hell	155
21	The Bowring Park Charioteer	164
22	The Elvi	168
23	Duke Street's Weeping Widow	173
24	A Dance with Death	178
25	Who Killed Julia Wallace?	188
26	Araminta	213
27	The Man of the Streets	224
28	The Summer of the Leprechaun	231
29	The Old Swan Mass Grave	240
30	Summon the Berserker	250
31	Voices	258
32	Strange Bird of Passage	264
33	Can You Keep a Secret?	276

34	Hilty	284
35	The Waterfront Ghoul	297
36	The Pellew Street Horror	304

ACKNOWLEDGMENTS

I would like to thank Kevin Roach of the Liverpool Records Office for some very interesting snippets and articles he has unearthed for me over the years, and also John Magin Kennedy, an ally in the quest for Manilu and other vampiric and paranormal entities.

A MARRIAGE MADE IN HELL

The following story allegedly happened in Liverpool in the 1960s. There are many fanciful versions of the tale that have been circulating the city for thirty years but this is the original version. It is the story of a young girl who was forever dreaming about marriage.

In mid-1960s Liverpool, a young woman named Collette worked in a textile factory near Wood Street in the city centre. Collette was a pretty but introverted girl who had no real friends at the factory. She just kept to herself and hardly ever spoke to the eight other women who worked with her.

Each day at lunch, the girls from the factory would go to a cafe in Bold Street but Collette never went with them. Instead, she went to a kiosk round the corner to buy cigarettes and would walk up Bold Street, window shopping. She always seemed to be in a world of her own. Every day, she would gaze through the window of a certain shop that had expensive wedding dresses on display. She spent almost all of her lunch-hour staring at these dresses in a dreamy state. One of her workmates named Chrissy used to see Collette wistfully gazing at the wedding gowns and she used to wonder what the lonely girl was thinking of.

Collette kept a diary and recorded all of her most intimate thoughts in her little black book. She used to fantasise over various film stars and wonder what type of man her future husband would be. She always imagined he would be tall, dark and very handsome.

Collette was attractive but she seemed to have difficulty meeting members of the opposite sex. One night at her flat in Huskisson Street, an old black woman named Mona who was a neighbour heard Collette sobbing. Mona tapped on Collette's door and asked if she was alright. Collette came to the door in a dreadful state. Mona took her down to her basement flat and gave the girl a cup of tea. Collette said she had asked a boy out and he had turned her down. Mona said he must have been a fool and boosted the girl's confidence by saying she was very pretty and that boys were ten-a-penny.

About an hour later, as Collette left Mona's flat, she met a sinister old man on the stairs who had only just moved into the flats. She only knew him as Mr Rose and he appeared to be very strange. He always dressed in black and was always accompanied by a black cat. "Hello, Mr Rose," Collette said, as she passed the old man on the stairs.

"If we meet on the stairs, we'll never meet in heaven," said Mr Rose, joking about an old superstition. Then in a serious tone he told her, "Collette, I couldn't help overhearing you and Mona before."

"Yes?" exclaimed Collette and she began to blush.

"I think I can help you. Come on," said the old man, and he beckoned the girl to come into his flat. Collette felt very nervous, and when she went into the old man's flat it was very dark. There were dusty old books on astrology and the occult everywhere. The old man even had a crystal ball on the table. He told her to sit at a table and handed her a piece of paper. "That's a pact with the Devil," he explained in a matter-of-fact way and offered her a pen.

Collette grinned and looked at the words scrawled on the paper. They seemed to be in Latin and were so small, she could not make head nor tail of them. "What does it say?" she asked.

"In return for your soul, you can have anything you desire. Just write your name at the bottom of the page," said Mr Rose and he uncapped an old fountain pen and handed it to the girl.

"I don't believe in all that. There is no Devil," said Collette.

"I know yes," said Mr Rose, "but just sign it anyway, go on."

"But..." stammered the girl.

"No buts. Just do it! Do it! Go on. You want to," said the old man, hypnotically staring at her.

Collette signed it and laughed. "I want to marry a man who's tall dark and handsome," she wished out loud, then left the room, giggling and trotted up the stairs to her flat.

On the following day during her lunchbreak, Collette was gazing in the window of the shop again, focusing on the beautiful satin and lace wedding gown. Suddenly, she saw a face reflected in the window. It was a tall dark-haired man with a handsome face. He was looking over her shoulder and his sudden presence naturally startled the girl. "Oooh! Who are you?" said Collette.

As she looked at the man, he grinned and he looked so handsome, but the pupils of his eyes suddenly burned with a dim red light.

Collette stumbled back in fear against the window. The figure then glided towards her without walking.

"Don't be afraid Collette. I want to marry you. I want you. You made your promise to me." said the weird stranger.

Collette let out a scream and ran up Bold Street in a state of terror. When she got home she barricaded herself in her flat and hid under a table.

At eight that night, the stranger called at her house in Huskisson Street. Collette looked through the window and he was in the street below with a brown paper parcel. She screamed, "Don't let him in!", but the old woman Mona let him enter.

He tapped on Collette's door, saying, "Let me in Collette, I love you. I'm your future husband," but suddenly turned nasty, shouting, "Let me in damn you!" Then there was silence.

Collette sat up all night drinking coffee and listening to her radio. As soon as morning came, she planned to leave her flat for good and she started writing down all the strange events that had happened in her diary. However, Collette never got to finish her entry for that day she dropped dead of a tremendous heart attack. Mona found the girl the next day with her eyes wide open, filled with terror. When the police called at the flat, they saw that someone had left a brown-paper parcel on the landing outside the girl's flat. What they saw was bizarre: it was a black silk and satin wedding dress, just like the one in the window in Bold Street but in black. When Mona read the dead girl's diary, she shuddered and decided to confront old Mr Rose, the man who had persuaded Collette to sign a pact with the Devil. But Mr Rose's flat was completely empty. Nobody had seen him leave and nobody ever saw that old man again.

SOMEWHERE ONLY WE KNOW

Have you ever suddenly recollected some unusual occurrence from your childhood, then thought, did that really happen or was it something I dreamt or some memory of an incident that happened on a television programme? I recall being visited by what I can only describe as a shadow-being when I was about two. It would sneakily slide out of the wall of my bedroom, almost immediately after my mum or dad had tucked me in and I vaguely remember pressing the tip of a butter-knife against my chest after some information was imparted to me from the silhouetted being which convinced me that I'd be okay if I died 'and went back'. My mother stopped me from doing any self-injury – or even worse – just in time. I think the shadow stopped visiting me some time after that. I have had the opportunity through my unusual work to talk to many people from all walks of life about the paranormal, and a lot of folk have told me of similar recollections of some very odd things which have lain buried in their memories for years. What follows is based on the recollections of two men who are, at the time of writing, what we imprecisely term as middle-aged. See what you think.

In the summer school holidays of 1972, two ten-year-olds from Bootle named Davy and Barry, were invited to go and stay with Barry's old Auntie Agnes, or "Aggie" as Barry called her, at a crumbling old house on Cambridge Street, just around the corner from the Oxford Street Maternity Hospital (now converted to house a suite of apartments known as Lennon Studios, as John Lennon was born there when it was a maternity hospital, as I was myself). Davy was from a rather clean home, and was quite shocked when he saw his first cockroach at Aggie's house, crawling on the floor of the kitchen, and he felt sick when Aggie halted in the middle of frying some sausages to stoop down and pick up the roach before tossing it out the kitchen window. When Davy told Barry about the disgusting way his auntie had continued cooking without washing her hands, Barry said, 'Don't start calling Auntie Aggie or you'll go home!'

Aggie was a widow who lived with a much older brother named Alf, who immediately struck Davy as a rather enigmatic man who knew something. 'Knows what?' Barry asked his best friend, but Davy just said, 'I don't know, it's hard to explain. I just think he knows things.'

And that teatime, Aggie and Alf and some jangling next-door neighbour named Queenie sat with the boys around the big table, eating fish, chips and peas, when Barry said, 'Hey Uncle Alf, Davy says you know things.'

Davy's face went pinkish-red, and he said to Barry, 'No I didn't, you.'

Barry grinned wickedly and said: 'You did, you said he knows things and you've gone all red, ha!'

'Stop talking at the table and eat your tea, Davy!' Aggie told her nephew sternly.

Barry licked the tip of his index finger and then placed it on his own face as he made a hissing sound as he looked at red-faced Davy. 'You've gone like a tomato!' he told Davy.

'Hey, Barry, be quiet and leave Davy to eat his tea!' said Alf, and he smiled at Davy and winked.

After tea, Barry and Davy left the house to go gallivanting. They played with a few children of an Irish family called the Ryans who lived locally, then went to explore the rocks outside the crypt section of the Roman Catholic Cathedral, which lay just a few hundred yards away. Around 10pm, as twilight fell, Queenie – Aggie's neighbour – could be heard, shouting for Barry in a yodelling type of voice. The two boys went to Aggie's house, and they were treated to cordial, jelly and cream, and then told to go upstairs to share the bath. The boys sat in the bath with their underpants on, flicking water and hurtling Crazy Bath Foam at one another, until Aggie came in and told them to dry and go to bed immediately. The boys did, and had to share an old double bed in a room with mildewed wallpaper and old fashioned furniture. Just after midnight, Davy and Barry were still awake, and telling one another stories, when Barry decided to go and root about in an ancient-looking mahogany cabinet. The two doors of the cabinet were adorned with what antique dealers would describe as foliate fretwork panels. Barry knelt down, opened the doors, and looked inside at the bundles of old yellowed newspapers. He shifted the bundles out the way and saw another door set into the back of the cabinet, and so he turned the handle to reveal a small flight of steps that went down into the darkness. 'Wow! Look at this Davy! It's a secret passage.'

Davy got out the bed and went to see what his friend was talking about. When he saw the steps, he had a bad feeling about the discovery, and advised Barry to close the inner door and put the newspapers back in place, but Barry was already crawling into the cabinet towards the stairs. 'Don't Barry, you might fall down a hole down there!' Davy warned, and then he saw an old candle in a holder on the cabinet, and he told Barry they should light it to show the way. Barry came back out the cabinet, and after he and Davy went downstairs to the kitchen to light the candle from the pilot light on the cooker, they returned to the bedroom and went inside the cabinet. Each boy was barefooted and Barry only wore his underpants, whereas Davy had old baggy pyjama bottoms on. They descended the ice-cold sandstone steps and came to a number of doors of different shapes and sizes. Barry carefully opened the first door, which was only about one-and-a-half feet high and two feet across, and the boys found themselves looking down at someone's parlour. An old woman was asleep in a high-backed chair in front of a fire, and her cat on the fireside rug was gazing up at the boys, who began to giggle. 'Whose house is this?' Barry asked and sniggered. The old woman started to snore, and Barry shouted: 'Hey love!'

startling the poor elderly thing. And then he slammed the door shut and went to look at the other doors. 'We should go back now,' Davy said nervously, his hand cupped around the candle, guarding it from draughts.

'No, this is great!' said Barry excitedly, and he pulled open a bigger door which was about three feet square to reveal a tunnel. The boys crawled down the tunnel and saw light streaming from a square on the wall which turned out to be a ventilator grille. They looked through it and saw a woman, aged about forty or less, sitting in the bath, reading a book. Davy was terrified of being caught as some Peeping Tom, and tried to back away on his knees, but Barry put his fingers to his mouth and whistled loudly through the ventilator, startling the woman. The boys heard an almighty splash and the woman shouted: 'Who's that? Who's there?'

The boys returned to the steps which led to the cabinet and fled up them to the bedroom. The inner cabinet door was slammed shut and the bundles of newspapers were put back in place. The boys laughed about their bizarre discovery until well after 1am, and then they both fell fast asleep. The next morning when they awoke they agreed not to mention the "secret passage" and the doors and tunnels to anyone. As the boys sat at the table for a breakfast of boiled eggs and fried bread (made with lard), Aggie said to them: 'What was that racket about in your room last night eh?'

'Wasn't us auntie,' Barry replied with a slight telltale grin on his face, 'we went to sleep straight away.'

'Well the bugs must have clogs on in this house then,' Aggie replied in a sarcastic tone.

That evening at 7pm, Alf gave Barry and Davy a

drawing pad each and some felt tip pens. The boys said they were going upstairs to their room to draw a comic strip, but this was just a pretence to go up to the bedroom to explore the tunnels leading from the cabinet again. On this occasion, the boys travelled some distance down a tunnel until they came to a normal-sized door, and when they opened it, they found themselves in a room lined with expensive-looking leather-bound books. The carpet was dark red, and from the ceiling hung an elaborate crystal chandelier. The boys entered the room and went to another door, and from behind this door came the most peculiar-sounding music they had ever heard. It sounded just like a piano playing in reverse. 'Let's go, quick, come on Barry,' Davy whispered as he watched his over-intrepid friend reach for the handle of the door.

Barry turned the handle, and there was a man sitting at a grand piano dressed in a black coat with hammer tails. His face looked very strange. He had a long aquiline nose, bulging eyes with dark circles around them, and protuberant teeth which stuck out as he grinned. He was hammering the keys with his hands and making an unholy racket. All of a sudden, the odd-looking pianist happened to glance over at the door, and he spotted Barry looking in on him. He stopped playing, got to his feet, and ran towards the boys. Davy was out of the library like a shot, and soon scrambling along the tunnel to the flight of steps. He heard Barry's screams echoing behind him and a man's gruff voice. Davy fell out of the cabinet and ran downstairs to tell Aggie what had happened but he collided with Barry's Uncle Alf on the bottom step.

'Hey! What's all this?' Alf said, leaning against the newel post with his hands clutching his stomach where Davy's head had winded him.

Davy rattled off an almost incoherent attempt at explaining what had just occurred and Alf ran up to the room, followed by Davy, who took slow, reluctant steps to reach the bedroom. When Davy entered the bedroom it was empty, and the cabinet door was wide open. He could hear Alf arguing with someone and the sound of Barry crying his eyes out. A few minute later, Barry came running out the cabinet with his shirt torn and his face was slicked with tears. He ran past Davy and out of the room. Then Alf came out of the cabinet on all fours with a cut lip, and without a word of explanation, he closed the inner door of the mahogany cabinet, then put all of the newspaper bundles back in place in the cabinet, and slammed the two doors shut with quite a temper. He then pushed Davy out of the room and said, 'You're going home!'

Down in the kitchen there was a blazing row between Alf and Aggie.

'They're nothing but trouble and they're going home tonight, so help me God!' bawled Alf.

'Over my dead body they are!' countered Aggie, and she hugged a sobbing Barry and said to him, 'Stop crying pet, you and your friend are staying here! Take no notice of your uncle!'

Alf stormed off out of the house but later returned and remained sulkily silent for an hour. After supper, the boys went up to their room and Davy asked Barry what had happened when the man who had been playing the piano had caught him. Barry said he had tried to bite his arms and legs but he had punched him and hit him with a chair, and Barry had hidden under the piano at one point, but then Uncle Alf came upon the scene and the two men started to punch one another. As Barry was telling an engrossed Davy about the incident, three raps sounded on the double doors of the mahogany cabinet, and Davy let out a yelp and sat up in bed, gazing at the source of the sounds. The doors opened, and a boy of around 7 or 8 years of age came out. He wore a dirty pale shirt with ho collar and a pair of trousers that ended just under the knees. He looked at Davy and Barry from the interior of the cabinet, and then this stranger and Barry posed the same question simultaneously: 'Who are you?' they said.

'You first,' said Barry, and he got out the bed and stooped down to look past the stranger in case that man was around, but the boy was alone.

'I'm Billy,' said the boy.

'Where are you from, Billy?' Barry asked him.

'From in there,' Billy said, pointing into the dark passageway behind him.

'Do you know who that man is who plays the piano?' Barry queried.

'Mr Wroot plays the piano,' said Billy, 'and he's trying to kill me.'

'Trying to kill you?' said Davy, feeling very unsafe all of a sudden.

'You'd better come in here then,' Barry advised Billy, and the young boy came into the bedroom and Barry went into one of the drawers in an dresser and found a pair of old brown nylon stockings that must have belonged to Aggie. He used one of the stockings to tie together the door handles of the mahogany cabinet –

just in case Mr Wroot tried to get into the room.

'Do you live next door?' Davy asked Billy, and the boy returned a puzzled expression.

'No, in there,' Billy nodded towards the cabinet.

'Yeah, we know you came out there, but where's your house?' Barry asked the barefooted boy. 'Is it in this street? Who made all those secret passages?'

Billy shrugged. 'I don't know. I live in there; that's where I live.'

'You can stay here if you like,' Barry told Billy, and pointed to the bed.

Billy nodded enthusiastically and soon the three boys were sitting on the bed, and Davy was showing Billy how to draw with the felt tips. Billy seemed fascinated by the pens, and he also seemed mesmerised by the bedside lamp, and burnt his fingers twice touching the bulb. At half-past one in the morning, there came a gentle tapping on the doors of the cabinet, and all three boys awoke with a start. Billy was sleeping at the bottom of the bed, top-tail fashion to the other two. He sat up with a look of fear on his face and gazed at the cabinet doors, which were bulging now as someone behind them pushed against them. Then a smarmy-sounding voice said, 'Billy? Are you in there?'

Billy recoiled with a yelping sound and backed away from the cabinet until he was seated between Davy and Barry.

'Is that him?' Davy whispered to Billy. 'Is that Mr Wroot?'

Billy was so afraid of the man behind those doors, he never heard Davy's question, and Barry, seeing how terrified the boy was, led him out of the room. All three went downstairs to the kitchen, where Barry armed himself with a huge carving knife, and Davy grabbed the heavy cast iron poker out the fire grate.

Billy started to sniffle, and tears rolled from his eye as he trembled.

'Don't be scared, Billy, he won't get you I promise,' Barry tried to reassure his new friend. 'Davy and I will kill him.'

All of a sudden, there came the sound of movement behind the walls of the kitchen, and the boys froze as they realised that Wroot was using some hidden passages leading to the kitchen. They heard loose powdery plaster behind the damp wallpaper trickling down, and it sounded like sand falling on the skin of a drum.

'He's here!' little Billy sobbed, looking about at the walls.

Davy and Barry were speechless with fear, and they were confused. How could this man move around the house behind the walls?

A deadly silence descended, and the only sound to be heard came from cats hissing and screeching at one another in the distance somewhere. The door of the cupboard under the sink flew open and that man Davy had seen playing the piano in that secret room – the one who had captured Barry and tried to bite him on the arms and legs – reached out with his arm and his large hand grabbed Billy by his left ankle. Before Billy could even cry out, Mr Wroot yanked at Billy's ankle and the boy fell forwards and cracked his forehead on the hard tiles as he fell face down. Billy was knocked clean out by the fall, and Wroot laughed as his other arm reached out and seized the other ankle of the unconscious boy.

'No!' Barry screamed and he wanted to stab Wroot but was too afraid to even try, and he and Davy watched in horror as the little boy was dragged into the cupboard under the sink. Wroot closed the door behind him, and then Barry and Davy heard the maniac move behind the wall as he returned to what was presumably his lair.

The door of the kitchen burst open, and Davy let out a scream. Aggie came in wearing a hairnet and nightgown, followed by her brother Alf, who was wearing red and white striped pyjamas. 'What's all this noise, eh?' Aggie yelled. Her eyes were all bloodshot.

Barry opened the door of the cupboard under the sink and pointed to the cylinder of Vim and bottles of disinfectant and Windolene laying on their sides in disarray. He spouted out the story of Billy coming out of the cabinet on the run from a Mr Wroot, and Alf stopped the boy's conversation stone dead by shouting at him to: 'Stop!'

'Come on you two, get to bed!' Aggie hollered at Barry and Davy. 'And put that knife back in the drawer,' she said to Barry, then took the poker from Davy's grip.

The boys begrudgingly went up the stairs to their room, and Davy whispered to Barry: 'I want to go home in the morning, I've had enough of this.'

'We can't go home and leave Billy with that man,' Barry told his friend, recalling the way he had tried to sink his teeth into him when he captured him in that room.

'I don't care about Billy, I hate this house!' Davy confessed.

At a quarter to four in the morning, the boys awoke

from their very light sleep, and heard distant screams. Alf knocked on the wall and shouted, 'I won't warn you two again!'

'It isn't us!' Barry shouted to the wall.

'Get to sleep now!' Alf cried out.

'Those screams,' Davy whispered, and his eyes seemed full of terror now; 'they sounded like Billy's screams.'

'We've got to help him,' said Barry, and he said this three times to Davy and elicited three shakes of Davy's head. 'Well I'm helping him!' Barry said, and he sneaked out of the room again and took ages tiptoeing down the stairs, avoiding the creaky steps, until he reached the kitchen, where he looked for some candles. The boy was terrified because he imagined Wroot would emerge from some cupboard and seize him in a flash, but he managed to obtain two candles and some matches before sneaking at a snail's pace back up the stairs to the room. He undid the stockings on the door handles of the mysterious mahogany cabinet and removed the newspaper bundles. The silver handle on the inner door was turned and the two boys bravely went in search of the little lad Billy.

They tried the door that led to that library, where the man they assumed to be Wroot attacked Barry, but it was locked. The duo tried another door, and looked in on the darkened parlour where they had seen the old woman dozing in the high-backed chair, but there was no sign of the woman, and the chiming of the clock on the mantelpiece striking the hour of four startled the boys. On the way back down the passage, Davy noticed a peephole in the door to the locked library, but it was too far up the door for either boy to look through, so Barry bent over and rested his hands on his kneecaps as Barry stood on his back, using him as a human step. Barry steadied himself, and looked through the hole. What he saw was so horrific, so shocking, he fell from Davy's back and ran off, unable to speak or cry out, leaving his candle in the holder on the floor.

'Wait for me!' Davy shouted after his terror-stricken friend, and he had the good sense to pick Barry's candle up off the floor before he ran after him. When Davy reached the bedroom he found it empty, and he heard a commotion downstairs. When Davy went down to the hallway he came upon Barry in tears, and he was illuminated by the light shining through the doorway of the parlour. In the doorframe, silhouetted, stood the boy's Uncle Alf with his coat on over his pyjamas, and he roared: 'Enough is enough! As soon as it's light, you two pests are out of here and I don't care what Aggie says this time! You could have caused a fire going round the place with candles all hours in the morning! Now get back to bed!'

And he lurched towards Davy, who backed away in fright. Alf snatched the candles from each of the boy's hands and told him to get to bed. 'Pronto! Go on! Get up there!' he barked.

Up in the room, Davy asked his friend what he had seen through the peephole in the door, and as Barry tied not one, but three stockings around the handles of the mahogany cabinet, he started to sniffle again.

'What did you see?' Davy pressed his friend, but soon wished he hadn't asked him.

Barry knelt there after tying the third knot of the stockings, and said: 'That weird man was sitting at a table, and he had one of those things tied round his neck under his chin...'

'You man a napkin?' Davy asked.

Barry nodded, and tears came streaming down his face. 'And there was all blood on it, and he had a knife and a fork and on the plate was Billy's head...' Barry started to cry again, and he buried his face in his hands.

Uncle Alf started knocking on the wall, and faint cries of: 'Shut up and get to sleep!' could be heard through the thin wall.

'What? Billy's head?' Davy recoiled in horror. A nervous twitch played in his cheek.

'He'd cut his nose off and he had it on the end of the fork, and Billy's eyes were gone as well...' Barry's voice trailed off into a whisper.

'Why would he do that to Billy?' Davy began to shake, and he looked at the cabinet then backed away and sat on the end of the bed – the end furthest from that portal to a very strange world of tunnels, doors and strange characters.

'Listen!' Barry suddenly said, and his eyes widened and turned right towards the bound doors of the cabinet.

Davy tried to stop breathing so he could listen more intently. Yes, he could hear it too. That peculiar piano and its odd-sounding music was playing faintly. Wroot was tinkling the ivories.

'Maybe we should leave,' Barry suggested, and Davy nodded enthusiastically.

The faint piano music stopped.

'How can we get home though?' Barry pondered, 'Bootle's miles away.'

'We should go to the police and tell them about Billy, and they'll lock that man up,' Davy said, still shaking from that mental image of Billy's severed had on the plate with no eyes and the bloody napkin and carved-off nose.

There came faint footsteps on the stairs outside. Barry and Davy looked at one another – two pallid faces barely visible in the bedroom, where the only light came from an old sodium light burning outside in the entry. 'Who's that?' Davy whispered.

The footfalls halted outside the bedroom door. The floor creaked outside that door.

Davy went to the dresser and picked up an old vase, ready to throw it at whoever was outside. He somehow knew – somehow sensed – that it wasn't Barry's Uncle Alf out there.

'Who is it?' Barry said to the door.

The door handle squeaked as it slowly turned, and the door opened a few inches.

'Uncle Alf, is that you?' Barry asked, and began to blink rapidly.

No reply came.

'Uncle Alf?' Barry asked once more.

'Get to bed!' came Uncle Alf's faint voice from next door. So, if Alf was in bed, who was coming into the room?

The door opened steadily and Barry and Davy backed away to the other side of the room, near to the window.

That man – the cannibal who had been seen eating Billy's head on the plate, looked around the door and even in the darkened room, the whites of the maniac's eyes seemed almost to fluoresce. He smiled, and ran the tip of his tongue around his lips.

'Uncle Alf!' Barry screamed at the top of his voice, 'Help! Murder! Murder!'

The man who the late Billy had referred to as Mr Wroot, gritted his teeth at the yelling boy and gave a threatening cut-throat gesture by drawing his index finger-tip across his fat adam's apple.

All of a sudden, Davy hurled the vase at Wroot and it smashed squarely in his face, and the fragments of the vase scattered everywhere. Wroot let out a loud grunt, and blood blossomed from a large cut on his forehead, just over his right eyebrow. He lunged across the room at the boys, and Barry dived onto the floor and scrambled under the bed, and a second later, Davy did the same. They then bolted like rats from under the bed and ran to the doorway with Wroot a few feet behind them. The boys ran downstairs and across the hall and tried to get out via the front door, but the old rusty bolt on the bottom of the door wouldn't budge. Davy slammed the vestibule door behind him and sandwiched between that door and the front door, he and Barry tried to yank back the bolt. Davy looked at the frosted glass of the vestibule door, expecting to see Wroot's evil sinister face peer through that pale pane at any moment.

'Help us open it, come on!' Barry groaned, putting all his might into shifting the damned bolt.

There came a steady thump on the carpeted stairs.

'He's coming!' cried Davy, and he tried with every ounce of his strength to pull that bolt back, and it seemed to be slowly moving.

Barry looked back at the vestibule door and saw a shadow on the pale grey glass window of the vestibule door. That door opened.

Both boys cried out in discordant skew-whiff harmony.

But thankfully it was only Alf, and although he was furious at the screams, he had obviously seen Wroot's blood from the injury he had sustained from the vase. 'Who's hurt himself?' he said, and he reached to the light switch and clicked it on. A small sixty-watt tungsten bulb burned its yellow light above.

The boys gave their account of the cannibal at large in the house and when Davy said, 'The man who gave you a fat lip is a cannibal Alf,' Alf became enraged and said to him, 'You will never, and I mean, never ever, set foot in here again! Pack your things you little runt!' This over-reaction to Davy's comments was incomprehensible to the lads.

And that morning, despite Aggie's loud and colourful protestations, Alf marched the boys to the house of a neighbour who had a car, and he got this neighbour to drive the boys to their homes in Bootle.

Barry's parent simply couldn't believe the far-fetched story of secret passages in Aggie's house and the cannibal who ate the little boy. Davy's parents just laughed and said he had a very vivid imagination when he gave his account of the strange and terrifying goings-on at the house on Cambridge Street, and gradually, over the years, the boys drifted apart, and whenever they told anyone about the goings on at that house in the summer of 1972, their accounts were met with scepticism and who could really blame anyone for disbelieving such a incredible and fanciful story? A few years ago, Barry, now a father of four in his forties, wrote to me to tell me about the extraordinary incidents from all those years ago, and he and I tracked down Davy, who was working in a call centre in Kent. Barry wasn't very computer savant, and never even bothered with email, and he wasn't aware that Davy had a Facebook page. When we caught up with Davy, he confirmed the story and the two men now stay in touch. I talked to a psychologist, and he told me that he knows of many people who suddenly recall very bizarre incidents from their childhood which they often dismiss as a faulty memory or a memory of a dream which has been filed away as a real occurrence. I mentioned this case briefly on a radio programme and did not mention Cambridge Street, and a woman later contacted me with a strange story which seemed to add some credence to Barry and Davy's frightening experiences. The woman, in her fifties, named Tina, who lived on Crown Street, Edge Hill, in the 1970s, said she used to be friends with a girl named Maureen who lived on Cambridge Street in the early 1970s, and she had heard the story of the secret passages under houses on Cambridge Street and once heard Maureen's grandmother talk about 'a dirty old man' named Wroot who was a well-known landlord of several house in the area around Cambridge Street. Wroot – and Maureen's grandmother would always emphasise the silent 'W' at the beginning of the man's surname, was said to lurk in the cellars of his house and stand under the aria grids so he could look up women's skirts. The other depraved things this man got up to could not be put into print in a book such as this or I would risk prosecution under the Obscene Publications Act. I asked Tina if Maureen's grandmother ever mentioned Wroot playing a piano, but Tina said she couldn't recall any mention of this. The period when this man was carrying out his disgusting activities would probably be around Edwardian times, and this leads me to believe that Barry and Davy, and Uncle Alf, must have been dealing with ghosts, so this makes me wonder if the secret passages were also ethereal, or whether a timeslip situation was the cause of the nightmarish phenomena.

GOLGON

This is alleged to be a true story from long ago, cobbled together from interviews with people involved in the tale, newspaper clippings, and reports gathered from readers of my columns and books. A few names have been changed to preserve anonymity and to disguise the locations of several graves. Do I believe in the following tale? I am not sure, but what I believe or choose not to believe is of no consequence; I am merely the person who collects, researches and documents these stories. You, reader, have to make up your own mind. Whether you are being asked to believe in a religious figure walking on water, or Lee Harvey Oswald assassinating the President of the United Sates with a cheap rifle, you and no one else should make up your own mind on what is fact and what is fiction.

On the Saturday night of October 19, 1963; a 23-year-old electronics student named Kevin Butterworth was sitting in his ground-floor flat on Gambier

Terrace, attempting to study a television repair manual – despite the noise from the swinging party next door. The satire programme - *That Was The Week That Was* - was on the TV in the background in Kevin's living room as a form of distraction from the high-jinks that could be heard all over Hope Street. The time was 11.15pm and a Beatles hit was being belted out by the Dansette record player next door now. A student in a cowboy hat, swigging a bottle of Lamb's Navy Rum, walked past Kevin's window, followed by a girl of about 19 wearing a pointy black witch's hat, and she was carrying a crate of Watney Mann beer bottles as she sung The Tremeloes' *Do You Love Me?*

Kevin was so envious of the partygoers. Here he was in the prime of his life, hungering for the caress of a female and a few well-deserved drinks, but instead he was sitting alone like some recluse, studying thermionic valves and resistor colour codes. He just felt like gate-crashing the early Halloween fancy dress ball, but he soon recalled how he had decided to knuckle down and learn a trade. He was determined to be a TV repair man, even if it meant forsaking Saturday nights to study schematic circuit diagrams. TV repair was where the money was. 'Willpower,' he muttered to himself, and then he glanced at the young singer Millicent Martin on the telly. She was one of his monochrome crushes of the moment. Oh how he would love to have a girl like Millicent. He sighed, and sat down to resume his studies with Woodbines and black coffee to get him through the hormonal surge that was threatening to sabotage his self-control.

Around midnight, as *The Third Man* detective series ended the BBC's Channel 1 for the night, Kevin heard faint voices – male and female – and a scuffle outside. He turned off his table lamp and went to the window, and he saw a man outside in the small garden patch. A tall guy in his thirties, perhaps older, obviously from the fancy dress party, because he wore a long black cape lined with purple satin, worn over a navy blue velvet jacket. Under this he wore a white shirt with a frilled collar and bow. In the arms of the stranger there was a beautiful red-haired girl of about twenty in a black polo neck sweater, short skirt and tights, and she was out cold, probably drunk. The man stepped into the shadows of the tall bushes and seemed to kiss the girl's neck. Because the couple were now standing in the shade of the bushes beyond the illumination of the lamp post, Kevin could barely see what was going on, but he could make out the man apparently inflicting a 'lovebite' in the redhead's neck. And then Kevin squinted because he thought he saw something dark trickle from the man's mouth down the girl's pale neck into the collar of her polo sweater. Kevin was naturally dumbfounded. This was taking the Dracula role a bit too far, the young man decided, and he slowly opened the window, ready to jump out and confront the costumed 'vampire' . Kevin wasn't sure if the act of biting the girl's neck was some sadistic action of the stranger or whether the girl was allowing him to carry out some extreme sexual fantasy, and for a moment, Kevin felt like some Peeping Tom – a loser of a voyeur. He heard the man in the long cape say 'Pandora, wake up!' in a deep rich well-spoken accent, but the girl never stirred, so the bloodsucker hunched over her to bite her once more. Kevin decided the creep was taking advantage of the unconscious girl, and he grabbed a poker and heroically jumped out the window, startling the neck-biting weirdo – who seemed very startled, and he turned to face Kevin with eerie blood-red eyes. Then the redhead in his arms suddenly woke up – and her eyes were of the very same blood-red. She smiled, revealing fangs, and Kevin backed towards the window, realising the couple were very unearthly. He reached for his penknife and instinctively placed it at right angles to the poker, forming a makeshift cross, and the vampiric couple hissed simultaneously. For a few minutes that felt like an eternity, Kevin yelled for help, and the vampires – or whatever they were - seemed determined to have him, and refused to flee – until some of the partygoers from next door came to see what the shouting was about, and they, and Kevin, saw the couple run off and jump clean over a ten-foot hedge. They landed somewhere on Hope Street and were heard running off at a phenomenal speed. Two of the students from next door said that the couple had come to the party just after nine. The girl, who gave her name as Pandora, had drunk a lot of wine, but her much older boyfriend never spoke once, and never touched a drop of drink. All he did for nearly three hours was sit in a dark corner of the room watching the female partygoers dancing with a fascinated look. Pandora had been very intrigued by the record player, watching it automatically drop stacks of forty-fives and lower its sapphire-tipped needle onto each record. Two female German students who were present said Pandora talked to her boyfriend in German as well as English, and she seemed to have a slight Germanic accent.

About a month after this baffling incident, Kevin Butterworth was once again sitting up late, reading an electronics textbook on television repair when he thought he saw something moving by his window. On this night the curtains were wide open and a full moon was shining down onto Gambier Terrace. Kevin looked up from his book and saw nothing out the ordinary, but when he commenced his studies, he once again saw movement out the corner of his eye. He slowly looked up, and there was the redheaded 'vampire' girl he had seen a month back, peeping into his room. Kevin pretended not to see her, and he gave a fake yawn, then put his hand over his eyes, pretending to rub them. He looked through his splayed fingers with his heart pounding. Yes, there was no mistaking that pallid face and reddish eyes – it was that female with the fangs. Kevin rose from his desk, and went into his bedroom. He pulled a large trunk from under the bed, opened it, and rummaged through it until he came to a rosary that had belonged to his late grandmother. He held the crucifix of the rosary and returned to the living room – to see two silhouetted figures at the window now, and one of them was much taller than the other. It was the caped stranger from the month before, and he was trying to lift the window open. Kevin held out the crucifix and rosary at the figures from inside the window, and he saw them back away, each with glinting red eyes as retro-reflective as that of a cat. The couple darted away into the moonlight and the shadows, and Kevin sat up until the dawn came creeping over Hope Street. Kevin went to see a priest at a local church and told him about the vampiric stalkers but the clergyman said there were no such things as vampires and assured Kevin that he was being hoaxed by some mischievous couple, but Kevin told the man of the cloth how he and many others had seen the couple jump clean over a tall hedge that was at least ten feet in height. The priest shrugged with a smile on his face and said, 'A trick of the light? We think we see all kinds of things at night.'

Kevin left the priest's house and went into the church to gather Holy Water in a little bottle at the font. He had seen the films about vampires like Dracula being repelled by blessed water and felt safer having it at hand in case the couple of neck-biters returned. Kevin also decided he'd try and get some company for tonight, believing there was safety in numbers. He called at the house of his old friend Roger Smithies off Brownlow Hill and told him about the weird couple. Roger's imagination was immediately captured by the accounts of the vampires. He had known Kevin since their days at infant school together, and his friend had never been one to tell lies, nor had he any interest in the supernatural, so he knew Kevin had definitely seen something strange. Roger had a week off work, and so he volunteered to spend that holiday at Kevin's Gambier Terrace flat, and one day during that period, he came home from a junk shop with a large crucifix. Roger also removed the leg of an old dining chair and laboriously shaved it into a fine-pointed stake with Kevin's penknife. Kevin started to wonder if the enlisting of his fanatical friend had been a grave mistake. Roger seemed to want to encounter the vampiric entities. He told Kevin he had always wanted to get behind a cause, to find a purpose and stance in life, and now he felt as if his role was 'to tackle evil'. The two young men went to Ye Cracke pub on nearby Rice Street, which was mainly the haunt of students from the "Inny" (Liverpool Institute on Hope Street). Here, over cider and bitter, Kevin and Roger discussed the vampires and how they would dispatch them if a confrontation took place. Outside it was a chilly rainy evening, and the pub was almost empty, except for three students and a man in his early sixties who wore a tweed trilby and sported an outlandish curled-up moustache. He had on a chocolate-coloured corduroy jacket, black trousers and black pointed ankle boots. He sipped a glass of gin and was casting a curious gaze at Kevin and Roger with his pale blue smiling eyes. The two young men noticed the way he was looking at them and found it rather unsettling. The man came over to their corner table and touching the vacant chair there, he said, 'May I join you chaps – just for a short while?'

Kevin nodded, lost for words, and Roger was equally surprised, but managed to mutter 'Yeah.'

The man took off his trilby to reveal a thick crown of white centre-parted hair, and placed the hat on the table. He then put his glass of gin beside it and pulled out the chair, which he slowly lowered himself onto with a grimace as if he had an arthritic back. 'My name's Roland Goddard,' the elderly man said once seated, and he paused with a half-smile on his face as if he thought his name might be recognisable to the young men, but he was met with blank stares.

'I've contributed many articles on the vampire in several periodicals pertaining to the world of the supernatural and the psychic,' Mr Goddard told Kevin and Roger, and the two younger men glanced briefly at one another, simultaneously realising that the visitor to their table had been listening in on their conversation about the vampire couple.

'Oh,' was all Kevin could say in reply to Goddard.

Goddard coughed to clear his throat and continued: 'From the sounds of it, the vampire you encountered is one Captain Rex Golgon, who was entombed alive in St James's Cemetery in the 1870s – and the girl with him is thought to be an incorruptible who was buried in the same cemetery in Edwardian times. She became of his kin around 1950.'

'His kin? I don't understand,' Kevin admitted bafflement at Goddard's words, 'And what's an incorruptible?'

'Not all bodies decay after death. We embalm bodies of course in an effort to stop or slow down decomposition, but for some unknown reason, through some mystery of human chemistry, a few people do not rot away in their coffins. Bodies that have been exhumed – usually in the course of a forensic murder investigation where the dead person is thought to have been poisoned – and these corpses have been found to be perfectly preserved, with peaches and cream complexions, looking as if they were merely asleep. These so-called incorruptibles – unless they are saints – like Bernadette of Lourdes or St Francis Xavier - are most prone to become vampires. This can happen when the wandering soul of an evil person invades the incorruptible's body – and takes it over. The body is then imparted with tremendous strength and it claws its way through the coffin lid and burrows its way to the surface after dark to go in search of *prana* – the very life-force of humans, which is mainly found in blood and other bodily fluids. The Pandora of which you speak was most likely Grace Eaves, a German-born teenager who committed suicide in Liverpool around 1902. Her coffin was opened by mistake in 1910 by police whilst they were attempting to exhume the body of a well-to-do woman to see if she had traces of poison in her corpse. They only realised they had opened the wrong grave when they saw that Grace had red hair and was much younger than the lady they had intended to exhume. Grace Eaves was warm to the touch, even though she had been dead for eight years, and this warmth is one of the four types of phenomena associated with the incorruptible. There is often bleeding from the orifices of the body, a sweet smell emanating from the mouth, and, most astounding of all – movement of limbs – as if the nerves to the muscles are intact. Rigor Mortis sets in to a corpse after about twelve hours and then the body becomes limp again, thirty-six hours after that, but the limbs of Grace Eaves were said to twitch eight years after her coffin had been lowered into the cold clay of St James's Cemetery. In some cases, corpses in coffins twitch so much after death, they actually have been found laying in odd postures, often face down, hence the old sayings about the dead turning in their graves.'

Roger was engrossed by Goddard's claims, but he was suddenly distracted by a small emaciated black and white mongrel dog which had sneaked into the pub as someone opened the door to leave the establishment. It left a trail of wet paw prints as it headed towards Roger with its tail wagging and its floppy ears pressed back against its rain-slicked head.

Goddard sipped his gin and continued: 'These things belong to a cult that is very extensive, and it stretches back into the mists of time; the promise of eternal life, promised by the Christians and other faiths, is offered by the vampire in this world, not the world to come. There are many moral weaknesses in man, and the threat of complete nothingness after death, and the annihilation of the soul and ego after death has driven many to try and achieve immortality by any means. Some have actively sought out vampires to join their ranks as immortals. I know of a killer, hanged many years ago in Walton Gaol, who rose from his grave in the prison graveyard where the executed are interred to rot in quicklime. No one knew that the hanged killer had been a vampire who had once had intercourse with a female sangu - a bloodsucker that is - in North Wales ten years before. The killer had voluntarily become a vampire because he knew the time would come when he would be brought to account for his heinous crimes and sentenced to hang. The revenant of this executed man was seen by two warders scaling the wall of the prison like a human spider one moonlit night, and they never dared report the incident, and who could blame them? We are a Christian country, and we say we believe that Christ left his own tomb three days after he was executed, and yet we deny the existence of the grave-defying vampire.'

'And this man, and the woman that I saw with him, they – they were vampires?' Kevin struggled to realise the uncanny far-reaching truth behind the encounters at Gambier Terrace.

'Yes, and – ' Goddard suddenly halted in mid-sentence and looked under the table - at the pied mongrel dog. He viewed the animal with obvious suspicion in his expressions, and as Roger was stroking the animal's head, Goddard took a crucifix from the inside left pocket of his jacket and thrust it at the dog.

The animal's eyes burned red, and it snarled at the vampire expert's hand, baring its teeth, then slowly backed away from under the table. Kevin and Roger regarded the animal's bizarre behaviour with great astonishment. Goddard rose from the table holding out the cross to the animal, and it darted across the floor and began to whine and scratch at the door in great desperation. A well-meaning drinker opened the door for the dog.

'No! Don't let it go!' Goddard shouted, and the young student who had unwittingly freed the creature, shot a bemused and puzzled look at the old man with the crucifix in his thrust-out hand.

'What was all that about?' Roger asked Kevin, and Goddard turned to Roger and gave a very unnerving answer: 'They use dogs, cats and even birds to look through their eyes and listen through their ears.'

Kevin and Roger secretly wondered if the old man was just some fantasist, and yet Kevin recalled the way the couple had cleared that tall hedge in a single leap; perhaps Roland Goddard really was telling the truth. Feeling uneasy and vulnerable now at the pub, Kevin invited Goddard to the flat in Gambier Terrace, and here, the old man revealed more of his incredible in-depth knowledge of the vampires, and how to fight them. He stayed until almost 2am, and arranged for Kevin and Roger to meet him at noon in St James's Cemetery, where they would investigate the white marble sepulchre of Rex Golgon to see if the alleged vampire and his mate were still there. And if the vampires were there, they would have to be dispatched. At this time in the early 1960s, St James's Cemetery bore little resemblance to the landscaped park it has become today, for all of the varied gravestones and palatial tombs of the Victorian and Edwardian dead were crowded closely together in those days, and few people ventured down into this necropolis. Five minutes before noon on the following day, Kevin and Roger arrived in the cemetery and found Roland Goddard already there, loitering at the shadowy northern end of the sunken graveyard. He had a Gladstone bag at his feet which contained the tools of his unearthly trade: garlic-based concoctions, a strong-bladed dagger (to decapitate the vampire if necessary), an old service revolver, several hawthorn stakes, bottles of blessed water, a copy of the Holy Bible, and even a small can of petrol to burn the decapitated vampire. As Kevin and Roger approached, Goddard raised his gloved hand and placed his index finger against pursed lips, gesturing for the lads to be quiet. He then pointed to the Victorian sepulchre and nodded with a chilling look in his eyes which said: they are in there.

Kevin and Roger slowed, but couldn't help but crunch the brittle fallen leaves of autumn underfoot upon their careful approach to the tomb.

Goddard picked up his bag and then he whispered 'Stay there.'

Kevin and Roger halted and Goddard walked to them as silently as a ghost. 'They are both in there, asleep.'

Roger gave a nervous smirk, and he muttered: 'Asleep?'

Goddard seemed irritated by this smile, and mistook it for mockery, and in a low voice he murmured to Roger: 'I'm serious; come and listen if you don't believe me.'

'I believe you Mr Goddard,' said Roger, but the old man took him by the arm and forcefully pulled him to the grand burial chamber. Kevin followed close behind. It was the most surreal, funny yet frightening sound the young men had ever heard. Strange snoring sounds could be faintly heard coming from the interior of the sepulchre. The low grey cloud over the cemetery suddenly scudded towards the tower of the incomplete Anglican Cathedral, and a welcome shaft of warm sunlight fell on the tomb. Goddard seized this opportune moment, and he opened his Gladstone bag and took out a long chisel, and he used this tool to prise at the marble slab door of the chamber, and despite the man's age, he managed to dislodge the door. Goddard swore and told Kevin and Roger to help him remove the slab, and as Roger used the chisel to lever open the door, Kevin put his fingers in the black gap at the side of the dislodged slab and pulled with all of his might – and that slab suddenly gave way. It fell towards him and caught Goddard on his shoulder as the old man tried to turn and get out of the way. The slab slammed into the floor and the resultant crash echoed about the cemetery.

As Goddard fell to the floor crying out in agony with a dislocated shoulder, Kevin and Roger looked into the square of blackness. Their eyes adjusted to the harsh sunlight streaming from the left side of their field of vision – and they saw not two vampires, but three. And they were awake now.

The tall man in the cape Kevin had seen twice before backed away from the opening in his sepulchre; it was Rex Golgon, according to Goddard, anyway. The red-haired young lady Kevin had seen before was there, wearing that same black polo neck sweater, but she was naked below, wearing no skirt, underwear or tights. This was probably the incorruptible Grace Eaves, given her rebirth name as "Pandora" by Golgon. The third figure was clad in what looked like off-white-coloured rags, most probably a tattered burial shroud, and was almost devoid of flesh, being mostly shrivelled skin and wasted muscle. It shrieked, and moved rapidly like an insect up the wall and pressed its body against the roof of the sepulchre. At the sight of this entity, Roger turned and ran off, leaving Kevin rooted to the spot, almost paralysed with fear. Golgon buried his face in his hands as if he could not bare the light of day, and Kevin then noticed something quite horrific: the face of the red-haired girl was falling apart. 'Help me!' she shouted, and suddenly ran out of the sepulchre and threw herself into Kevin's arms. Kevin fell backwards and landed on his backside, trying to get the girl off him as he screamed. He pulled at her long red hair – and that hair became detached from the head as if it was some wig. It remained attached to the powdery red scalp, but the eyes of the girl plopped out onto Kevin's coat and shirt, and her lower jaw dropped and dangled. Kevin threw the crumbling corpse aside, and he watched as Goddard got to his feet in great pain. Roger suddenly returned, panting, and he tried to pull Kevin away from the nightmare, but Kevin swore and told him to help Goddard.

Goddard took the revolver from his Gladstone bag and aimed it at the wiry creature stretched out on the ceiling. He fired all six shots at the thing, and it hissed at him and vile green fluid ejaculated from its mouth, hitting the old man in the face twice. Goddard wiped the olive green spittle from his eyes with his sleeve and delved into his bag to take out a lighter and the can of petrol. He began to toss the contents of the can into the tomb, and Golgon and the thing in rags began to howl in blood-curdling harmony, as if they knew what was about to happen. Goddard lit his lighter and hurled it into the sepulchre, and a fireball exploded in the chamber and blew outwards through the hatch, burning Roger's face superficially, leaving him with no eyebrows and a smoking fringe. Roger cried out and staggered blindly to the cemetery's old spring, where he took handfuls of the mineral water and bathed his face in it. When he turned to behold the scene of mayhem behind him, he saw a man in a long cape on fire, rushing out of the sepulchre, followed by the ultra-agile skeleton in rags, which was now charred and smouldering. The abomination fell down onto the ground and Goddard poured a bottle of Holy Water on it until the thing lay motionless. Kevin went to chase Golgon, and almost lost him in the forest of gravestones and tombs, but he and Goddard found the remains of the 'arch-vampire' as Goddard called him, laying close to Huskisson's grandiose mausoleum. All that remained was his hair, his cape, and a brown fat-like substance similar to watery excrement. A police whistle sounded in the distance, and Goddard slapped

Kevin, and then Roger, on their backs and said, 'Get out of here, quick! Go on! I'll be alright! Go!'

Kevin and Roger ducked down as they hurried off between the gravestones until they reached the arched entrance of the tunnel leading to Upper Duke Street, and from there they ran pell-mell all the way to Kevin's flat on Gambier Terrace.

On the following evening in the *Liverpool Echo*, Kevin read of the desecration of a tomb and the fire within it, thought to be the work of Satanists, according to the authorities, and he felt butterflies in his stomach. Roger told his mother what had happened, and fortunately, she never believed him. Kevin told him to never tell another soul what had happened, but Roger did, although no one ever believed him anyway. A year after the incident, Kevin was dating a girl in Oxton, and one evening as he was waiting for the train home at Birkenhead train station, he bumped into Roland Goddard. Goddard hinted that he and a fellow vampire hunter – a certain Victor Mordelly – were now stalking a 'fiend' which was said to have its lair in Flaybrick Cemetery. Kevin asked Goddard if he could help him and his friend, and the old man shook his head and smiled, but Kevin persisted, even missing his train as a result, and Goddard relented and said Kevin could be of some assistance as long as he told no one about the unearthly mission. Kevin became that wrapped up in the vampire-hunting, his girlfriend chucked him, but he thought it was worth it to confront his fears once again. He went on to join Goddard and Mordelly in many battles with what we would term as vampiric creatures, and these adventures could fill a book – and one day they probably will.

TERROR ON THE M62

The following mysterious incident was related to me in September 2001, by a well-known Liverpool comedian whom I cannot identify. He stipulated that he would only relate the full facts of the bizarre and scary tale if I would give him my word that I would never identify him. I shall therefore have to call the comedian 'Bob'.

In the early 1990s, Bob drove up the M62 to Manchester, where he was due to perform a comedy routine as part of a cabaret show. As usual, Bob's performance was very warmly received by the audience, and, in appreciation, he decided to go back onstage for a further twenty minutes. While he was performing his additional material, he noticed a beautiful-looking woman of about 25 or 30 years of age, sitting at a table. She was smiling at Bob, and she reminded him of the Seventies film actress, Farrah Fawcett Majors. After he had finished his comedy act and had basked in the audience's enthusiastic applause,

Bob went backstage and changed, then the manager of the club escorted him to a specially-reserved table for a meal and a drink.

Just before the next performer took to the stage, Bob made his way over to the table where the woman was sitting alone, and asked her if she would care to join him. The woman smiled, and accepted without any hesitation. She was very tall and looked even more attractive at closer quarters. She had sapphire-blue eyes, and long blonde hair. In a soft voice, she said, "My name's Danielle." Her accent was not a local one, but was difficult to place.

Bob ordered champagne and was soon flirting with Danielle. The woman, however, refused the champagne and preferred to sip mineral water. There was a 'stay-behind' at the club, and it was not long before Bob and Danielle were dancing slowly, tightly embracing each other. He learned that the reason Danielle was on her own was that her boyfriend had arranged to meet her at the club, but had not turned up for some reason. She told him that she lived in St Helens, and Bob said that, as she had not been drinking, she could drive him home to Merseyside in his car. Danielle was not keen and instead preferred that Bob stay overnight at her home until he was fit enough to drive in the morning. At 3am, Bob and Danielle left the club in Manchester and walked through the chilly night air towards the club car park. Danielle shivered in her sleeveless top, so Bob gave her his leather jacket. Danielle had to strap Bob's seatbelt on for him because he was so intoxicated. Minutes later, the couple embarked on the return journey down the M62. During the journey, Bob fumbled for the controls of the car radio, but Danielle's hand intercepted his, and so, the couple sat in silence as the car sped along the motorway.

Suddenly stirring from his alcohol-induced doze, Bob turned to look at Danielle and saw something that still gives him nightmares to this day. The girl's beautiful features had contorted into what can only be described as a demonic scowl. Her head swivelled towards him and her eyes turned blood red, and her mouth opened wide - twice as wide as a normal mouth - to reveal a fearsome array of pointed teeth.

The comedian instantly became sober, but felt faint and breathless with the shock. The girl sitting in the driving seat of his car must be some sort of supernatural entity and was driving him goodness knows where. As if it was able to read his mind, the thing in the driving seat screamed with manic laughter and suicidally zig-zagged between the lanes of the motorway. Bob was not a religious man, but he suddenly found himself imploring, "Jesus, please save me".

The car screeched into a 180-degree turn and slid off the hard shoulder onto a slip road, then veered into a ditch. Bob opened the door and tried to get out, but in his blind panic, he forgot to unclick his seatbelt. He cried out desperately for help and looked back in terror at the seat beside him; it was empty, except for his leather jacket. There was no trace of the fiend who had been masquerading as a woman.

The police found Bob wandering along the hard shoulder of the M62, and he gabbled out his bizarre tale, but was not believed. The police checked the club, and the management confirmed that Bob had left with a woman and that she had driven him home. Not one person at the club had any idea who 'Danielle' was. Bob was badly shaken by the spine-chilling incident, and has never appeared at the Manchester club since.

Postscript: Shortly after this story was published, a number of people got in touch with me and told me that the comedian in the story (whom they all correctly identified) had quite a skeleton in his cupboard, and this related to a despicable incident 'Bob' was allegedly involved in many years before the encounter with the demonic being. It has been alleged that the encounter was payback for something sordid the comedian had done in his past.

THE STORY OF SPRINGHEELED JACK

In Victorian times, Barnes Common, an isolated tract of land on the southern bank of the Thames, was a place to avoid. Travellers foolhardy enough to cross the common during twilight hours, were often attacked and robbed.

One evening, in 1837, a businessman, who had been working overtime at his office, decided to risk a short cut across the common on his way home. A figure suddenly vaulted high over the railings of the cemetery - as if propelled from a springboard - and landed with a thud in front of him. The businessman turned and fled when he saw that the mysterious leaper had pointed ears, glowing eyes and a prominent pointed nose.

Three girls encountered the same sinister figure the following night. Again, he made his appearance by bounding over the railings of the cemetery but, on this occasion, he displayed a violent streak. One of the girls had her coat ripped by him, but managed to flee, closely followed by one of her screaming companions. The third girl tried to scream as the unearthly-looking stranger grabbed at her breasts and began tearing off her clothes, before leaving her unconscious.

During the following month, the leaping terror struck again. This time the venue was Cut-Throat Lane, Clapham Common. After visiting her parents in Battersea, Mary Stevens, a servant, headed back to her employer's household on Lavender Hill. As she strolled through the entrance of Cut-Throat Lane, a tall figure, dressed in black, jumped out of the darkness and threw his arms around her, holding her in a vice-like embrace. Before she had a chance to scream, the stranger kissed her face, then dipped his hand into her cleavage, before laughing hysterically. The girl screamed and the stranger released her and ran off into the darkness. A number of men hurried to the distressed girl and, after calming her down, they listened to her account of the attack. The men immediately searched the neighbourhood for the mysterious assailant, but without success. The following night, the attacker appeared again, not a stone's throw from the house where the servant girl worked.

That night, the demonic figure bounded out of the shadows into the path of an approaching carriage. The horses pulling the carriage bolted in fright and a terrible crash ensued, injuring the coachman. The mayhem-maker then seemed to defy the law of gravity, as he jumped effortlessly over a nine-foot high wall. Not long after that superhuman feat, a mysterious high-jumping man with a cape attacked a woman near

Clapham Churchyard.

Gradually, the news of the satanic superman spread and the public gave him a name - Spring-Heeled Jack. In February 1838, 18-year-old Lucy Scales, and her sister Margaret, were on their way home in the evening, after visiting their brother's house in the Limehouse area.

Suddenly, the terrifying cloaked silhouette of Spring-Heeled Jack leapt out of the darkness and exhaled a jet of blue flames, from his mouth, into Lucy's face. The teenager screamed, her legs collapsed under her and she fell to the ground, blinded. Jack jumped high over his victim and her sister, landed on the roof of a house and bounded off into the night.

A pattern was emerging. Jack seemed to like molesting and terrifying young females. His next attack, which took place two days later, was also on an 18-year-old girl, Jane Alsop. Jane's house was in Bearhind Lane, a quiet back street in the district of Bow, where she lived with her father and two sisters. She was spending the evening reading when, just before 9 o'clock, there was a knock on the front door. Jane answered and outside in the shadows stood a caped man. He said to Jane, "I'm a policeman. Bring a light! We've caught Spring Heeled Jack in the lane!"

Jane ran excitedly back into the house and returned with a candle. Offering the candle to the caller, she beheld a nightmarish sight. The flickering light illuminated the face of the man purporting to be an officer of the law. It was Jack and he grinned as he studied the girl's shocked expression.

Before she could move, he spurted out a phosphorescent gas, which partially blinded Jane, then started tearing at her clothes. Jane punched his big nose and managed to give him the slip but the enraged Jack bolted after her and stopped her from re-entering the house by clutching her hair. His claw-like hands scraped her face and neck but Jane's screams alerted her sisters, who came running out of the house and they managed to drag her from her attacker. The three sisters retreated indoors, with Spring-Heeled Jack in hot pursuit and, in the nick of time, the door was slammed in Jack's face. The trembling, whimpering girls then listened in horror to Jack's talons clawing slowly down the other side of the door. These scratch-marks left by the fiend were visible for years.

When Jane was quizzed by the Lambeth Police Court about the assailant's appearance, she described a very unusual person:

"He wore a large helmet and a tight-fitting costume that felt like oilskin. But the cape was just like the ones worn by policemen. His hands were as cold as ice and like powerful claws. But the most frightening thing about him was his eyes. They shone like balls of fire."

Two days later, Jane's description was strengthened by the testimony of a butcher from Limehouse. He was the brother of Lucy and Margaret Scales - the victims of the Green Dragon Alley attack.

Accounts of Spring-Heeled Jack's cowardly assaults on the ladies of South London soon spread, scaring many into staying indoors after dark, while others decided to organise vigilante patrols.

A week after the attack on Jane Alsop, Jack called at a house in Turner Street, off Commercial Road. A servant boy answered the door, and Jack, shielding half of his face with his cloak as he stood in the shadows, asked the boy if he could talk to the master of the house. The youngster was turning, about to call for the master, when Jack made the mistake of moving out of the shade into the lamplight. The boy recoiled in horror when he saw the caller had bright orange eyes. As he stood there in a state of shock, he noticed two other details about the mysterious caller; he had claws for hands and, under his cloak, an intricate embroidered design that resembled a coat of arms. Below this design, the letter 'W' was embroidered in gold. The boy had heard all the spine-chilling rumours of Jack's 'eyes of Hell'. He let out a terrific scream and, within seconds, windows and doors all over the neighbourhood were opening. Jack waved his fist threateningly at the boy, then rocketed over the roofs of Commercial Road.

When the boy regained his senses, he was cross-quizzed and interrogated repeatedly by the authorities about his hair-raising encounter. His inquisitors wondered what the significance of the embroidered 'W' was and some conjectured that it was the initial of the Marquis of Waterford, widely known as a mischievous prankster. The Marquis was also something of an athlete, but his physical capabilities could obviously not be equated with Jack's superhuman stunts. Even the fittest man on earth could not leap 25 feet into the air, as Jack was alleged to have done many times. In 1859, the Marquis met his death after falling from a horse but the reports of the 'Leaping Terror' continued to pour into London police stations and newspaper offices. Spring-Heeled Jack was still at large.

He made an appearance in Lincolnshire one evening,

where he shattered the rural tranquillity by leaping over thatched cottages wearing a sheepskin. A mob confronted the laughing leaper and blasted him with shotguns at point-blank range but their firepower had no effect. When the buckshot hit Jack, it sounded as if it was hitting a metal bucket.

One night, in January 1879, a man driving his cart across a bridge on the Birmingham and Liverpool Junction Canal on his way home from Woodcote, Shropshire, was startled when a black, hideous creature, with large luminous eyes, leapt out of a tree and landed on the horse's back. The man tried to knock the beast off the horse with his whip but the creature managed to hold onto the frightened animal, which broke into a wild gallop. When the man got the cart back under control, the 'thing' darted high into the air and disappeared into the trees.

By the end of the 19th century, the geographical pattern of sightings of Spring-Heeled Jack indicated that he was moving in a westerly direction across England, towards Lancashire. In 1888, the blackguard turned up in Liverpool, where he was seen hurtling down from the roof of High Park Street reservoir. Soon afterwards, Jack gave a typical performance when he was seen clinging to the steeple of St Francis Xavier's in Salisbury Street. Before the awe-struck crowds filling the streets below, Jack jumped suicidally from the steeple and landed somewhere behind a row of houses. The mobs stampeded to see where he had landed and a rumour spread that he had killed himself. The Evertonians were subsequently startled when a helmeted, egg-headed figure in white, suddenly ran down the street towards them. As several women in the crowd screamed, Jack lifted his arms and flew over William Henry Street. After that memorable night, Jack made himself scarce for years.

Then late one evening, in 1920, a man dressed in a radiant-white costume, was seen by scores of witnesses in Warrington's Horsemarket Street, jumping back and forth from the pavements to the rooftops. He finally cleared the town's railway station in one mighty leap and was never seen in the north of England again. In 1948, the last recorded sighting of a sinister leaping figure, took place at Monmouth in South Wales. Locals who saw a strange-looking man leaping over a stream near Watery Lane, surmised that he was the spectre of a man who had drowned in the stream but the few Welsh folk who were unfortunate enough to encounter the leaper at close quarters, swore he was too solid to be a phantom.

Who or what was Spring-Heeled Jack? Many bizarre theories have been advanced to answer the question. Some said he was an insane acrobatic fire-eater, others believed him to be a dressed-up kangaroo, or a mad inventor who had built an anti-gravity device. One theory that does fit the facts is the alien hypothesis. If we suppose that Jack was from another planet, this would explain his alien appearance, behaviour, his jumping ability and his longevity.

The descriptions of Spring-Heeled Jack's fiery gaze seem to indicate that he had retro-reflective eyes, similar to a cat, which would suggest he was ideally suited to a nocturnal environment. His fire-breathing is not easily explained. Perhaps what Jack really breathed into his victims eyes was not real fire (for none of those attacked suffered burns, nor did the 'fire' ever singe a single hair), but a type of phosphor.

Another unanswered riddle is the fate of Jack. If he was a misunderstood alien, marooned in our world, was he finally rescued, or did he die a lonely death here? We will probably never know.

A PICTURE OF EVIL

Early in March 1995, a young couple, Denise and Joe, moved into a house in Liverpool. The house dated back to early Victorian times and had a welcoming atmosphere with a lovely panoramic view of the river from an upstairs window.

A fortnight after they had moved in, the couple heard strange noises coming from the attic. Denise was naturally scared but Joe pointed out that it was probably just the wind rattling the windows and he went up with a torch, just to make sure. He was right, the wind was rattling the loose frame of the skylight; there was nothing ghostly about the sounds after all. Denise came up into the attic and Joe remarked, "God, this place has a real musky smell."

Noticing a large wooden tea-chest, Denise grabbed the torch and, aiming its beam at the chest, opened it. The box contained bundles of cobwebbed documents and two pictures framed with ornate gold borders.

One was of a slim man, about 30, with dark hair and a Van Dyck beard, the other was of a plump-looking woman with honey-blonde hair and a cheerful, rosy-cheeked face. As Denise shone the torch at these paintings, the attic door burst open and a terrific howling sound, like a gale-force wind, whistled through the doorway. The door then slammed shut with such a force that dust and loose plaster fell from the ceiling of the attic. Denise trembled and Joe hugged her reassuringly.

"It's okay, Denise; it was just a draught, that's all."

Denise swore. "That was not a draught! Let's get out of here."

She dropped the paintings back in the large tea-chest and left the attic.

In bed that night, Joe was soon asleep but Denise lay awake, startled by a distinctive creaking noise; the sound of a floorboard outside the bedroom door. She peered over the duvet, staring in horror as the handle of the bedroom door twisted and the door slowly opened a few inches. She screamed and shook Joe awake.

"Someone's outside on the landing. They opened the door," she gasped. "Don't go!" Denise pleaded as Joe went over to the door and peeped outside. He looked both ways but there was only darkness. However, Joe did notice a peculiar musky smell. Assuming that the gales outside had opened the door, he grumpily returned to bed.

A few days later, when Joe was at work, Denise was lying in bed with influenza. Feeling really ill, she tried to read a book but, around three in the afternoon, something weird began to happen. Denise heard the faint sounds of music coming from somewhere nearby. She put the book down on the floor and listened to the faint strains of a harpsichord. Suddenly, a strange darkness came over the room. All light from the bedroom window seemed to fade, as if a black cloud had descended on the house, so dark she had to switch on the bedside lamp. To her horror she heard the floorboard creak outside her bedroom door. At that precise moment, the bedside lamp went out with a clinking sound, as if the bulb had gone.

Denise felt fear course through her body. She sat up in bed, staring at the bedroom door, as the handle began to turn, just as it had done the other night. She felt her heart pounding as the door creaked open, wider and wider.

As the figure entered the room, Denise recognised him immediately as the man depicted in the oil painting in the attic. He had straight black, shoulder-length hair, dark menacing eyes with thick eyebrows, a Van Dyck beard and he wore a black velvet coat with white cuffs. She was so afraid, she could not speak. The stranger's teeth were yellow and crooked. In a refined voice he whispered, "Hello, Miss."

He walked across the room and leaned over Denise. Terrified, she could not turn away. The man's dark eyes seemed to have a hypnotic pull on her. She noticed the dank, musky smell he gave off, the same odour of decay that had greeted her when she had opened the large tea-chest in the attic. The stranger stooped down and kissed Denise's face. She trembled as his ice-cold face pressed against hers, his beard and moustache bristling against her cheeks as he caressed her. Suddenly, the intruder announced, "Oh, to be alive again, that *would* be something," and he kissed and bit her neck. Denise suddenly regained the power to move and, picking up the bedside lamp, tried to hit her attacker on the head with it.

The stranger glanced up, his eyes glaring with a look of pure evil. He clenched his crooked teeth and snarled, "Don't you dare!"

At that moment, the doorbell rang out and the startled stranger fled from the bedroom in one swift movement, like a shadow. Denise ran out of the bedroom in her nightdress and almost fell down the stairs. She opened the door and saw, to her relief, that it was Joe, who had been sent home because he, too, seemed to be coming down with the flu.

When Joe saw the state Denise was in - and the large lovebite on her neck, he became concerned. "Denise? What's going on?" he asked, and by the angry look on his face he was demanding an answer.

Denise gave him a blow-by-blow account of the assault and said she was leaving the house that very moment. Joe persuaded her to stay and phoned the police. Having searched the house thoroughly to find there was no stranger on the premises, the police suggested that Denise had a high temperature and had probably hallucinated the whole incident.

"Then who did this then?" She screamed and pointed to the red lovebite on her neck.

The police said nothing but one of the officers glanced at Joe and smiled.

"I didn't do it," Joe assured the presumptive officer, and watched the policemen leave.

That evening, Joe and two of his friends searched the house again. One of his mates, Alex, opened the tea-chest and looked at the paintings.

"What are these?" he asked.

Joe recalled that Denise had told him that the attacker looked exactly like the man in the painting. "One's of some weird-looking fellow and the other's of a woman."

"No, this one's blank," Alex replied and showed the painting to Joe.

It was just a dark green background. The man with the Van Dyck beard had vanished from the painting. Joe tried to rationalise this bizarre occurrence and wondered if fungus had recently corrupted the painting but he knew that was impossible. On the back of the painting, a label with faded writing said, 'Richard Brownrigg, musician'.

Joe remembered that Denise had heard the eerie harpsichord music before the man came into her bedroom and, that night, the couple left to live with Denise's parents until they found accommodation in another area of the city. The house where they lived is still said to be haunted, according to the present residents, who are not aware of the weird paintings in the attic. Recently, at 2 o'clock in the morning, the faces of a dark, bearded man and a blonde woman were seen staring out of a second storey window...

THE BLACK ELVES OF BLOODY ACRE

This is a very puzzling tale that has never been satisfactorily explained. It concerns one George Winter Warr, who was the Vicar of Childwall, at All Saints Church, from 1870 until his death at the age of eighty-one in 1895. Reverend Warr was known for his fire and brimstone sermons, many of which were addressed specifically at the drinkers of the parish, because Warr was a strict teetotaller.

In September 1874, there was nothing short of an epidemic of drunkenness in Liverpool, which spurred on the self-righteous reverend to increase his efforts to reform his parishioners. No one was spared, and he aimed one of his firebrand sermons at several professional parishioners, including a doctor, and a local police detective, whom he accused of drinking on duty. Facing All Saints Church, there was, and still is, a beautiful old pub called the Childwall Abbey Hotel, but our reverend deemed this drinking establishment to be too near the church for his liking. Whenever

Warr walked past the pub, he would look through the latticed windows to glare and fume at the 'sinners' within, and the parishioners enjoying a drink in the Childwall Abbey would turn guiltily away.

One Sunday, in the spring of 1874, Warr delivered a damning sermon, in which he actually named the Childwall Abbey pub as a den of iniquity, and he told the congregation: 'When the wine is in, the wit is out! Bacchus [the god of wine and alcoholic beverages in general] has drowned more men in this town than Neptune!' On the following Wednesday, an anonymous letter, obviously penned by some prankster with the design of invoking a reaction, was received by the fanatical vicar. It read:

Your Holiness,

You are forever condemning the drinkers of your parish, but people close to you know you're but a hypocrite of the worst type, and we know you've emptied many a bottle of wine behind closed doors after Mass. Your fine words dress ill deeds! Pretended holiness is a double iniquity, and there is no rogue like the Godly rogue! You live off the very people you condemn, but you're quick enough to pass the basket among us, aren't you? You're like a fox in the pulpit, preaching to the geese!

He who buys land buys many stones, he who buys meat buys many bones, and he who buys eggs buys many shells - but he who is wise enough to buy good ale, buys nothing else.

May the Lord reveal your many sins to the parish,

(signed) One Who Tells the Truth

Instead of ignoring the anonymous letter, the vicar became so enraged by its contents, he left his house and stormed into the Childwall Abbey pub, which was only playing host to a handful of drinkers at that time, and most of them were farmhands slaking their thirst at noon after a heavy morning in the fields. Few of them were literate enough to write their own names, never mind pen a vitriolic letter of such savage criticism. Warr ranted and raved and promised eternal damnation for the 'faceless coward' who had written the poison pen letter, but his bombastic accusations were met only by blank stares and bemused expressions from the bumpkins.

One Sunday evening in the late summer of that year, at around 9pm, an Irishman named Michael Maloney came stumbling into the pub, his face as white as a sheet, and his hands trembling as he placed his money on the bar counter. He said he'd just 'seen things' across the road in a field adjacent to the graveyard of All Saints Church. Maloney had foolishly taken a short-cut across 'the Acre' as the locals called it. This was a mysterious acre of land that had always been left uncultivated, because of an ancient law that strictly prohibited its use. Weeds, brambles and wild flowers run rampant there, even today. Some call this field the Bloody Acre, but no local historian can tell you why. Even Romany people travelling through Childwall have refused to camp upon the Bloody Acre. Perhaps the gypsies, with their well-reported powers of clairvoyance, can sense something very unsavoury about the field.

Everyone in the pub urged the Irishman to tell what he had seen, but he just kept repeating, 'I couldn't describe 'em, and I'm too scared to say what I seen, in case they comes after me.'

In the end, the curious locals plied Maloney with sufficient drink to loosen his tongue, enough for him to make a peculiar claim: 'I saw the black elves, over yonder in Bloody Acre, sure as I'm standin' 'ere.'

There was a ripple of hollow forced laughter from a few of those present, but then a cold draught wafted through the pub, across the back of everyone's neck, and silence descended on the assembled company. Maloney was a religious man and always wore his rosary, and he undid the top buttons of his shirt, clutched the rosary beads, and said, 'I swear upon these 'oly beads that I saw black elves... 'orrible they were!' And there were gasps from some of the drinkers, for they knew now that the Irishman was telling the truth.

Maloney downed a shot of whiskey, then, full of dutch courage, suggested a midnight torch hunt for the elves. Many of the drinkers, also full of ale and spirits, obtained flaming torches, and en masse invaded the cemetery across the road. Staggering and swaying, they walked in a disorderly procession along the low sandstone cemetery wall to see if any of the black elves were knocking about. A fox bolted past the motley file of torch-bearers, and a man fell off the wall in fright, landing amongst a tangle of brambles.

Suddenly, Reverend Warr turned up in his pyjamas,

giving them all the fright of their lives. Infuriated by the midnight hunt for elves, of all things, he drove the superstitious locals out of the churchyard, telling them there were no such things as black elves in the Acre and to stop being so stupid and gullible.

'Well, I begs to differ there, you see, Father Almighty!' said Maloney, almost setting fire to a friend's clothes with his wavering torch. Reverend Warr accused the Irishman of blasphemy, but Maloney went on unabashed, 'I am prepared to swear on a stack of Bibles ... go and get 'em, Vicar, go on! I, Michael Patrick Maloney, swear by Almighty God that I was chased by elves dressed in black, and armed to the teeth they was, in that field yonder!'

'There's nothing in that field but hares and foxes you stupid drunken Irishman!' said Warr.

Maloney took offence and hopped down from the cemetery wall. 'Oh, I'm not 'avin' that, your holiness. Stupid Irishman, eh? Well, put your money where your mouth is and go across yon acre yerself then! Go on! Prove me a liar!' Maloney said, laying down a challenge, which the vicar had no choice but to accept, because over twenty parishioners were present.

'Very well,' he replied, 'I shall go forth into the Acre tomorrow evening, and put an end to all this silliness; now kindly leave this hallowed ground and get to your beds like good Christian men.'

At around 10pm on the following evening, Warr, true to his word, entered the Bloody Acre from the eastern side, via a farmer's field where Hartsbourne Avenue now runs. As a concession, he was allowed to carry a torch which had been dipped in tar. About thirty people watched the vicar squeeze through a gap in the hedge as he entered the mysterious field, which was an overgrown jungle choked with ferns, nettles and weeds. At the other side of the acre, on Score Lane, Maloney waited with a hip flask of whiskey on this cold evening. Dozens of locals waited with him, expecting to see the brave vicar emerge from the field within a few minutes. An enterprising baker sold cakes (still hot from the oven) to the curious mob, and Mrs Rimmer, the landlady of the Childwall Abbey, served alfresco ale to the crowd. It was turning into quite an event and everyone was enjoying the party atmosphere.

Just a few minutes after he had ventured into the acre, the flame of the vicar's torch went out. Half an hour went by, and Reverend George Winter Warr still hadn't shown up. A smug Maloney addressed the crowd. 'Didn't I tell yous there were evil tings afoot in that field? And didn't the Reverend call me a liar? So 'e did.'

A soldier named Talbot, a policeman named Jones, and a butcher named Williams, eventually went into the acre to search for the overdue vicar, but they couldn't find any trace of him. Others joined in the search, but were forced to give up by midnight because of an unseasonal downpour.

That night, the Childwall Abbey pub did a roaring trade, packed with members of the search party, and hordes of curious people who had come to learn more of the vicar's seemingly supernatural disappearance. Michael Maloney didn't have to put his hand in his pocket once that night, because everyone who wanted to hear first hand what he had seen in the acre bought him a drink. Maloney chalked his impression of the black elves on the darts Scoreboard, and started to tell ghost stories as the winds of Childwall wailed like a banshee and the rain battered the pub windows.

At nigh on three in the morning, Mrs Rimmer was telling the drinkers they'd have to go home, when there was a loud knocking on the pub door. Everyone went deathly quiet. A tall tailor named Loftus peeped out the window - but could see no one at the door. Yet three more knocks came in quick succession, followed by a groaning voice. The bolt was drawn back by Mrs Rimmer, and everyone backed away from the door.

'Who is it?' Mrs Rimmer called out. There was no answer. She slowly opened the door. Michael Maloney hid behind the bar counter, then peeped over it at the door that was steadily opening. 'They've come for me! Don't let 'em in!' he cried in a slurred voice.

The Reverend Warr lay on the ground outside the pub door in a sorry state. A long tail of his grey hair, which was usually neatly combed over to conceal his extensive baldness, was dangling on one side of his head, and his trousers were missing, as were his shoes and one of his socks. His black clerical jacket was slashed in several places and his white collar was all askew. The crucifix which he always wore round his neck had somehow had its crossbeam broken off and the upright was bent into a horseshoe shape. Warr's eyes were bulging with fear.

Three burly drinkers picked the vicar up off the road and carried him as decorously as they could into the pub, and gently placed him in a padded-leather fireside chair, where, against his will, they administered brandy to him. When he had regained his senses he began to mutter strange things. 'The devils!' he kept repeating over and over. Then, all of a sudden, a hush came over the pub as a rain of taps was heard on the front door. Mr Loftus looked out the window and yelled, 'Gloriana! Look at this!' Everyone rushed to the windows.

In the pale summer predawn light, hundreds of tiny figures, all about three feet in height, were swarming down the cobbled road, some of them carrying spears. They were as black and shiny as a death watch beetle in their strange armour, as they streamed past the pub, headed for the acre, and when they reached that accursed piece of land, they disappeared into it.

From that day until the day he died, in December 1895, aged eighty-one, the vicar refused to tell anyone what had happened to him that evening when he tried to cross the Bloody Acre in Childwall.

Bloody Acre is still uncultivated, and few will venture into it, even today.

THE OLD SWAN VAMPIRE

As astonishing as it sounds, Liverpool has quite a history of those mysterious fanged creatures of the night - vampires. At the junction of the city's Rupert Lane, Breck Road, Heyworth Street and Everton Road, there lies the skeleton of a man who bit his wife, drank her blood, and, until he had a wooden stake thrust through his body, and was re-interred face down, allegedly rose regularly from his crossroads grave after dark, to terrorise his victims. Thankfully that was all back in 1680, but I have in my files dozens of such reported incidents, stretching right up to the present day.

In the summer of 1866, a gory, shocking murder took place in Liverpool at 14 Wood Grove, which now exists only as a weed-carpeted cul-de-sac off Edge Lane, beside a derelict garage. Yet it was here, in May 1866, that one John Thomas Moss, an outspoken twenty-seven-year-old denouncer of the Christian religion, stayed with his beautiful twenty-five-year-old cousin, Mrs 'Nan' Train, a woman who felt abandoned by her husband Thomas Train, a ship's purser. Moss was rumoured to be a vampire, and people claimed that they had seen his eyes 'light up' like burning coals at the mere mention of Jesus Christ. Despite this, women found themselves unaccountably attracted to him and some even offered to walk out of stable marriages, just so they could wait on him.

For many years Moss lived in Sydney, Australia, as a cigar manufacturer, but then something must have happened to him, because the John Moss who returned to Liverpool in the early 1860s was not the same happy young fellow who had gone to seek his fortune and a new life in Australia. Very strange stories began to circulate about a suicide attempt at the Albert Dock, and how Moss's lifeless body, dredged from the salty mud at night by some watchmen, was apparently revived by moonlight - one of the many uncanny biological capabilities of a vampire.

Mrs Train had lived under the same roof as Moss for a few years as a lodger, before he was to horrifically murder her. In the Spring of 1866 she and her cousin moved from Elm Vale in Bootle, to Wood Grove, in Liverpool's Old Swan district, and even Mrs Train's husband did not seem to mind Moss's constant presence in their household. It appears that when the cousins were children, they vowed never to separate and, pricking palms and mixing their blood, they ritually sealed their promise.

The only witness to the ghastly murder was twenty-year-old Margaret Golding, Mrs Train's loyal maidservant. She had bravely stayed with her mistress as an enraged Moss had pursued her around the Old Swan residence wielding a hatchet. Mr Train, as usual, was away at sea when these events took place, and Mrs Train was slaughtered because she refused to give Moss a ring, and, more importantly, would not desert her husband and marry him. He ranted on about Hell and the Almighty, loudly rejecting both, and the maid Golding trembled in a corner as his eyes began to glow "as if on fire".

In the frenzied attack, Moss brought the hatchet down on his cousin's head repeatedly, taking off her nose as the blade embedded itself deep in her skull. During one of the ferocious hatchet blows, Mrs Train's eyeball flew out its socket. The maid was so traumatised she was unable to scream, and she found herself running down the stairs, almost in slow motion, as terror got the better of her legs. Behind her, she heard what she would later describe as the sound of a butcher's cleaver hitting bone. When the neighbours and police stormed the house, they found Moss lying in an immense pool of blood on the kitchen floor. He had slit his own throat, and according to the coroner, he had known exactly which arteries to cut in his neck to affect an instantaneous death.

Rumours of vampirism, the stigma of suicide (deemed unholy in those times), and the brutal murder, led to John Thomas Moss's body being buried in unconsecrated ground between St Anne's Church, Stanley, and the cattle market. The body was staked, they say, with wood cut from the oldest tree in Liverpool - the Allerton Oak, in Calderstones - which still stands to this day, estimated to be aged over a thousand years old. However, despite these precautions, as you may have guessed, that was not the end of Moss.

Moss's caped form was seen over many evenings in June 1866, lurking in St Mary's Cemetery, Kirkdale, the resting place of his beloved murder victim Mrs Train. A teenaged courting couple, kissing beneath a willow tree in the cemetery, were attacked by the cloaked fiend, but they both managed to make their escape and raised the alarm at a nearby inn. A small posse turned out to hunt down the ghoul, who was seen jumping straight over a five-foot wall at the cemetery, his cloak billowing out behind him.

He also stalked the young maid Margaret Golding in December of that year. The maid had been having terrible vivid blood-spattered nightmares in which she relived the horrors of seeing her mistress being hacked to death. One night she awoke in the early hours in a bedroom at a friend's house in Liverpool's Aigburth district, and felt a strong urge to go to her window. Through a glacial fog, she could see a pale-faced man in black, wearing an opera cloak, but no hat on such an inclement night, standing on the pavement, staring fixedly up at her window. Margaret's heart almost stopped when the man's eyes started to pulsate with a glowing reddish orange tint. Oh, no! Not again, she thought as she recognised John Thomas Moss. As the girl turned and ran out of the room, she heard the window rattling violently behind her, as if someone was trying to prise it open from the outside, but she was too afraid to check, and she awakened the entire household with her screams.

Understandably, Margaret's friend believed the poor

girl had suffered nothing more than a particularly lucid nightmare, caused no doubt by the traumatic memories of her employer's horrific murder, but over the next three fog-bound nights, the evil-looking shade of John Thomas Moss was seen by other members of the household, looking in through a basement window of the house, and, according to a neighbour, the cloaked stalker had even been seen on the roof of the Georgian dwelling, apparently trying to break open the skylight window. In the end, a local Catholic priest blessed the house, sprinkled Holy water over the threshold, and gave Margaret a Bible and a Rosary to keep on her bedside table at all times. That seemed to do the trick, and Moss relinquished his sinister pursuit of the former maid.

The Reverend Thomas Gardner, incumbent of St Anne's Church, Stanley, which overlooked the site where Moss had been buried, staked and face down in an unmarked grave on wasteland, warned his congregation in a chilling sermon, about the dangers of succumbing to the dark powers of evil as Moss had. He talked of lost souls wandering the darkest reaches of the earth after death, of demonic persecution and possession, and that other nerve-jangling topic that was doing the rounds in his parish - vampirism.

People living within a mile of the site where Moss lay in his unchristian grave took to taking crosses with them to their beds and hanging garlic from their bedposts, and for many months the churches of the district were guaranteed to be packed every Sunday, as parishioners sought divine protection from the self-resurrected Moss. Eventually the vampire mania subsided, but even today, there are occasional sightings of a solid, carnate ghost in a cloak, who has been seen in the area of Edge Lane, close to the street where Moss butchered his cousin and then took his own life.

OF UNSOUND MIND

One afternoon in April 1967, thirty-five-year-old Marianne Hill entered her Dovecot home laden with carrier bags after a trip to the shops. She unpacked the shopping and put it all away and then went upstairs to get something from her bedroom, little suspecting that she was in for the shock of her life. For there, hanging from the light fitting, was the body of an eerily familiar woman. In fact, that woman looked exactly like herself and was even wearing her clothes. Mrs Hill shot out of the bedroom, down the stairs and out into the street, quite unable to scream.

An off-duty postman came upon his distressed neighbour wandering in the road, occasionally gazing up at her bedroom window with an expression of utter terror.

"Hey! What's the matter, love?" he asked. "You look like you've had a bit of a fright, you alright?."

"In my bedroom ... woman ... hanging ... she's in my

bedroom ... hanging" said the distraught woman, incoherently, pointing to her upstairs window.

"What's in your bedroom, Mrs Hill," coaxed the postman, gently. "Come on now, you can tell me all about it."

"She's hanging from the light - and she looks - she looks just like me!"

After Mrs Hill had finally managed to stammer out this somewhat unintelligible reply, the postman gently shepherded her into his own house, and then ran to the nearest telephone box to alert the police and summon an ambulance - just in case the hanged woman - if indeed there was one - was still alive.

Having left his wife looking after Mrs Hill, the postman then went across to her home and upstairs into the bedroom, where his neighbour's 'look-alike' was supposedly to be found hanging. He braced himself against what he thought he might encounter. But there was no corpse dangling from the light, or anywhere else for that matter, yet he did come across something very bizarre and equally creepy. Hanging by a flex noose from the light fitting was a mannequin of some kind. It had on a wig that mimicked the exact same hairstyle and hair colouring as Marianne Hill, and the clothes which the dummy wore had been removed from her wardrobe - right down to the underwear and footwear.

The police turned up and because they couldn't find any evidence of a break-in or other crime as such, they dismissed the whole thing as a rather distasteful practical joke, presumably perpetrated by someone with whom Mrs Hill had had an argument. It was April after all, commented the postman, who also concluded that the whole thing must have been some late April fool stunt.

When Mrs Hill was sufficiently recovered, she was persuaded to return to the house, accompanied by the postman and his wife for moral support. They went up to the bedroom with her and there she studied the mannequin's face. Whoever had put the mannequin there had gone to a lot of trouble to make it look authentic. They had not only stuck a pair of her false eyelashes on it, but had even carefully coated the dummy's lips with Marianne's own lipstick.

Not surprisingly, Marianne was very badly shaken by the hanging dummy incident, and slept on the sofa that night, leaving the lights on in the hall, living room and kitchen. Throughout the night she had the pricklish sensation of being watched by someone, and she kept the curtains and blinds drawn until well after sunrise, but otherwise, the night was uneventful.

Three days later, an electricity man called at 2 o'clock in the afternoon and told Marianne that he had come to change her meter under the stairs. She was glad of the company, as she was still feeling shaky and she offered the electrician a cup of tea. He politely declined, then asked her if she had left any electrical appliances on all night, as he scrutinised the dials of the electric meter. She nodded and admitted that she had left the lights on in the hallway, kitchen and living room throughout the last three nights.

"What for?" asked the electricity man. "D'you always do that? It must cost you a fortune when you get your 'leccy bill."

"No, I usually switch all the lights off when I go to bed, but something terrible happened the other day and now I'm afraid of the dark. I know it's silly."

Mrs Hill went on to describe the shock of finding the mannequin hanging in her bedroom, and the electricity man, a small square-shouldered individual, with shoulder-length raven hair and a thick black 'gunslinger' moustache, was rather unsympathetic and couldn't help but grin when she mentioned the underwear. She was cross at first, but then realised that it must have sounded comical to him.

"Yeah, I suppose that would have given me the creeps as well," he said, suppressing a smirk as he checked the fuse-box.

"Do you think it's been somebody's idea of a joke?" asked Marianne rather tetchily.

Despite being rather annoyed that he seemed to think the whole business funny, she found herself being strangely attracted to the electricity man, which surprised her, as she usually went for much taller men.

"Probably," the electrician replied, whilst opening a small canvas tool bag. He rummaged around in it for a while and then said, "Do me a favour, will you, love?"

"Yeah, sure, what?" said Marianne squinting into the dark cubby hole under the stairs.

"Can you go into the kitchen and make sure nothing's plugged in, and wait there till I shout you?"

"Yeah, sure."

Marianne Hill went off straight away and checked each of the electrical gadgets. She had to pull out one or two of the appliances to get at the plugs and the last thing to be unplugged was the electric toaster. She had been in the kitchen less than three minutes in all when she returned to the hallway, even though she hadn't heard the electrician call her - but he was nowhere to be seen. She went into the living room and looked out of the window, perhaps hoping to see him fetching his tools, or the replacement meter from his van. But there was no van outside and no electrician.

"I've turned everything off in the kitchen, like you said," she shouted, but there was no reply. She opened the front door, stepped outside, and looked both ways. He was still nowhere to be seen.

Marianne went back into her house, utterly perplexed, and went to look round upstairs. Perhaps he'd gone the toilet? No. the toilet was empty. She opened her bedroom door and gasped. There, on the bed, someone had carefully laid out her navy skirt and matching jacket, with a pair of her stockings positioned so that hey led from the skirt to a pair of shoes. The handle of what was subsequently identified as a long chef's knife, protruded from the bed. The blade had been driven through the front of the navy jacket and into the bedding. On the floor lay a collapsed hollow 'face'; the rubber mask, with a fine head of black hair attached and a moustache, had obviously been discarded by the so-called electrician. On the dressing table mirror, scrawled in lipstick in capital letters were the words: 'C*nt! They put me away because of you!'

Dizzy with fear, Marianne Hill backed out of her room, expecting the unbalanced impostor to come chasing after her. Steadying herself on the banister she descended the stairs and groped her way with difficulty to the front door. She tried to open it, but it had been bolted at the bottom. Then she heard the sly chuckling behind her and felt the sweaty hand grabbing at her hair. She screamed, bent down, and somehow managed to slide the bolt sideways and yank open the door. As she did so, the eerie voice behind her cried, "Now, now!"

Mrs Hill shot out of the house like a cork from a bottle, with just one thing on her mind - escape. She was oblivious to everything around her and was almost run down by a passing motorcyclist who had to swerve to avoid her. Passers-by went to her aid and the police arrived at the house within fifteen minutes. Who could blame them for being sceptical about the story? Just three days ago they had been called out to a suspected suicide, which turned out to be nothing more than a dangling mannequin. The knife in the mattress of Marianne's bed was dusted for fingerprints, but none were found. These days, the knife and discarded rubber mask would no doubt have provided the police with DNA samples, but in those days no such technology existed and anyway, it was all deemed to be an attention-seeking hoax, unworthy of such serious investigation.

But that is not the end of the story. Mrs Hill left Dovecot and moved to St Helens, where she stayed with her ex-husband for a while before moving to the Dingle. She wrote to me at BBC Radio Merseyside to try and make some sense of her experiences, and I must admit that I did not know what to make of it, and it stayed on my file, metaphorically gathering dust, as one of the many unsolved mysteries which come my way. However, three years afterwards, my interest in Marianne's story was revived when fifty-five-year-old Sheila emailed me with an another intriguing story...

In April, 1987, a little old lady knocked on the door of Sheila's Dovecot home one evening. She seemed confused and asked Sheila - who lived alone - if she could use her toilet. The old woman said she had been looking for an old friend's house and had lost her bearings - and apparently her memory. All she could remember was that her house was in a road in Huyton near Woolfall Heath. Sheila told her that she would phone her son and he would drive her home. She put the kettle on after waiting outside the toilet door for the old woman to come out.

"I'm just washing my hands," the old lady called from the other side of the toilet door. "I had a fall you see, dear."

As the kettle was beginning to boil, Sheila hurried up the stairs again and knocked on the toilet door, but got no answer. Fearing that the elderly visitor had collapsed, she tried the door, and it opened. The toilet was empty but the hot water tap was running in the wash basin. Sheila began to get suspicious about the old lady, and wondered if she was only pretending to be confused, when in fact she was actually a thief in disguise. So, Sheila crept on tiptoe towards her bedroom door. She turned the handle, trying not to make a sound. As the door opened a small white feather drifted on to her face. The Dovecot widow looked in dismay at the state of her room. The pillows had been ripped open, and the feathers were drifting down like a small blizzard - suggesting that this frenzied act was very, very recent! In the middle of the bed, a long carving knife had been plunged into the mattress.

What was going on? Where had the old woman disappeared to? Then Sheila noticed something out of the corner of her eye - lying on the floor was a crumpled head and neck, with stringy grey hair attached. Sheila recoiled but soon realised that the 'head' was actually a thin latex mask of an wrinkled old woman's visage, with a wig of grey hair attached, partially tied up in a small bun.

Something else troubled her. There was something missing from the room. A sickening thought suddenly crossed Sheila's mind. Her old cat Fifi was nowhere to be seen, yet she invariably slept curled up on her bed in the evenings. The fear she felt was so intense it was physical, and yet she was also furious at having been duped and her beloved pet threatened. Picking up a heavy metal framed picture of her late husband, she prepared herself to strike out at this weirdo who had invaded her house and taken advantage of her by pretending to be an old woman.

Steeling herself against what she might find inside, Sheila flung open her wardrobe doors, but there was nothing there except her clothes and shoes and a couple of handbags. Then she gingerly lifted the bedcovers and looked underneath the bed, dreading finding the creepy intruder. Instead, she found Fifi, cowering behind some old suitcases; the only other witness to the horrors of that evening.

Sheila cradled the cat in her arms and smothered her with kisses. She carried her downstairs, and then took her across the road to her friend's. The police were called out, but they couldn't find the intruder, despite going through the house with a fine-toothed comb. Sheila could not get her head round the way the impersonator had managed to get out of the house without passing her. He or she had definitely not escaped via the upstairs bedroom window, because it was still locked from the inside, and no one had been heard coming down the stairs.

About six months later, Sheila's son had to go into hospital for a minor operation, and one evening after visiting him, she boarded the bus, as usual, back to Huyton. Sitting on a seat facing her was an old man and there was something vaguely familiar about him. Sheila racked her brains but couldn't place him, but judging by the way he was looking at her, he certainly remembered her from somewhere. The old man suddenly got up, and she saw that he was very small for a man, and he disembarked at the next stop.

As the bus drove on, Sheila felt butterflies in her stomach, because it suddenly came to her where she had seen that man - he had undoubtedly been the person who had worn that thin latex mask that evening in April, whilst pretending to be a distraught old woman. His eyes had been the dead give away, together with his small build. When Sheila reached her stop, she hurried home, looking behind her every few seconds, in case the old oddball had followed her, and she sat up most of the night with the doors bolted and the windows securely locked. However, that night her fears proved groundless.

Indeed, she saw no more of the sinister female impersonator, but in the following year, on 14 February, she received a Valentine's Day card from someone who signed himself as, 'You know who (three sheets to the wind) xxx'.

'Three sheets to the wind' is an old expression, originally meaning 'very drunk' but in Liverpool the phrase is usually used to denote lunacy, and Sheila believes that the strange old man she saw on the bus that night was definitely of unsound mind.

Sheila has since moved to Crosby, and as far as I know, there have been no further strange intrusions into her former house in Huyton.

So what is the connection between Marianne's and Sheila's stories? I hear you asking. You have probably already guessed. Yes, that house is the very same one where Marianne Hill lived twenty years before Sheila. Their experiences, taken together, make a very unusual case, but someone out there with knowledge of that building can probably throw some light upon it.

SHIP OF THE SEVEN MURDERS

On 9 May 1828, a ship called the *Mary Russell* sailed from Barbados to Cork carrying a cargo of sugar. Her captain, William Stewart, was known as a very kind and gentle man, but for reasons that are still a mystery to this day, in mid-ocean, William Stewart lost his sanity.

His mental deterioration appeared to have started with increasingly frequent and terrible nightmares. He claimed that something evil was hovering over his bunk when he woke up. His devastating nightmares grew progressively worse, and the captain's mental health became increasingly unstable.

On 22 June, Captain Stewart summoned his crew, one by one, into his cabin. Each member of the crew was in turn bludgeoned to death by the crazed skipper. The only survivor was a Liverpool man. Stewart was found guilty of the seven murders but was declared insane and committed to an asylum.

People wondered what had happened to the so-called Ship of the Seven Murders. In actual fact, the ship was renamed *Rose Hart*, but such was her reputation, no one would buy her. She was finally sold at Cork Harbour to a young mariner named Captain John Delaney, who was from Douglas on the Isle of Man.

In July 1832, the newly-named *Rose Hart* sailed from

New York to northern Italy with a cargo of petroleum and a crew of eight. One of the crew was a thirty-seven-year-old Liverpool man named Richard Davies. Captain Delaney was reading his bible in his cabin around midnight, halfway through the voyage across the Atlantic, when a Force 8 gale struck the ship, and forks of lightning danced around the dramatic seascape. There were unholy screams from the captain's cabin. When the cook went to investigate what the matter was, he discovered Captain Delaney convulsing and shaking on the floor, foaming at the mouth. What was most disturbing was the fact that his eyes had turned entirely white; his pupils and cornea were no longer visible.

Three more members of the crew entered the cabin to investigate the piercing screams that were echoing along the ship's corridors. The first mate, a Mr Gill, bent over Delaney, when suddenly, the captain leapt upright and punched him directly in the face, shattering his nose. The captain then managed to bolt from his cabin and made his way frantically into the cargo hold. There, he grabbed the ship's axe and tried to smash the hull. He tried to hole the ship whilst simultaneously yelling out dementedly and incoherently.

The ship's cook attempted to wrestle the axe from Delaney. During the struggle, the captain managed to grab hold of some sort of docker's hook and shoved its point under the cook's chin, its sharp tip dimpling his flesh. Suddenly the tip of the hook protruded obscenely from the cook's screaming mouth, like a fish on a line. Delaney seemed to be possessed with double strength. He roared as he lifted the cook high above his head and hitched the hook over a ceiling beam. The cook's shrieks wilted as he passed out in agony, his body limp and hanging grotesquely for all to see.

Another crewman went down into the hold and was horrified to discover the cook's swaying and blood-soaked body dangling before him. Delaney grabbed the axe again and launched it directly into the crewman's back. He died a bloody death in minutes.

Crewman Patrick Render then tried to attack the rampant captain with a knife. The enraged Delaney swiped again and sliced off Render's kneecap with the axe, and in an appalling act of sadism, he stabbed his finger through Render's eyeball as he writhed in agony before him. Before Render passed out with shock, he managed to ram the knife between Captain Delaney's shoulder blades, but the captain appeared not to feel a thing and remained undeterred, without any sign of weakening. He lunged forward, unstoppable, and attacked Render's groin. His inhuman attack was extended far beyond obscenity as he chopped and hacked at his victim to perform a brutal castration.

While the captain was engaged in this hideous and savage rampage, his face appeared unfamiliar to those who witnessed it. It seemed to have somehow changed, as if he was possessed. After just thirty minutes, there were only three crew member's left surviving. In sheer, petrified panic they fled on to the deck, closely chased by the demonic Captain Delaney. These poor remaining men were Gill, who attempted to stifle the blood pouring from his broken nose; a young crewman named Williams, who had lost two fingers in the axe assault; and the Liverpool shiphand Richard Davies.

As the thunder rolled and the lightning flashed through the torrential rain, young Williams slipped on the rain-lashed deck, impeding his desperate getaway. Captain Delaney lifted the axe, poised and ready to kill him, but first mate Gill rushed forward and attacked Delaney, punching him twice in the face and somehow managing to dislodge the axe from his menacing and manic grip. Gill was out of breath but mustered enough strength to swing the axe at Delaney, but his grip was not tight enough and it slipped from his hand. The unleashed axe flew through the air and over the rails, flailing into the raging sea. What happened next made young Williams and Mr Davies queasy and faint with fear.

Delaney's frenzied attack had not lessened in its ferocity and he seized Gill's head in a vice-like grip. Violently forcing his hand in to the man's mouth, with a great effort he wrenched Gill's jaw wide apart. The jaw cracked, sinews were uprooted, and Gill's body dropped down hard, twitching spasmodically as his tongue writhed uncontrollably.

Delaney's rage was still not quenched. He moved on to his next casualty and picked up the young cabin boy Williams. Throttling him, he threw the boy's weakly resisting body over the rail into the storm-tossed sea as if he were a rag doll. The mad mariner then closed in on Richard Davies and the Liverpudlian stumbled backwards on to the bowsprit, the long beam at the front of the ship. He crawled along it away from Delaney, who was more manic than before and foaming at the mouth again. The man's hands were heavily bloodstained, and his protruding eyes had heavy, dark circles around them. To Davies, he looked like the devil himself. The captain followed closely and climbed on to the bowsprit. Davies retreated away from this lunging beast until he was clinging on to just the ropes. He could go no further - there was just a watery grave below him now.

"Lord, please deliver me from this devil," Davies howled in desperation.

Almost immediately, before Davies' fearful eyes, the captain's face seemed to alter. His expression dropped and softened and he appeared dazed and confused, as if he had just snapped out of a hypnotic trance. He limply slid back down the bowsprit and landed on the deck, weak beyond exhaustion.

Back on land, Delaney was charged with the murders, and so was Davies, because the court believed that two men must have been jointly responsible. At the subsequent trial, the jury asked: "How on earth could one man wipe out seven men single-handedly?"

In the end Davies was cleared due to a technical point and Delaney was deemed insane and committed to an asylum in London. One night he was heard screaming in his cell, and when the warders looked through the peephole in the door, they discovered that some kind of invisible force was hurling John Delaney up in the air and against the walls. A week later he died in his sleep. During the post mortem, the coroner was puzzled to discover a strange red marking outlined on the dead captain's back which resembled a long claw-like hand.

REAPER AT THE ROADSIDE

The rainy Sunday night of 12 August will remain embedded in the memory of a certain retired bricklayer named Gene until his dying day. Upon that Sunday, at ten minutes to twelve, Gene swiftly drank his last vodka and tonic and left a public house in the district of Thingwall. He walked unsteadily through heavy rain to his Ford Cortina in the pub carpark, a little the worse for drink. He'd been drinking with friends at the pub since 7pm, and now, dangerously over the limit, he was to embark on the journey home to Noctorum.

After stalling the vehicle as he was leaving the car park, Gene switched on the car radio, which was tuned to Radio City. As the booming tone of the radio presenter's voice echoed around the empty car park, he quickly restarted the engine and was soon travelling up Barnston Road. Not only was he drunk, Gene was also speeding along as the rain lashed down. Suddenly, he noticed a man in black standing at the roadside, about two hundred yards up ahead of him. The figure looked like a policeman to Gene, so he slowed down and quickly turned down the volume on the radio. The car neared the silhouetted figure, and Gene was able to see that the person standing at the roadside was a black man, dressed in a black suit and a black polo neck sweater. He raised his arm as Gene's Cortina approached. The high intake of alcohol had made him feel quite charitable, and he did what he normally would never have done when sober - he stopped for a hitchhiker.

Before Gene could even lean over to unlock the passenger door, the man in black had entered the vehicle, yet he was certain that the passenger door had been locked. The stranger slammed shut the car door and relaxed back into his seat.

"Where do you want to go?" Gene inquired, with a slight slur in his voice.

"The roundabout, up ahead," the stranger answered, speaking in a low voice, without even turning to face the driver.

Gene clumsily fumbled with the clutch control, and as the Cortina shuddered and moved off, the man announced: "I have to pick a child up as well."

"You what?" Gene muttered, confused.

"I'm Death."

The man turned at last to face Gene.

Gene realised that he had foolishly let a stranger into his vehicle, and that, worse still, he had obviously picked up a man with a serious mental problem. Gene immediately started to think of ways to get rid of his deluded passenger, who was beginning to make him feel very uncomfortable.

"You die tonight, Gene," he said. "And you kill a child at this roundabout."

Gene was more than uncomfortable by this stage

and desperately wanted to let the man out. He attempted to brake, but the car refused to stop. The gear stick was somehow locked in position, as was the steering wheel, which refused to turn, even a fraction of an inch. Gene swore, fear and panic rising up inside him, as he kept trying to stop the vehicle. No matter what Gene tried, the speedometer stayed at a steady 55 miles per hour. He took his foot off the accelerator pedal completely, but the car continued to speed along, heading straight towards a junction. Beyond that was the long stretch of Arrowe Park Road - then the roundabout. Beads of sweat formed on Gene's face and forehead, and an icy chill coursed through his body. It all felt like a nightmare, but one in which the dreamer cannot wake. He contemplated jumping from the vehicle and tried the door handle, but like the steering wheel, it refused to budge.

What unsettled Gene even more, was the car radio, which, instead of playing pop music, was now emitting dreary funereal organ music. Worse still, before him in the windscreen of the doomed Cortina, Gene could clearly see the faint images of two coffins materialising. One of the coffins was small, and Gene understood that it must be that of the child he was about to kill in the accident. With terror gripping his heart, he let go of the wheel and turned to the man who was undoubtedly the Grim Reaper himself, and pleaded for mercy.

"What about my children? My wife and kids?" sobbed Gene, verging on hysteria. But his desperate words fell upon deaf ears. Not a trace of mercy could be detected in the poker-faced personification of death, who simply replied: "At the back of your mind you knew this would happen. You knew that drinking and getting behind the wheel of a car would come to this one day, so you obviously think nothing of the people you are going to leave behind."

"Please, I'll do anything," Gene begged, staring in dread through the swaying windscreen wipers at the dark and dismal road ahead. The ghostly coffins then appeared to melt away to reveal the crying face of a distressed little girl. Gene's insides churned over. It was the face of his own, darling, seven-year-old daughter, Emily.

"When you die, your wife gradually gets over it, and she marries again. The man she marries ends up beating her, and also abuses Emily. Emily starts drinking, and she also ends up as an alcoholic."

The blunt delivery of such an awful scenario tormented Gene to breaking point. "Please, let me have another chance," he cried.

The Grim Reaper said nothing and Gene suddenly felt resigned to the terrible fate ahead of him. "Is there an after-life?" he asked, his voice quivering.

Again, his question was not answered. The cruel silence was almost palpable. Then, as the Cortina sped past the grand gates of Landican Cemetery, the sinister passenger suddenly spoke. "Here it comes," he said.

Up ahead, Gene could make out several cars which were proceeding round the roundabout and heading to various exits. He could clearly see a Give Way line on the road ahead, but still he was unable to stop the car. As it hurtled towards the roundabout, out of control, three boys suddenly ran out of a field opposite and raced across the road. The last boy was just not quick enough, and in a second he was caught squarely in the headlights of the speeding Cortina. He turned and froze, his eyes wide in complete horror. Through the blinding glare of the oncoming headlights, the boy thought he saw two people; the driver, with his hands over his face, and the dark outline of a passenger. "Noooo ... !" Gene screamed.

In that moment, the hand of the mysterious passenger grabbed the wheel before Gene's eyes could even register the action. The wheel was jerked to the side, and within a heartbeat, the car swerved and so narrowly missed the boy, that the atmospheric wake of the Cortina nearly knocked him off his feet. There was a sharp, gut-churning screech of tyres, and the Cortina suddenly shuddered to a halt along Church Lane - minus one passenger! The lugubrious stranger had vanished. Gene shakily parked his vehicle and jumped out. The rain had stopped, and he started to walk homewards, a sober man. The three boys who had foolishly hurried in front of the Cortina ran after him.

"You fucking nutter!" shouted the boy who should have died under the wheels.

As delayed shock set in, Gene turned to the boy and, ignoring his taunts, asked: "Did you see a man in that car with me just then?"

"Yeah, so what?" said the boy, taken unaware by his odd manner.

He backed away from Gene, calling him a dickhead as he scurried back to his waiting pals, but his insults seemed to fall on deaf ears, because the man who had almost ended his life, walked silently away up the dark road, staring vacantly ahead.

Gene was so badly affected by the terrifying paranormal experience, that soon afterwards he gave the Cortina away. After breaking down in tears upon his return home to his terraced home in Noctorum, Gene told his wife about his unbelievable encounter with Death. She had never known him to lie, or to hold the remotest interest in the occult, so she believed his strange tale.

Nowadays when Gene has a drink, he makes sure a taxi takes him home.

MANILU - THE LODGE LANE VAMPIRE

I remember taking calls at BBC Radio Merseyside after a programme I'd broadcast on vampires, and I talked to about a dozen callers who claimed they had been bitten in the neck during the night, and had woken up with bloodstained pillows and bedclothes. A majority of these people lived close to one another off Liverpool's Earle Road, and I visited a few of these 'victims' and found them all apparently sane enough. These night-bites continued for about six months and then ceased as mysteriously as they had started. Around that time, there was a strange rumour about a vampire named "Manilu" being on the prowl in the area around Lodge Lane. People claimed to have actually seen him, and described him as a bald-headed man with a pale, foreign-looking face, dressed in black. A 67-year-old woman told me how she had been walking along Hartington Road with her Jack Russell dog Simon one summer evening at 10pm when a weird-looking man picked up the dog with both hands and sunk his teeth into it. The dog yelped and almost died from blood loss. That same week in 1997, the same man, who matched the aforementioned description of Manilu, was seen prowling nearby Toxteth Park Cemetery on Smithdown Road. A heroin-user who often injected in the cemetery during twilight, saw a tall bald "ghoul" creeping among the gravestones, muttering to himself in a foreign language. A gang of children were roaming the cemetery several nights later when the tall peculiar stranger chased them, and allegedly grabbed one young lad by his ankle and threw him perilously high into the air as if he was a doll. On another occasion the heroin addict was spotted by the graveyard prowler, but he did nothing, as if he realised the drug user was not a threat, and simply walked off into the darkness. The reports of Manilu date back at least to the 1940s, and may simply be urban legends, but I feel there is much more to him than that.

In 1894, a 60-year-old woman named Emma Furnival, who ran a bakery at 13 Lodge Lane, was visited by a sinister abnormally tall man in black with "foreign features" and peculiar dark eyes. The man entered her shop to buy a loaf, and he spoke in broken English with an East European inflection in his voice. At this time, there were queer rumours about a vampire being at large in the south of Liverpool after a child and a number of women living near Sefton Park had awakened in the morning to find strange puncture wounds on their necks. Bram Stoker had not yet written *Dracula*, his Gothic masterpiece, but the habits of vampires were well-known, and one of them was the drawing of blood from the neck. The vampire was also believed to originate from Eastern Europe, from places such as Transylvania and Hungary, and when the tall thin foreign man with staring eyes remarked upon the beauty of Mrs Furnival's neck, she became so frightened she ran through a door to a back room on the premises and locked herself in. The man in the black homburg and frock-coat made himself scarce, but was later seen prowling nearby Toxteth Park Cemetery at twilight. Two policemen chased him but he somehow managed to evade them among the forest of gravestones. Weeks later, two spinster sisters, surnamed Bould, awoke at their home on Earle Road to find the tall silhouette of a man standing in their bedroom. One of the sisters screamed and fled from the room, but the other one remained in her bed, frozen with fear. The intruder assaulted her, bit her neck, and drew off blood, before fleeing through a window. The assailant was never captured, and his bloodsucking fuelled the vampire 'mania' prevalent in south Liverpool at that time. The reports of the vampiric man then subsided for decades, but in the late 1940s, dark rumours about a vampire who prowled the area bounded by Lodge Lane, Smithdown Road and Ullet Road began to circulate in postwar Liverpool. According to the rumours, the vampire was well over 6 feet in height, and was named Manilu. Some said his first name was Nathan. He was said to have lived at a crumbling Victorian house off Lodge Lane for over forty years, and at this old abode he had accumulated a handful of disciples who had been initiated into his personal religion by participating in blood-drinking rites. Of course, the vampire stories may be nothing more than hearsay, urban myths and exaggeration, yet I believe there is more than a grain of truth in the stories of Manilu. In the 1980s, a wave of vampire reports rippled across several parts of Liverpool, originating in Lodge Lane. A highly-controversial self-styled vampire-hunter, Victor Mordelly, set out to confront the vampire and lay it to rest. Equipped with hawthorn stakes, holy water, crucifixes – and a profound knowledge of these creatures of the night – Mordelly allegedly traced "Manilu" to his lair. I will now relate the shocking outcome of this vampire hunt, according to Mordelly's testimony.

In February 1983, a young single mum living in a bedsit off Lodge Lane with her eight-month-old baby had the feeling that she was being watched. She was not the superstitious or paranoid type, but from the day she moved into the bedsit, she had the horrible sensation of being observed by someone or something next door, especially at night. In the end, the edgy electric atmosphere in the bedsit became so intense that the woman went to Wavertree Road police station and told a bemused constable about the interminable feeling about being watched by something evil in the flat next door. The policeman said there was nothing he could do, but the girl began to sob, and she hysterically begged him to send an officer to the flat adjacent to her bedsit, for she felt as if something sinister was going on next door - but it was hard for her to put her fears into words. To calm her down the police officer promised he'd send someone around to look into the matter, and that night as the young woman was watching *News at Ten* to take her mind off the eerie predicament, she was startled to hear loud thumps coming from the flat next door. She looked out the window and saw a police car down below in the street. Then she realised that the police constables had responded to her plea, and were inspecting the next-door flat; they had been the source of the banging noises. The police later revealed to her what they had found in the flat next door, and the revelation resulted in the girl packing her bags. After they had broken into the flat, the two policemen saw that the previous occupier had painted all of the walls black. These walls were dotted with mysterious pentagrams and other occult symbols. In the middle of the floor there was a coffin which looked over a hundred years old. It had probably been stolen from a tomb in a local graveyard, but it was empty and there were no traces of the corpse it had contained. The nameplate was too rusted to be identifiable. Next to the coffin was a mysterious ancient mildewed handwritten book on occultism, and next to this tome was an empty milk bottle - which contained a small amount of human clotted blood.

No one in the street could remember who the occupier of that flat was, and he or she never returned, but even the hard-boiled streetwise policemen said they experienced an icy chill in that flat. Understandably, the young mum left the bedsit that very night and went to stay with her auntie on the Wirral. The 50-year-old self-styled 'vampire-hunter' Victor Mordelly committed the crime of trespass to investigate this peculiar incident. He examined the flat with the black walls and ceiling. He looked into a wardrobe in the room of the flat and discovered a hole in its floor. This hole led down into the cellar, and from the cellar, a tunnel ran into the darkness. Mordelly explored this tunnel, armed with his vampire-hunting kit – which contained a mallet, hawthorn stakes, holy water, cloves of garlic, and a crucifix.

He bravely negotiated the winding tunnel for a mile or two, until he came upon a large vault coated with fungus, lichens, stalagmites and stalactites. Set into the limestone-encrusted floor of this vault was a block of sandstone, upon which someone had placed two rusted candlesticks streaked with black wax. Mordelly had seen such subterranean 'altars' before in tunnels leading from Beeston Castle in Cheshire, and also in the caverns beneath places as far apart as Billinge and Kirkby Lonsdale. Mordelly could see tell-tale dark stains of mammal blood on the altar, but no sign of the Sanguinarians (Mordelly's term for vampires) responsible for the sacrifices. The courageous stalker of vampires raked the darkness ahead with the beam of his torch as he trudged through a tunnel that became increasingly more waterlogged with each step. After almost an hour he came upon a glimmer of light in the roof of the tunnel. Pale wintry daylight bled in through a crescent opening in the roof, and Mordelly could see the grim grey tenements known as Fontenoy Gardens through the aperture. He consulted his A to Z map book and deduced that the secret passage had led him into a disused railway tunnel. The only exit from this tunnel was blocked by a landslide of discarded rubbish, so Mordelly was forced to go back the way he had come. When he passed the altar, he heard a sound reverberate through the tunnel, and at first it sounded like the dripping of water that had percolated through the sandstone stratum. Clouds of his exhaled breath bloomed in mid-air in the glare of the torch as he became anxious – then he saw Manilu.

Mordelly claims in his unpublished books on vampirology that some of these underground bloodsuckers living in perpetual darkness were devoid of eyes, but the vampire standing inert before him had large expressive red watery eyes. Mordelly slowly reached into a satchel to retrieve a revolver loaded with hollow-point bullets tainted with hawthorn berry powder. With an extraordinary swiftness the vampire flew at him, knocking Mordelly on his back with a bony fist. The thing held him down by the throat and bared its long fangs.

Mordelly lay on his back with the strong iron-grip hands of the blood-sucking fiend Manilu around his neck. The vampire knelt with his legs on either side of Mordelly as he opened his mouth, ready to pierce the carotid artery. Mordelly felt the ground in desperation, seconds from a choking death, hoping to find the revolver loaded with hawthorn-tipped bullets, but it wasn't there. Instead, Mordelly's hand located a sharpened hawthorn stake which had fallen out of his satchel, and in one swift movement he pushed its pointed end into the vampire's gaping mouth until it was impaled in the palate. The creature screamed as blood dripped and sprayed from its mouth and it released its deathly grip then rose up trying desperately trying to pull out the stake. Mordelly pushed the soles of his boots into Manilu's chest and sent him flying backwards into the darkness. Mordelly saw the revolver by the light of the torch lying in a puddle, and he seized it and began to fire at the tall wiry bloodsucker. After the third shot the unearthly figure flitted into the shadows with the agility of a startled spider. Mordelly turned and ran back down the tunnel until he reached the cellar of the house off Lodge Lane. He rented a flat on Picton Road in Wavertree, and wrote an account of his encounter with vampires in Liverpool and elsewhere. He went to a local paranormal investigation group and asked them to assist him in his vampire hunt, but they mocked him and decided he was crazy. Mordelly claimed that the network of tunnels excavated by the "Edge Hill Mole" Joseph Williamson under Liverpool in the early 1800s were now being used by light-fearing vampires, and even controversially suggested that Williamson himself may have been a dhampir (having a vampire father and human mother). John Burns, a member of the ghost-hunting group, initially believed Mordelly was a crank until late one night in 1983 when he pulled into a filling station in Wavertree. Burns saw Mordelly running from a lane, pursued by two strange-looking men in black - each about 6ft 5 in height. Burns watched as one of these tall skinny men picked up Mordelly and threw him with great force onto a rubbish skip. Burns went to Mordelly's aid and saw from closer quarters that the eccentric man's attackers were pale-faced with joined-up eyebrows and long pointed fangs. One of the sinister figures lunged towards Burns, but was struck by a car. Despite appalling injuries, the figure got to its feet and gave chase with its weird-looking comrade. Mordelly ran with Burns to his car and managed to escape. According to Mordelly, the two figures were centuries-old vampire confederates of Manilu. Burns realised that Mordelly was not a crank at all, and decided to join him in his quest to fight the Sanguinarians. I could fill a book with the tales of Mordelly and Burns, and who knows? Perhaps I will one day, although I doubt many would believe my accounts of their nocturnal adventures. Believe it or not, vampires are still being reported today. In January 2005, vampire mania swept Birmingham after the newspapers reported a Dracula-like attacker on the loose. The "Birmingham vampire" was even reported in the high-brow pages of *The Guardian*. The vampire reports are also available to see online. According to Mordelly, Manilu is still at large across the north-west after dark. I remember an incident many years ago, in the 1990s, in which a Tuebrook man was going to a filling station at three in the morning to buy cigarettes, and whilst on his way, a black limousine pulled up, and two tall men in black suits seized him by each elbow and pushed him into the back of the vehicle. The man resisted but felt an electrical jolt through his chest; perhaps from a stunner. He became groggy and the limo was driven to somewhere in the Toxteth area, because the captive remembered passing Lodge Lane Library. The abducted man was taken into a house and down into a spacious cellar, where a man sat on what could only be described as a throne. It was a high-backed seat of marble, featuring strange gargoyles and carvings of serpents. The man seated on it was bald, and although he was sitting down it was clear, from the unusually elongated proportions of his torso and limbs, that he was very tall. His face was so pale it looked as if he was wearing make up, and his eyes protruded from their dark-lined sockets. On one of his fingers he wore a large ruby ring, and his suit looked as if it was made of black velvet. His shirt was dark blue and satin. For a few tense moments he surveyed the captured man trembling between the two heavies before him, then announced, 'That is not Cavaleri [or what sounded like that name].'

The man on the throne waved the frightened Tuebrook man away and the two tall muscular henchmen dragged the abductee up a flight of stone steps and back to the limousine. The man was dropped off on Binns Road without a word of explanation or apology. The gargoyles on the throne and the serpents indicate an occult element. Was the man seated on that throne the legendary Manilu?

WITCHES STAY AWAY FROM MY DOOR!

The pub sign of the Swan may say it was established in 1898, but back in the 1850s there was a tavern on the spot. In those Victorian times, the Swan Inn had a serious rival, which existed thirteen doors away at 58 Wood Street, and this competing pub was a tavern known as the Ruthin Castle, run by a man named Joe Asbery, who tried all sorts of underhand tricks and devious antics to draw drinkers away from the Swan to his public house. Drink-price wars between the two pubs erupted, but the clientèle of the Swan remained remarkably loyal. The Ruthin Castle had cheaper beverages, dirt-cheap mussels, and occasionally free jellied eels, but even in Victorian times, the Swan Inn had a distinctive welcoming atmosphere and stronger ales than its rivals, and at this time (in the 1850s) the pub was managed by Ann Duncan, a very charismatic woman in her thirties who treated the drinkers like family members. Late one midsummer evening around

1853, the Swan Inn was packed with drinkers, many of whom were dancing to an Irish band of musicians, when a window was smashed. Ann Duncan and several of the drinkers went outside and saw no one on Wood Street except a group of warehouse men harnessing horses at the far end of the street, near Hanover Street. The only other figure that was noticed on this night was a drunken vagrant, and he was sitting in a doorway in the moonlight, almost opposite the pub. Mrs Duncan went over to him and asked the tramp if he had thrown the stone, and he said he had, but it had been thrown with the best of intentions. Mrs Duncan was furious at the down-and-out's admission and asked him why he had smashed the pub window.

The tramp said he had been aiming the stone at the 'witch' who had been writing something on the doorstep of the Swan. The scruffily-dressed Ishmaelite knew the woman was a witch because she had jinxed him many years ago and caused his business to fail.

Ann Duncan and the gaggle of drinkers went to inspect the stone step in front of the Swan Inn, and sure enough, someone had chalked seven strange words upon it, and one of the words was 'Astaroth'. One of the drinkers, a tobacconist named Jack Denman, said he possessed a smattering of knowledge concerning the occult, and believed the chalked words formed a curse invoking the demon Astaroth – one of the infamous 'Dukes of Hell' who causes havoc once he has been summoned up. 'Wash it off!' Mrs Duncan told her brother Robert, but Mr Denman advised the landlady not to, for washing such a 'witch-graffito' away was known to only make the invisible effects of the curse harder to remove. Denman instead suggested that Mrs Duncan should seek 'wise counsel' from someone who knew how to remove such curses in a proper and effective manner. Mrs Duncan asked who could do such a thing, and Mr Denman said he knew of a man, a real-life warlock, who was well-versed in such arcane matters. His name was Patric Shalos (pronounced Shayloss), and he lived in a cottage in the district of Thingwall, over on Wirral. 'Oh, we shan't be needing someone like that,' said Mrs Duncan with a dismissive smirk, 'I'll tell a priest to bless the beer house.'

'This curse is from an ancient religion that was here long before Christianity,' Denman told the landlady, and many of the drinkers recoiled at the blasphemous assertions of the tobacconist.

'Fiddlesticks!' Mrs Duncan said, and she went to fetch a sponge and bucket of water. Mr Denman took out a pencil and a scrap of paper and scrawled down the seven strange words. Then the landlady came out and washed the cryptic words away. As she did, the full moon slid behind a cloud, plunging badly-lit Wood Street into an eerie gloom, and in this darkness, the sounds of a dog howling could be heard somewhere in the twilit distance.

'There, all the codswallop's gone now,' announced Mrs Duncan, and she stood up and walked back into the Swan Inn. Then she cried out and fell down unconscious. When the landlady came to, she said someone had struck her on the back of the head, but not one of the drinkers had been close enough to strike her as they entered the pub, although several of the regulars claimed they had heard the thumping sound of something hitting Mrs Duncan. Over the next few days, more strange incidents took place in the Swan Inn. The ales began to taste sour, and the best and most expensive brandy began to smell like vinegar. Drinkers who went to the pub toilet found they couldn't stop urinating and their streams went on for inordinate lengths of time, and the Swan's cat, Shamrock, kept hissing at something in the bar no human eyes could see. There was a crash upstairs in the evening, and Mrs Duncan saw her best crockery in pieces on the floor. Then a plate sailed past her and smashed against the wall. That same evening, one of the drinkers requested a glass of gin, and as Mrs Duncan tilted the bottle to pour the drink, the glass was seen to dart away a few inches, and the gin spilled onto the counter.

A priest from St Peter's Church on Church Street was informed of the supernatural goings-on at the pub, but condescendingly sneered at Mrs Duncan's account and suggested that the incidents were probably down to 'hallucinations born from the bottle'.

Mrs Duncan stormed away from the priest's residence and paid a visit to Jack Denman. She told him about the strange phenomena that was playing havoc with her business, and asked him to enlist the help of the 'warlock'. On the following day, before dawn, Mr Denman travelled to Thingwall, and somehow managed to persuade Mr Shalos to accompany him back to Liverpool, where Mrs Duncan provided the Cheshire occultist with his own quarters and allowed him to drink and eat as much as he required during his stay. When Shalos arrived in a carriage at the Swan with Denman, Mrs Duncan noticed her rival, Joe Asbery, standing across the road, watching proceedings from under the brim of a wide felt hat.

Over breakfast, Patric Shalos surveyed the words of the chalked spell that Jack Denman had copied down. It was a particular nasty spell in his experience, and to countermand it he had brought along the esoteric tools of his trade in a satchel. Some of the requests Shalos made were met with bemused looks from the landlady and her drinkers. He asked for hanging baskets to be hung on chains on either side of the entrance to the Swan, and this was done. Shalos then uprooted vervain plants in the wild fields of the suburbs and put them in the hanging baskets. Vervain is a plant of great magical protection from evil, known as the "tears of Isis" by the ancient Egyptians, and was once traditionally gathered around the time of midsummer, when the star Sirius was prominent, and, furthermore, it was also used to cleanse the altars of Jupiter in ancient Rome. Daughters of the Druids were also crowned with blue and purple vervain after initiation ceremonies. The ancient Picts even revered the juice of the plant as a healing ointment.

At noon, as the hanging baskets were being woven and the chains were being fastened to the walls of the pub, the front door of the Swan burst open, and a howling vortex of wind hurtled through the premises, overturning tables and chairs before blowing itself out. People were naturally afraid, but the warlock Shalos told them it was just the work of desperate witches who were now angry because they knew their powers would soon be overcome. Inside the Swan Inn, over the entrance of the door, Shalos drove an iron spike into the wall and attached a three-legged symbol known as the Triskelion – which we today would associate with the symbol of the Isle of Man. This powerful iron symbol hung in the Swan for many years, until it was removed around 1900 by the landlady of the pub at that time, a woman named Ada Allison. After its removal, bad luck plagued Mrs Wilson until the symbol was re-mounted. It has since been lost.

After the purple vervain had been put in the baskets, the warlock Shalos happened to glance over at the mirror behind the bar, and there he saw the ghostly faint vision of a pair of pale oval faces. They were of two women of about thirty, and their eyes resembled black almonds. They both scowled as the warlock looked on. Jack Denman followed the magician's line of sight and saw what he was looking at. 'The witches?' he whispered, and Shalos nodded. The faces quickly vanished. Shalos had the mirror covered up with a sheet of tarpaulin, and explained to Mrs Duncan how a looking-glass could be used as a spying-glass by certain witches who practised the Dark Arts.

The next plan was to identify the witches if possible, and once their names had been discovered, there were two courses of action. To either kill them, or banish them. Shalos preferred to kill the witches, as in his experience, Hell had no fury like a witch who had suffered the humiliation of banishment, and he told Denman how a coven of blackballed witches had managed to overcome a banishment ritual to kill a warlock on the Thor's Stone on Thurstaston Common in Wirral. This stone, which is over 230 million years old, is still used by real witches today.

'If you kill them you'll be hanged,' Jack Denman

warned Shalos, but the warlock shook his head and said the bodies of the witches would never be found after he had finished with them.

'I won't help you to murder women, witches or not,' Denman said sombrely.

'What's all this talk of murder?' Mrs Duncan, the landlady of the Swan, approached the table.

Shalos explained the two choices as to the treatment of the witches, and Mrs Duncan said, 'No, you can't kill anybody Patric. All I require is to keep the witches from my door.'

Shalos and Denman tried to discover who the witches were, and even went in disguise into the Ruthin Castle tavern in an effort to eavesdrop on the conversation of the landlord Joe Asbery, but the strangers, being outsiders, soon aroused suspicion among the regulars and were told to leave. The unexpected break came from Mrs Duncan, who told Shalos about the tramp who had smashed the window of her pub as he tried to throw a stone at the witch who had scrawled the spell on the doorstep. The vagrant had recognised the witch as the woman who had jinxed his business years before. The vagrant was traced a few days later, and brought to the Swan Inn, where Shalos and Mrs Duncan quizzed him over the witch who had chalked the malevolent spell. The vagrant, who was only known as Morris, said the witch was not known to him by name, just by sight, and four years ago she was living with her sister in Wolstenholme Square at the end of Parr Street. Mrs Duncan promised the tramp five shillings if he would show Mr Shalos where the 'witches' lived. The vagrant cheerily agreed to the offer.

Under the cover of night, Patric Shalos, Jack Denman, and the tramp Morris loitered in the shadows of the trees in the park that was situated in the centre of Wolstenholme Square. The vagrant squinted at the motley row of lamp-lit houses and warehouses before pointing at a thin dark-bricked terraced dwelling. 'I think that's the house there. I'd say I'm sure of it in fact,' he said.

It was fast approaching midnight, and the three men waited for a while as three old stragglers, all old men, stood talking on a corner nearby. Judging by the way the trio were swaying, they'd just returned from a tavern. They each bid one another goodnight as a clock chimed midnight, and when the last one had gone into his home, Shalos walked alone to the house that the vagrant had pointed out. He stooped upon reaching the three stone steps and took a small strong-bladed knife from his belt. He engraved something on the top step with the point of the knife, and moments afterwards, a policeman entered the square – and he was heading in the direction of the self-proclaimed warlock.

Jack Denman told the vagrant to stay behind the tree, and not to move an inch. The tobacconist then started yelling, 'Police! Stop thief!' before he ran off pell mell out of the square.

'What is it?' the policeman shouted over to the retreating figure.

Denman stopped, and gestured for the policeman to follow him with a wind-milling motion of his left arm. 'I've been robbed!' Denman shouted, 'And he's ran off down here!'

Patric Shalos, meanwhile, finished etching his

powerful spell into the doorstep. Any witch within that dwelling would now be housebound. Unless she had someone to bring her food or water, the witch would die of thirst or hunger, and sometimes, if the witch happened to be asleep at the time when the spell was cast, she would remain asleep as if in a coma.

The policeman suddenly realised that Denman was merely trying to distract him, and refused to follow the tobacconist. He turned to see Shalos, walking from a house – as he slid a knife into a sheath on his belt. That naturally struck the officer of the law as highly suspicious, and so he gripped the handle of his truncheon and challenged the stranger.

'You! Stay where you are!' he shouted.

Shalos did as he said, and turned to face him. 'I've done no wrong sir,' he told the policeman.

'You have a knife there,' said the policeman, 'have you just used it?'

Shalos gazed into the policeman's intense dark eyes, then probed his logical but limited mind, and easily took control of it. He reached out and placed his thumb between those eyes, at the top of the officer's nose, and the lawman's eyes gently closed. Shalos walked away to join the other two on Parr Street, and when they looked back, the policeman was still standing there in the square, as stock-still as a statue.

The witches were never heard from again and their malign influence never touched the Swan Inn again. They say that Joe Asbery, the landlord of the Ruthin Castle, brought the witches food and drink at first and tried to remove them from the house on Wolstenholme Square, but it proved to be impossible, for the sisters experienced agonising pains in their uteri when they tried to leave the house. There was talk many years later of two skeletons in tattered clothes, with nests of rats in their rib-cages being found in a derelict house in Wolstenholme Square.

The Swan Inn thrived, Joe Asbery died, and the Ruthin Castle closed down for good when its customers deserted it. Shalos lived at the Swan Inn for many years as a honoured guest, and during his stay, Mrs Duncan prospered well.

Now, before I end this tale, I must mention the following. A man once contacted me to tell how, during the 1930s, his father Brian Hedges had been hired by a brewery to repair the sunken cellar floor of the Swan Inn. During the excavations to strengthen the foundations, Mr Hedges unearthed the remains of a rusted helmet and a long granite tablet with characters upon it. A young worker wanted to take these relics home, but Hedges told him to leave them where they had been found as he had a bad feeling that some supernatural harm would result if they were taken from the cellar. The young man who reluctantly put the items back, copied down the inscription on the length of granite stone, and he later discovered that the glyphs of the inscription were runic. The inscription proclaimed: *Dedicated to Woden*. There are Viking relics to be found all over the north-west. In 1828, navvies working for the railway engineer George Stephenson were making excavations for the foundations of the railway bridge on what is now Archway Road in Huyton, when they discovered the remains of a Viking ship. Archaeologists were baffled as to how a ship, over a thousands years old from Scandinavia, could be found about fifteen feet underground in the middle of

Huyton. The clue was the River Alt, which ran close to the site of the railway. It's now known that the River Alt was much wider thousands of years ago and a huge lake existed in Huyton, where the Hag Plantation now exists. Sand has also been found beneath Huyton, proving it was once a landing place for ships in ancient times.

The meaning of the Viking relics found beneath the Swan Inn are still unknown, but if that granite slab's inscription is to be taken at face value, it would mean that the Swan is the only pub in the world to be dedicated to the Norse god Woden, even though the pub didn't exist when the slab was left at the site!

MR BILL

The following story concerns one of the strangest and creepiest incidents I have ever investigated and I have been involved in some spine-chilling cases. As I write my account of the following tale I am on my own and, although I consider myself to be a seasoned, almost shock-proof ghost investigator, I feel distinctly uneasy, and during this paragraph I have already glanced over my shoulder twice.

Before I relate the eerie story of Mister Bill, a word of warning. After you have read this tale, either move on quickly to another story, or watch a soap, or listen to your iPod, maybe. Surf the net, or visit a friend, but whatever you do, do not lie in bed tonight dwelling on what Mister Bill is, and if possible, do not even mention him again.

First, here's a case which may throw some light on the true nature of the uncanny Mister Bill. Many years ago, in 1972, an American psychiatrist named Wilson

Van Dusen was working at Mendocino State Hospital in California. He treated a number of patients who said they were being stalked by phantom people. Van Dusen specifically sought permission to interview these supposedly schizophrenic individuals to fathom out the nature of the psychoses which were causing them to experience such persecution complexes. As his examinations progressed, he was not prepared for what he uncovered.

Firstly, a young female patient visited the doctor and claimed that she had a phantom lover. By asking a series of probing questions, Van Dusen tried to elicit exactly what she meant. She sighed deeply and nervously explained in a timid voice how it had all been a joke at first. Apparently all of her friends had been dating someone, and she had no boyfriend, and so, out of sheer wounded pride, she had invented Stephen, "just for heck of it", she said. Her tone hardened and her expression changed as she went on to say that now she could not get rid of him. She shook uncontrollably as she confided in the doctor, explaining that she had told him repeatedly it was over, but that he would not take no for an answer.

Van Dusen calmly asked her where exactly Stephen was. He inquired politely whether he was nearby in some location, or whether he was just in her mind.

"He's standing next to you right now," she stated curtly.

"Would I be able to have a little chat with, with um, Stephen?" Van Dusen asked carefully.

"Sure," the girl replied, flashing her eyes up at the person only she could see.

Van Dusen proceeded to ask Stephen what he was,

and why he would not break up with his patient; and the girl relayed everything that her unseen and unheard companion told her. She had never read a psychology book in her life, yet she elaborated in amazing detail as she forwarded Stephen's replies to the psychiatrist's questions.

Van Dusen began to feel very uneasy as he gradually received a strong impression of a presence in the room. He definitely felt as if someone was standing just to his left. At one point in the interview the girl made an unexpected announcement.

"Stephen has just told me that you were reading a book on Greek myths yesterday."

Van Dusen immediately visualised the copy of the Greek text sitting far away in his house on his bedside table, where he had placed it the night before. He was shaken to the marrow, as there was no way his patient could have possibly known that. He was still digesting the implications of all this when she came out with the following statement:

"Stephen says he started off as some hallucination in my mind, but he was able to evolve a consciousness of his own."

Van Dusen was a man of science and reason and could not accept the concept of possession, but he felt that the girl he was interviewing was somehow possessed by an exterior intelligence. In the end, the psychiatrist reached a dead end in his investigations and was sadly unable to help the troubled girl. In an endeavour to understand her psychological state, he subsequently interviewed a series of apparently schizophrenic patients, and discovered that many of them were well-balanced and far from mentally dysfunctional. It seemed as if they too were actually being shadowed by independent entities of some sort. Again, on interviewing these patients, it transpired that these invisible stalkers exhibited a remarkably wide range of knowledge that encompassed psychiatry, literature, astronomy, religion and musical composition.

Van Dusen was so fascinated by the experiences of his patients, that he wrote about the phantom individuals in his book, *The Natural Depth of Man*, in 1972. The book truly is a fascinating read in terms of psychological exploration and theory. The strangest fact that comes to light in Van Dusen's investigation is that many of the menacing entities share distinctive names that are reported by patients living in many different areas of the world. One of these names is 'Mister Bill'.

Out of all of these inexplicable 'hallucinations', Mister Bill has one distinctive attribute: he has allegedly been seen by people other than the person who is supposedly hallucinating him. Even more frightening is the fact that he has been seen in the United States, Australia, Japan, Europe and even right here in Liverpool as well. His appearance is very sinister indeed. He is always seen wearing a black, tight-fitting garment, not unlike a body stocking, with a black balaclava-like headpiece which gives the bizarre apparition a somewhat medieval look. The face of Mister Bill is said to bear an uncanny resemblance to the old glove puppet, Punch, with a prominent and ruddy-coloured nose; his eyes have black borders and are often described as being evil-looking, whereas his voice sounds contrived, like the shrill projected sound of a ventriloquist.

Now, in the occult world there are intriguing things known as 'tulpas'. These are solid, tangible projections that are born of human imagination, but gradually manifest themselves on the physical plane. They are also known as 'thought forms'.

In the 1920s, a remarkably tough-minded and highly independent Frenchwoman named Alexandra David-Neel, undertook a long and hazardous journey into Tibet on a pilgrimage to seek out the fabled practitioners of the ancient art of magic. She was a wise traveller and knew a charlatan when she saw one. On her travels, Alexandra visited many strange and intriguing places and met various magicians, gurus and accomplished yogis, who demonstrated their perplexing powers. The Frenchwoman was very impressed with one particular magician who not only gave a demonstration of levitation, but also showed her how to construct a quasi-solid form that he had generated through sheer willpower. The Tibetan magician called the apparition he had created a tulpa, and seriously warned Alexandra how these 'children of the mind' often escaped out of the control of their maker to become independent beings, often becoming mischievous and even murderous.

The magician gave Alexandra the specific instructions which enabled her to create her own tulpa. Alexandra was completely intrigued and decided to create a harmless character: a short fat monk who looked innocent and jolly. For a period of several months, the westerner shut herself away to concentrate her thoughts and practise the rituals prescribed by the magician. In the end, and much to her amazement, she succeeded in creating the phantom mirthful monk, but found the astounding exercise in willpower mentally draining. The corpulent monk would follow Alexandra about, but in time he started performing various actions his creator had not commanded him to carry out.

What was even more disturbing was the fact that the tulpa was not a subjective hallucination; it was seen on many occasions by everyone else besides Alexandra. Gradually, over the weeks, the monk became more troublesome. He developed a sarcastic, mocking personality as a decidedly evil streak began to surface. In the end, Alexandra David-Neel spent six long, hard months trying to rid herself of the terrible monk.

Perhaps something similar happened when the ubiquitous Mister Bill turned up in the house of a family in Liverpool. This tulpa, if that is what it was, turned up on a photograph taken on the Christmas Eve of the year 2000. A 45-year-old man named Jimmy had taken a photograph of his family and friends in his living room. In January of the new year, when the developed snaps came back from Max Spielmann's, Jimmy smiled as he shuffled through the glossy prints because of the memories they triggered. His smile faded abruptly when he noticed on one print a strange figure in black standing in the hallway in the background, just visible through the doorway.

The looming figure was not noticeable on any of the other photographs. It looked like someone in a grotesque mask, depicting a weird, big-nosed character. The presence of the figure really unnerved Jimmy, and he showed the photograph to his wife, who thought it was extremely creepy. Both were unsettled by the intrusive presence in the picture and decided not to show it to their young son, just in case it frightened him.

Well, the photograph was later sent to me. I placed it on a computer scanner at high resolution and zoomed in on it. I agreed it was an eerie figure, but asked Jimmy and his wife whether they could be absolutely sure that someone in fancy dress had not been standing in their hallway when the picture was taken. They were absolutely positive that no one other than close family members had been at the house that day. Furthermore, no one present had been remotely dressed like the peculiar man in black.

Then the mystery took on a new and terrifying dimension. The couple's eight-year-old son, Danny, began to wet his bed. He told his mother that he had started to wake up in his bed in the early hours of the morning, unable to move a muscle. Sometimes he complained of a 'horrible man in black', who appeared in the room during these frightening night-time periods of paralysis. Danny was asked to draw the scary after-dark visitor, and his parents immediately recognised that the drawing matched the likeness of the black-clad weirdo in the Christmas photograph which, of course, Danny had not been shown.

A few weeks later at four o'clock in the morning, Danny ran screaming into his parent's bedroom. He cried out that the figure in black was in his room again, sitting on top of his wardrobe. Jimmy grabbed the baseball bat which he kept under his bed - reserved for any late night intruders. He told his wife to dial 999 and then stormed towards his son's room. Jimmy stopped in his tracks for a moment as he heard very faint singing coming from inside Danny's bedroom. He kicked open the door and paced his way in, only to find that there was nobody there. The only indication of any disturbance was the heavy wardrobe, which had somehow toppled over onto the bed.

It took a week before the family finally calmed down. Danny was most unsettled, and when a doctor examined him he informed his concerned parents that he was a highly-strung child, who was possibly hyperactive. Racking his brains for any cause for his distress, Jimmy wondered if the troubled child had heard them talking about the man in black captured on the Christmas photograph. Maybe he had, and maybe that had triggered a series of vivid nightmares.

Things seemed to settle down over the following weeks, until Valentine's Day, 14 February. Jimmy's wife was gift-wrapping a boxed set of CDs which she had bought for her husband, when she distinctly felt someone breathing down her neck. She turned round, fully expecting to confront someone, but there was nobody there. Feeling jittery and on edge, she went to check the kitchen door which led to the yard and found that it was fully locked. When she returned to the living room, she noticed that there was now childish writing on the blank gift tag which she had been about to write; it rested on the parcel containing the CDs. Vividly upon the tag, in blue ink, someone had scrawled the words, 'Mister Bill'. Naturally, she was bemused and more than a little unsettled.

When she mentioned the name to me, I wondered if it was a mere coincidence. Perhaps Danny had written that name on the parcel, maybe as some Freudian protest because he wanted his mother to give the gift to him, instead of his father. But the creepy events did not cease there.

The next day was a Thursday and that evening the window cleaner called to collect his payment from Jimmy. He also had a strange tale to tell. He said that on Monday afternoon, while the house was empty, he had been cleaning the living room windows and had seen something which made the hairs on the nape of his neck stand on end. A man in black, whom he thought looked like something from the Middle Ages, had been sitting on the sofa in the parlour. He was bolt upright and gazing straight ahead at the clock on the wall. The window cleaner described to them how he had banged on the window, expecting a response, but apparently the figure had remained stock still and did not even blink. The window cleaner had become suspicious and called his colleague from across the road to come and have a look at the stranger in black; he too saw the man and was equally intrigued. They called over Jimmy's neighbour, but when she looked into the parlour through the bay windows, she saw nothing, there was definitely no one in the room.

Understandably, Jimmy and his family have now left that cursed house in Liverpool and I remain curious about the mysterious Mister Bill.

Now forget everything you just read.

THE ST LUKE'S ABDUCTION

The following weird incident took place in Liverpool in the early 1990s and it has never been satisfactorily explained. It all started one foggy December evening in 1991.

It was 7pm on the Friday evening before Christmas when the Edwards family, of Dovecot, decided to go and do a bit of late Christmas shopping in Liverpool city centre. Mr Edwards drove his wife and four children to town in his old Volvo estate and, as usual, finding a place to park proved to be very difficult. Mr Edwards drove around, searching desperately for a parking space, as his three sons and daughter gazed excitedly at the spectacular Christmas lights and decorations lining the streets. The youngest of the Edwards children was Abbi, who was only six years old. She loved Christmas and for days she had been pestering her mum and dad to take her to see the big fir tree, covered with coloured lights, in Church Street.

As Abbi's dad was grumbling about finding a place to park the Volvo, her Mum suddenly pointed to a secluded side-street called Bold Place, which runs from Berry Street, past the back of St Luke's Church, up to Roscoe Street. Mr Edwards sighed with relief and turned left into the poorly-lit cobbled road, which lay on a bit of an incline. As soon as the car was parked, the four children eagerly jumped out of the vehicle and started pestering their parents about what they were getting for Christmas. Meanwhile, an icy fog rolled down the street.

After checking that the doors of the car were locked, the two adults had a quick discussion about where they were going to first. He wanted to go to a shop in Bold Street, to buy his father a cardigan, but she insisted on going to Dixons first, to buy a CD player for her sister. The children then started arguing too; naturally, their first priority was to visit the various toy stores. Their father's temper finally snapped.

"Alright, that's enough, will you all just shut up!"

The whole family immediately responded to the stress in his voice and quietened down, ready to set off. Suddenly, Mr Edwards noticed something - and his heart skipped a beat. With a look of dread, he glanced frantically about Bold Place and yelled, "Where's Abbi?"

Everyone joined in the search for the lost child, anxiously looking through the windows of the car, but finding no one there.

"Where on earth's she gone?" her mother pleaded, with a trembling voice. The three boys looked desperately about, but the street was totally empty.

At this point, they all heard a faint voice screaming out in the distance. "Daddy!" The voice sounded like Abbi's and it came from the top of Bold Place, towards Roscoe Street. The family rushed up the cobbled road with the father leading the way.

"Abbi!" he called, "where are you?"

The gates at the back of St Luke's were open and he surmised that his daughter must have wandered into the precincts of the old church. He hurried into the grounds, followed closely by his wife and their sons, and, once again, they all heard Abbi cry out for her father. But the little girl was nowhere to be seen and the fog was getting thicker by the minute.

Mr Edwards was reluctant to alarm his wife and children, but he secretly wondered if some perverted lunatic had grabbed his daughter and taken her into the ruins of the old church. He handed his wife the car keys and asked her to go and bring the torch from the vehicle. When she returned, he climbed up onto the ledge of a church window and shone the flashlight into the deserted ruins. The interior was deserted, with nothing but rubble scattered about. He knew that the church of St Luke had been gutted by an incendiary bomb during the Second World War during the Blitz. Only the shell of the building survived and the church had been deliberately left that way, as a reminder of the War. And yet it sounded as if Abbi's voice had come from inside the church.

As Mrs Edwards helped her husband down from the window, she put her fingers to her lips, "Listen!" she whispered. The faint eerie sound of a church organ were just audible and it seemed to be emanating from the church.

"Sound can play funny tricks at night," replied her husband dismissively. "Come on, let's go and get the police." When his wife began to cry, he tried to reassure her. "It'll be alright. We'll find her, love. She can't have gone far."

They set off to the police station in Hope Street and reported their lost daughter to the desk sergeant, who alerted all the patrol cars in the area and told officers on the city centre beat to be on the lookout for the girl. The family then rushed back to Bold Place to resume their search for the girl. They scoured the grounds of St Luke's once again and, after 20 minutes, they were about to return to their car, when something happened which continues to puzzle them to this day. A tall man, wearing a top hat and a long black calf-length coat, came out of the grounds of St Luke's and walking with him was little Abbi, holding his hand.

When Abbi caught sight of her mum and dad, she ran to them and started to cry, as her father picked her up. The sinister man in black looked like something out of the Victorian age. He had long bushy sideburns, a pallid face and staring, ink-black eyes. He stood like a statue outside the gates of the church and, in a creepy low voice, the outdated-looking stranger addressed them.

"Please accept my sincere apology for any distress caused."

He then turned and walked silently back towards the rear of the church ruins.

Mrs Edwards grabbed Abbi from her husband.

"Are you all right? Where have you been?" she asked her frantically.

"I'm fine, mummy."

Mr Edwards was furious and he shouted after the man: "Oi! Who are you? What's your game, eh?"

Then a police patrol car came tearing down the road and he told the officers about the stranger who had returned his daughter. Three of them bolted from the car and rushed into the grounds of the church wielding their batons.

But the police found no one. The grounds were completely empty. Reinforcements turned up and the grounds were searched repeatedly with powerful torches, but the place was deserted. However, several police officers also heard the faint strains of a church organ playing somewhere nearby, but they were unable to determine just where the strange music was coming from.

One of the policemen asked little Abbi where she had been and the child gave a strange account. She claimed that an old woman in a shawl had grabbed her hand and dragged her into the church, where a mass was being celebrated. In the church, there were many people dressed in old-fashioned clothing. The women wore big hats and the men were all dressed in black. Abbi had screamed for her father, but the old woman had put her hand over her mouth to silence her. Sometime later, a tall man entered the church and pulled Abbi from the old woman's clutches. He had been the man who had delivered Abbi back to her parents.

The intrigued policeman continued to interrogate the child and he asked her if the man had spoken to her about the strange incident. Abbi shook her head, then added that he had said that he had been 'a long time dead'. Everyone went quiet when they heard the child's strange reply. Since the disturbing incident, the Edwards family refuse to go anywhere near St Luke's Church, especially during the Christmas period.

After recounting this unusual story on the radio, I received a lot of letters, phone-calls and e-mails, from people who had weird tales to tell about St Luke's. A man who worked in Rapid Hardware in Renshaw Street told me how he had been driving to work early one morning, when he saw St Luke's lit up on the inside by quaint-looking chandeliers. He could even see stained glass windows and decided that the church must have been renovated. However, when the witness glanced at the traffic lights, out of the corner of his left eye, he watched the illumination from St Luke's start fade. He turned to look back at the old church and noticed that the windows had now gone and the place was in darkness once again. This was just one of the many accounts I received regarding the church.

A woman who worked in the Leece Street Job Centre, up until the 1980s, recently told me that during her lunch breaks, she would often cross the road and enjoy a sandwich or a cigarette in the quiet grounds of St Luke's Church. On many occasions, this woman, and several other people present, distinctly heard the faint hum of a church organ's bourdon note, the drone bass which always precedes a piece of organ music, which would drift and reverberate around the shell of the empty church. I even received an alleged tape recording of this music and it certainly did sound quite eerie.

THE DEVIL IN THE CAVERN

The following story is a particularly strange one. It concerns three men who used to visit the Cavern Club in Mathew Street, way back in the days before Merseybeat, when the Cavern was a jazz club. The story is told all over Liverpool and has been in circulation since the early 1960s. Nobody knows whether there is any truth behind the tale or if it is just a so-called 'urban myth'. Strangely enough, in every version of the story, the names of the characters are always the same. Furthermore, according to an article in the *Liverpool Echo* in the late 1950s, the manager of the Cavern claimed that there was a ghost that haunted the ladies' toilets...

Around 1957, a man named Alan Sytner opened the Cavern Club in Liverpool to provide a venue for the then thriving jazz scene. As most people know, the Cavern was basically a collection of arched warehouse cellars in the heart of downtown Liverpool where the Beatles first came to prominence.

In the late 1950s, three men went to the club one evening with their girlfriends and had a great time listening to the jazz bands. The men were Johnny, Tony and Peter and, at four in the morning, when most of the clubgoers had gone home, the three men and their girlfriends sat at a table, smoking and chatting away. The conversation turned from sport, to politics, to religion, to the meaning of life and finally resulted in an argument about the occult.

At this point, one of the men's girlfriends, a girl named Rita, said that one of the toilets in the Cavern was supposed to be haunted, but Peter, who was a hard-boiled sceptic, said the ghost story was probably just a publicity gimmick invented by the Cavern's owner. One of the members of management overheard Peter's remark and insisted that there really was a ghost. He said that one of the bouncers had recently seen the ghost, a man dressed in black.

At this point, Johnny suggested that everyone present should gather round the table and join hands to summon the ghost up, claiming that he knew the actual words to evoke a spirit. The girlfriends thought it would be exciting and urged their boyfriends and the bouncers to join in. Everyone thought it was a joke except a young man named Tony, who was not exactly religious but said the occult should not be regarded in such a light-hearted manner. He sat at another table, lit up a cigarette and watched the proceedings nervously.

With everyone but Tony gathered around the table, Johnny said, "Right, turn the lights off. Get a candle or something."

A candle could not be found but someone brought a small electric torch to the circle, switched it on, and then placed it in the centre of the table. The lights were switched off and all the people around the table joined hands.

There was a scream. One of the bouncers had put his hand up one of the girl's dresses for a laugh. Johnny said, "Stop messing about. We need absolute silence."

There were a few sniggers but then a strange silence descended into the cellars. After a minute, Johnny called out, "O Lord of darkness, I invite you into the Cavern. Give us a sign so we may believe."

One of the girls said, "And get a move on 'cos I wanna go to the friggin' toilet."

A shadow walked across the darkened room. It was a tall man wearing a black suit and a black polo-neck sweater, hardly in fashion at the time. His black fringe was combed back into the style of the so-called 'DA (duck's arse) cut' popularised by the film star Tony Curtis. All the girls looked at him but none of them were scared. They thought the stranger was just a clubgoer who had been part of the stay-behind. All the girls later said that the man was very attractive and had magnetic dark eyes.

Tony, who was seated at the other table on his own, thought the man was evil from the moment he set eyes upon him and noticed that the stranger seemed to come from the direction of the toilets.

"I am Lucifer," said the man, in a rich deep voice. He then smirked and studied the shocked expressions of the people at the table.

"Stop messing about,'said Johnny, "we're trying to

hold a séance here."

"You idiot," replied the stranger, "I am Lucifer. You didn't expect me to have horns, did you?"

"Oh, you're the Devil, like?" sneered one of the bouncers trying to impress the girls.

The stranger nodded, "I haven't got hoofed feet either."

"Johnny, I'm scared. Turn the lights on," cried Rita, shaking hysterically.

"Relax, my dear," said the stranger, "I'm really not as bad as I'm painted."

The sceptical Peter retorted, "There's no such thing as the Devil."

"If you believe in God, you must believe in me too," said the man in black, "unless you are an atheist, of course."

"Yes I am, actually" Peter responded in a matter-of-fact way.

"Then if you don't believe in me, can I have your soul?" asked the stranger.

Peter laughed nervously, "But I don't believe..."

"Give me your soul then!" shouted the stranger.

The atmosphere was tense with a mounting sense of terror. Some present detected a peculiar sweet smell reminiscent of church incense.

"Okay, take it then." Peter grinned but he seemed to be very uneasy.

"No! Don't, Peter! Don't!" shouted Tony from the other table. He stood up but was afraid to come over.

"Thank you," said the stranger reaching out in the direction of Peter with his hand and clutching at something in the air.

The torch started to fade. Within seconds it was just

a dim orange filament, then the Cavern was in complete blackness.

"That was one amateurish set-up," said one of the bouncers, almost falling over the table in the dark. He went to switch on the lights but they did not go on. "Oh, don't tell me the fuses have gone again," said the bouncer groping in the darkness. Such sudden blackouts were a common occurrence in the Cavern in those days because the condensation generated by the clubgoers' perspiration would short the wires in the lighting circuit.

During this time, a voice whispered in Tony's ear, "*I'll be back for you one day and your god won't be able to save you.*"

Tony cried, "In the name of our saviour Jesus Christ I tell you to leave."

Suddenly the lights came on and everyone rose from the table. All but Peter who slumped forwards, hitting his face on the table-top. He seemed drunk but, when his friends took him home to his flat in Smithdown Lane, he did not seem to be breathing. He was taken by a taxi to the Royal Infirmary on Pembroke Place and was certified dead on arrival. The coroner who performed the post-mortem examination later said that Peter, who was twenty-seven, had the body of an eighteen year-old and seemed to have been in perfect health. A verdict of death by natural causes was recorded but all the people who attended the frightening séance believed that Peter had died because he had foolishly given permission to the Devil to wrench his soul from his body.

A SINISTER SHADOW FALLS

A soft night wind stirred a teenaged girl's long black hair as she sat on a bench on Speke Boulevard. In her hand she clasped a can of lager. Her two male friends were both aged about fourteen. The lads were smoking, as they periodically swigged vodka from the plastic soft drinks bottles. The boys had an arrogance about them, convinced that their underage drinking was well disguised.

A further group of teenage girls gathered on the secluded stretch of the Boulevard, and the rowdy bunch of underage smokers and drinkers laughed and argued and boasted among themselves. There was all the usual torn foolery associated with such gatherings, including offensive gesturing at passers-by and traffic.

It was a sight Craig was sick of seeing through the closed-circuit television cameras of the factory at which he worked each long and tedious night. Most mornings at one o'clock, a fellow security guard named Ken came into the room to break the monotony with a pot noodle or a pack of sandwiches, and he would also look at the images of the juvenile delinquents on the monitor screens of the security surveillance room.

Weekends and the school holidays were the worst, when gangs of kids reaching numbers of up to thirty or more would rampage on the Boulevard, and the police cautions and patrols seemed to do nothing to deter the wild children from their antisocial antics. They continued to congregate near the factory, often scaling the fences and sitting on the walls surrounding it. Craig had asked the factory owners to attempt some kind of deterrent such as topping the walls and gates with barbed wire and anti-vandalism grease, but the guard's requests were never responded to.

In June 1998, Craig was at the bank of monitors, manipulating the remote-controlled cameras. A radio was turned down low in the background, churning out a tinny echo of music. As he observed all of the focused areas, he caught a glimpse of something that chilled him to the bone and set the hairs on his neck on end. Some kind of shadow moved rapidly from the darkness at the side of a building and flitted into another patch of blackness in the space of a second. The dark penumbra seemed to stretch and disguise itself as the angular shadow of a shed when it reached its destination.

On the monitor, Craig could see Ken walking through the yard and straight towards where this unidentifiable dark 'thing' was lurking. As soon as the security guard passed through the yard and turned a corner, the shadow of the shed peeled itself quickly off the ground, and appeared to slide up the wall, before vanishing over it.

The unusual sighting all happened so fast, Craig just sat there, gazing at the monitor, trying to take it in and make some sense of the puzzling phenomenon. After a moment's pause, he lifted his radio transceiver and spoke into it. At first his voice was caught. Still unnerved, Craig cleared his throat and attempted to speak again. "Ken, come up here a moment," he demanded, with a note of urgency in his voice.

Ken acknowledged the request and entered the monitor room. He found Craig analysing the screens with a disconcerting expression on his face. Craig turned to face him and explained what he had seen as accurately as he could, more than aware of how bizarre his experience sounded. Indeed, Ken was more than a little sceptical, until Craig rewound the security camera tape and played it back for his colleague.

Watched at normal speed, the mysterious shadow was so fleeting in its movements, that Craig had to replay it several times so Ken could see what he was talking about. However, when the tape was played at a slower speed, the shadowy entity looked even more sinister and was more easily visible. Ken and Craig agreed that the black shape was definitely not some trick of the light or an optical illusion; it was some sort of amorphous black entity that displayed an intelligence of some kind.

When Ken saw himself walk past the entity on the television monitor, he shuddered and turned cold.

"What could it be?" Craig asked, as he rewound and replayed the tape again and again, frame by frame.

Over the next month, the menacing shade was not

only captured by the closed-circuit television cameras, it was seen by Ken at close quarters, and the experience really shook him up. The frightening encounter took place at 3.20am one Thursday morning in July 1998. Ken was walking down a narrow passage between two buildings near the perimeter walls of the factory yards, when he saw what looked like a black ground mist rolling towards him. He quickly realised that it was the eerie shadow he'd seen in the footage of the TV security cameras. Ken turned on his heels and ran to a nearby hut, where he stayed for half an hour, until he was sure that the dark cloud had gone.

The most chilling incident concerning the vaporous being took place days later, when Craig was once again at the bank of monitors, checking and rechecking the screens, when suddenly he noticed a solitary girl, aged about thirteen or fourteen, staggering past the front gates of the factory with a small bottle in her hand. The girl was violently sick, and she threw down the bottle, smashing it into pieces all over the ground, before tottering away up the road. The teenaged girl didn't get far before she fell flat on her face. Craig zoomed the camera in on her and alerted Ken and another guard named Robbie to the collapsed teenager. The guards made a beeline to the gate, and as Ken left the factory to tend to the girl, Robbie telephoned the paramedics and the police. Ken ran down the lonely, poorly lit lane, then turned a corner. He shone his flashlight at the girl - and saw that the shadow entity was covering her. The murky life form was star shaped now and spread across the unconscious girl, who was shivering, as if she was having a seizure.

Of course, people under extreme stress behave out of character. Ken panicked and let out a string of expletives before charging at the shape. The murky entity darted away from the girl and crossed Speke Boulevard, where it melted into the darkness of a field. Minutes later, Robbie joined Ken at the scene and shortly afterwards, an ambulance arrived. The girl was taken to hospital and her stomach was pumped, because she had taken unidentified pills and washed them down with scotch after having a row with her mother. Luckily, she later made a full recovery.

The shadow was seen no more at the factory in Speke, but in 2004 I was giving a talk at Woolton Hall, when a young man approached me with a videotape. He said he was a security guard at a factory in Speke - not the same one where Craig, Ken and Robbie worked - and he told me that something very strange had been captured by a closed circuit television camera at his factory. The guard wanted my opinion on what the thing that had been captured on camera could possibly be. I viewed the tape with natural curiosity when I got home, and found it to be a large shadow that was moving around in some loading bay at a factory complex, and the thing appeared to be mimicking the shadows of buildings. I am sure the black cloud-like entity is the very same one that haunted the other factory in Speke, but just what it is I cannot say. I still have a video cassette that shows the shadow on the move. Sometimes I wonder if these unearthly entities come from some crack between our world and another one that is separated by a wafer thin dimension of space and time.

I shudder when I think what would have happened

to the prostrate, unconscious teenager, had Ken not challenged the vaporous fiend.

The shadow entity in Speke is reminiscent of a similar incident that allegedly took place at the Royal Liverpool Hospital on Pembroke Place in Edwardian Liverpool. A man named Charles Shaw was recovering from a serious operation. His hospital bed was situated at the end of a ward which contained seven beds. Mr Shaw suffered from insomnia, unable to sleep due to his extreme pain. One moonlit night, after the gas lamps had been turned off, the patient caught sight of a black flat object, about four feet in diameter, sliding along the floor, near to the bed at the far end of the room.

Shaw squeezed his eyes shut, willing the presence to disappear, but when he looked back at the unusual object, he found it was still there. He knew that he was not seeing things. The shadow then eerily somehow crawled on to the bed at the end of the room, and covered the face of a another male patient. Shaw felt an intense ominous fear and rang a bedside bell, summoning the nurse. Before the nurse entered, the black creeping entity slipped silently off the man's face and vanished under his bed.

As the nurse tended to Shaw and attempted to calm him, she was not able to take his account of the shadow seriously. The nurse then proceeded to perform her nightly checks on her patients, and examined the man in the first bed, only to find that he had passed away.

Over the remainder of the week, the shadow being

returned, and Shaw watched in terror as he saw it crawl over each bed, sometimes settling over a patient's face until the inmate of the ward woke up coughing and fighting for breath.

On Shaw's last night at the Royal, he had his closest encounter with the terrifying black liquid-like life-form. The time was half-past midnight, and he felt a sharp coldness on his foot that startled him. He looked towards the bottom of the bed and saw the black and doom ridden, shapeless object rippling as it moved across the covers towards his face. It stood up, inches from his face, as if it was ready to try and smother him, and before he lifted the blankets and let out a scream, Shaw saw two eyes slowly open up in the blackness of the entity.

Two nurses came running to Shaw's aid. They were not amused by his constant claims about the so-called shadow and they grumpily told him that they would be glad when he was discharged.

Charles Shaw's accounts were dismissed as hallucinations induced by the pain-killing medications with which he was dosed, but in the light of the similar case in Speke that we have looked at, it would seem that these sinister shadow entities have been around for quite some time. Google "shadow people" to see what I mean.

BLOODY MARY

This is a grisly tale, told from two different sources; a man who worked at the Geemanco factory in Barlow's Lane, Fazakerley in the 1960s - and a ouija board. Before I begin, just let me issue a warning to the idly curious about misusing the ouija. Just as astronomy books warn amateur astronomers not to glance at the sun through their telescopes, I am warning novice dabblers to steer clear from meddling with the power of the ouija.

I have seen so any lives wrecked by the upturned glass and even one suicide, that I must dissuade people from playing about with forces they do not comprehend or respect.

Now that I have got that off my chest, let's get on with the story...

In early 1996 I was observing a ouija session in south

Liverpool. The glass kept spelling out a specific girl's name. The surname of this girl was very unusual and stuck in my mind. I scribbled the name down together with what her spirit had to say, with my usual unbiased attitude. The girl described how she was caught between this world and the next because she had died after being struck on the head in a factory in Fazakerley in the late 1930s.

I decided to research the story and, a week later, I was tracing people who had worked at this factory through a friend, who put me in touch with a man named John who had worked there in the 1960s. At that time it was called Geemanco and it was a printing works. John remembered that when he started at the factory, the guards seemed afraid to go near an old storeroom after dark, referring to an apparition they nicknamed Bloody Mary. John was curious about the nickname and asked why they called the ghost by that name. An old guard replied, "Oh, you'll see, lad, you'll see".

About a fortnight later, John was working on the night shift and could not help noticing that his workmates and manager were becoming increasingly uneasy as the night closed in. John needed to go into the old, poorly-lit storeroom at around 1pm to fetch a carton of paper - and there she was! A young woman, with a chalk-white face and blonde hair, standing there in clothes that belonged to the 1930s. Her blonde hair was soaked in blood and there were scarlet streaks down her face and neck. Her eyes rolled upwards and her mouth quivered. John still recalls the paralysis which gripped his legs.

"They just turned to jelly and I seemed to turn away

from the ghost, which was about ten feet away, in slow motion. All I could say was 'No!'"

John finally regained control of his legs and described how he sped out of that storeroom at such a rate that he would have put Linford Christie to shame. The manager and his workmates calmed him down and reassured him that the storeroom was empty but he noticed that none of them would volunteer to go down to the room to switch the light off. For weeks after the encounter, John experienced terrible recurrent nightmares about the ghost, often waking in the night, in a cold sweat, screaming out loud.

When I told him about the girl's name coming through the ouija, John poured himself a large Scotch with a trembling hand and gulped it down in one go. He had given up cigarettes for six months, but was suddenly rifling through his wife's handbag for her packet of 20 Embassy Regal. I went on to tell him that, back in the 1930s, a girl had been killed in that storeroom. She had been a factory worker, operating a large machine with an enormous eight-foot-long lever. This lever had developed a mechanical fault in its spring and one day it came crashing down, without warning, on the girl's head. One witness graphically described how the heavy lever had smashed in her skull, as if it were an eggshell. Amazingly, the girl did not drop dead on the spot but staggered around for a full ten minutes in a cataleptic state. Blood was gushing from the open wound in her head and her eyes were rolling about. The poor thing was unable to speak and presented a gruesome spectacle, terrifying her workmates.

A priest and a psychic were sent to the factory site

recently and between them managed to induce her troubled spirit to move on from the place of her traumatic death, to what we would call the 'other side'. The terrifying ghost of Bloody Mary has not been seen since.

THE WINSFORD VAMPIRE

When I was a child, adults confidently reassured me that vampires, such as the legendary Dracula, do not and never did exist. Today I know they were wrong to dismiss the bloodsuckers. Believe me, vampires do exist but there are two varieties of them nowadays; fake and genuine. Firstly, there are cults in several major cities, notably San Francisco and London, in which members drink each other's blood and the blood of sacrificed people and animals. Not a very sensible idea in the AIDS era but a cursory browse of the Internet will list hundreds of these vampiric sects. Many of the blood-drinkers undoubtedly indulge in this type of vampirism for erotic reasons but, throughout history, from the days of the ancient Egyptians to the present, there have been many well-documented reports of real vampires attacking and subduing victims.

We don't have to go back thousands of years to examine reports of these strange beings, because there have been several vampire alerts in modern times and they are still being reported today.

On 16th April 1922, a man was admitted to London's Charing Cross Hospital with a strange, deep wound in his neck. All he could remember was that he had been turning a corner off Coventry Street, when he felt an agonizing stabbing sensation in his neck which caused him to pass out. He saw no attacker, so the police had nothing to go on. A few hours later, another man was brought into the hospital with a similar wound. He, too, had felt a sharp pain in his neck before losing consciousness, at the very same turning off Coventry Street near Piccadilly Circus. This second victim was also unable to give a description of his assailant because there had been no one within twenty feet of him. Incredibly, a third patient was later taken to the hospital and he, too, had a deep neck wound which he had received at the same spot.

The *People* newspaper covered the strange story and rumours of a vampire, at large in the West End, spread like wildfire. Alas, the invisible Coventry Street attacker was never apprehended by Scotland Yard but the case has all the hallmarks of a true vampire assault. You see, contrary to popular belief, vampires do not turn into bats and fly off in search of victims; that was the invention of Bram Stoker, who created the anti-hero, Dracula, in his 1897 novel. From the data we have on actual vampire attacks, it would seem that these strange, bloodthirsty beings have the ability to 'teleport' themselves about, either in physical form, or by somehow projecting their wraith, or astral body, to the victim's home. Furthermore, the genuine vampire rarely bites the victim to imbibe blood. Instead, it usually draws off the very life-energy of the victim, leaving him physically ill and mentally exhausted.

In fact, the symptoms of a subtle vampire assault, are identical to a condition that is becoming increasingly prevalent in the civilized world: ME, short for myalgic encephalomyelitis. This is a benign but debilitating (and often long-lasting) condition, which allegedly occurs out of the blue, causing headaches, weakness, muscular pain, extreme fatigue and even fever. Over 150,000 people in Britain are affected by this puzzling condition and, for some reason, most of the sufferers are women. The medical authorities still cannot agree amongst themselves about the nature of ME. Some doctors think the condition is psychosomatic, while others believe the syndrome has a link with the coxsackieviruses in the human body. Whatever the cause, the strange, incapacitating condition is reaching epidemic proportions world-wide.

No one had even heard of ME in 1970 but, in the summer of that year, Judith, a 19-year-old Winsford girl, was stricken with ME-like symptoms. A doctor examined the teenager and initially diagnosed flu but the girl returned a week later, accompanied by her mother. She was very pale and lethargic and had a number of purple marks on her neck and breasts. The GP identified the discolorations as 'love bites' and concluded that the girl was suffering from a form of glandular fever which is commonly spread from 'French-kissing'. However, Judith's mother went on to tell the doctor about her daughter's screaming fits in the dead of night and the strange lucid nightmares which haunted her sleep. Judith's own accounts of these night terrors resulted in her being referred to a psychiatrist, Dr Dwerringwood. She told him that once midnight arrived, she felt a sinister, cold presence invading her bedroom. Then, a young man in black would appear at the foot of her bed, leering at her as she lay paralysed with fear. Asked if she could identify him, Judith claimed it was a foreign-looking art student from her neighbourhood named Lazzlo, who, although attractive, had a creepy presence about him. She then gave details about the first 'assault' in her bedroom.

'I was just nodding off, when I felt a cold hand stroking my breasts. I opened my eyes and the room was in darkness but someone was on top of me and he was kissing and biting my neck. I was so frightened, I couldn't move or cry out. I closed my eyes and hoped I was just having a nightmare but, when I opened them, he was still there. From the light of the lamp post shining into my bedroom, I saw his face. It was Lazzlo.'

The young man in question, Lazzlo Ordog, was a 23-year-old Hungarian art student. He was quite tall; over six feet in height, with olive skin and black, slicked-back hair and a lively pair of dark brown, probing eyes.

Dr Dwerringwood quizzed Judith about her relationship with her father, as he suspected he might be the nocturnal culprit but he had died several years before. The psychiatrist therefore asked if any uncles or male relatives were staying at Judith's house. Only her 6-year-old brother, Graham, who had no time for girls. Then came the bizarre twist in this intriguing case. Another girl in the neighbourhood was also referred to Dwerringwood. The girl, Zara, had just turned sixteen and her body displayed the same cluster of love-bites on the neck and breasts. She also exhibited the same apathetic symptoms as Judith and, stranger still, this girl also nervously related how, on some nights, a 'ghost' got into bed with her and tried to have sex with her. Dwerringwood asked Zara to describe this ghost and her descriptions matched Judith's in every detail. The apparition was handsome but spooky, with black hair and penetrating eyes. The psychiatrist also suggested that perhaps it had been a nightmare but the girl insisted she had been awake throughout the nightly ordeals, which stretched back months. He then asked if the man resembled anyone she knew. She revealed that she had spotted someone who was identical to him. Zara didn't know his name but she knew which street his lodgings were in - the very same street where Lazzlo Ordog lived.

The police were powerless to quiz the Hungarian on the strength of such a bizarre testimony but Dwerringwood decided, out of curiosity, to break with protocol and pay a visit to Lazzlo. The landlady who ran the small boarding house admitted the psychiatrist into the hall and summoned Mr Ordog. The student crept silently down the stairs and, with a furtive half-smile on his face, gave the disquieting impression that he had been expecting Dwerringwood to call. The psychiatrist introduced himself and asked if he could speak to him in private for a few minutes. The student simply nodded and beckoned him up to his attic quarters.

Lazzlo was evidently using the room as his studio. There were several canvasses propped up on easels. All were of female nudes and most were incomplete but Dwerringwood was intrigued to see two finished watercolours lying side by side in a corner of the room. The subjects were two girls who bore an uncanny resemblance to Judith and Zara. Dwerringwood asked who had posed for the two paintings but Lazzlo claimed he had painted the girls from imagination.

The psychiatrist got straight to the point and told Lazzlo how he was the bogeyman haunting the dreams of two troubled teenagers. He added that both girls had identified Lazzlo as the nocturnal visitor and then asked him if he had any theories as to why they might be dreaming of him.

The Hungarian suddenly couldn't maintain eye-contact with the psychiatrist and, after shrugging off Dwerringwood's question, he busied himself with the arrangement of his paint tubes. Then, in an irritated manner he blurted out, 'Girls are crazy!'.

The psychiatrist now felt very uneasy being alone with the art student and decided to leave. As he reached the door, Lazzlo turned to him and asked, 'What do you think of the girls' stories? Do you believe them?'

Dwerringwood felt the hairs stand up on the back of his neck. He didn't turn around. Instead he left, mumbling, 'I don't know.'

When he returned home, Dwerringwood found his cat lying dead on the doorstep. There were no signs of physical injury on the cat's body, so he took it to the vet, who was a friend of his. The vet could not establish the cause of death and the psychiatrist felt his pet's death was somehow connected to the sinister Hungarian painter. On the following night, as he was watching the late news on TV, the mirror above his fireplace split in half with a loud crack. He could not explain the cracked mirror and later that same night, when he retired to bed, he distinctly caught a glimpse of a man's silhouette standing at the top of his stairs. The shadow-like figure vanished a split-second after Dwerringwood glanced at it, but it looked like Lazzlo Ordog's outline. He knew he had not imagined the figure, even though its transient appearance flew in the face of reason.

Dwerringwood never told his fiancée, Glynis, about the strange incidents or about the mysterious Hungarian but, one night they were lying in bed together, when she woke up choking. She felt a pair of powerful, ice-cold hands wrapped around her throat, throttling her. As soon as she managed to scream out, the strangling sensation ceased. She was so sure there was an attacker in the bedroom, that she jumped out of bed and rushed to switch on the light, but there was nobody there. On another occasion, Glynis experienced someone performing cunnilingus on her – while she was lying wide-awake in bed - alone. Dwerringwood racked his brains, wondering what he was up against. He was a man of scientific rationality and he felt out of his depth tackling the menacing Lazzlo Ordog. One afternoon, a bizarre thought dawned on him: what if the Hungarian was some sort of vampire? It was a far-fetched idea but the more he thought about him, the less ludicrous his theory seemed. He obtained two copies of the Bible and bought three small crucifixes. He left one copy of the Bible in Judith's bedroom and the other in Zara's bedroom. He also gave the girls a crucifix each and told them to wear it when they went to bed.

Dwerringwood wore the third crucifix on a chain about his neck and. when he went to bed, he turned off the lamp and settled down ready to sleep. Then a low gruff voice, seething with hate, whispered in his ear: *'I'll break your neck one day.'* The voice sounded as if it came from someone standing at the bedside.

For as long as Judith and Zara wore the crucifixes and left the Bibles in their rooms, they enjoyed a quiet night's sleep, regained their zeal for living and the purple contusions quickly faded from their bodies.

Some time later, Dwerringwood went to the lodging house to interview Lazzlo again. This time, he carried a Bible and wore his crucifix, ready to confront the creepy young man but Lazzlo had left. The landlady said he had moved out during the night, without leaving a forwarding address.

Dwerringwood's experiment with the Bibles and crucifixes seemed to do the job and yet, for many years afterwards, he struggled to rationalize the whole vampire episode and wondered if it had just been a case of hysteria, autosuggestion or coincidence.

Curiously, in October 1991, there was an intriguing haunting reported in Winsford. In the very house where the teenager Judith had lived in the 1970s, a young woman awoke one morning at 4am and was confronted by a man in black, with his arms stretched out, floating close to the ceiling directly above her bed. The woman was naturally terrified by the floating phantom and she hid under the covers, quaking with fear. She summoned enough courage to have another peep at the ceiling and found that the black-clad figure had vanished. Was Lazzlo on the prowl again?

According to the acupuncturists of ancient China, the health of a person depended on the life-force ch'i. If ch'i did not flow smoothly and harmoniously through the body, physical and mental sickness were said to result. Ch'i was regarded as the very essence of the soul, circulating under the skin through a series of specific channels known as meridians. Recent scientific research has proved beyond doubt that the human body is buzzing with electric fields and, furthermore, any interference with these fields can have serious medical repercussions. It has been proven, for example, that children living in close proximity to electric pylons and substations, are more likely to develop leukaemia because strong electromagnetic fields have a detrimental effect on the body's immune system. Perhaps this is how Lazzlo and others like him prey on their victims; by sapping the very essence of their life-energy, or ch'i.

For all we know, parasitic vampires may be at large at this very moment in our society, draining the energy of their unsuspecting victims. Would this explain the explosion in recent years of ME cases? Have you been feeling run-down lately?

THE WIND FROM HELL

The longer revenge is delayed, the crueller and bloodier it will eventually become, both in this world and in the world of the supernatural. Where blood has been unjustly spilt, the tree of forgetfulness can never flourish, and this is the grim theme of both this and the following story - supernatural vengeance and retribution from beyond the grave.

In the autumn of 1838, John Hunt, a well-to-do middle-aged cotton-merchant of Ashton-under-Lyne, residing at Canning Street, became engaged to twenty-seven-year-old music teacher Anne Jones, who lived in the Toxteth Park area of the city. Hunt seems to have had something of a chequered past, but he covered it up to some extent by occasionally embroidering a false history of his life.

One day a man named Scott recognised Hunt as he and Anne stood near the Old Infirmary amongst the crowds watching the foundation stone of St George's Hall being laid; an event simultaneous with the coronation ceremony of Queen Victoria. When Scott accosted him, Hunt swore he had never set eyes on him in his life, and when he accused Hunt of committing an outrage against a serving-maid at the Old King's Head public house in Chester, the devious businessman stormed off in a rage, dragging a bemused Anne behind him.

Anne was a highly naive and gullible young woman and seemed to be totally blind to the inconsistencies in John's account of his past life, despite the fact that she had been betrayed once before, by her previous fiancé. She did not even suspect him of having not one, but two, affairs behind her back.

During Christmas 1837, Anne received an anonymous letter claiming that John Hunt had, since the summer, been having an affair with a poverty-stricken gypsy girl of sixteen named Maggie. The girl scraped a living by selling bunches of lavender, heather and shamrock, as well as peg-dolls - anything to survive. At first, she succumbed to his charms and fell madly in love with John, but her Romany intuition soon warned her that he had a dark, unfaithful side. They say love can be blind sometimes, and Maggie made the fatal mistake of initially doubting her grave suspicions about her lover, for she desperately wanted to stay with him. She chose not to believe the letter's contents and threw the anonymous warning on the fire, for she also wanted to remain his wife-to-be.

Then one day Maggie was on Duke Street, selling her little wares, when she was shocked and then utterly heartbroken to see John Hunt walking along with Anne Jones on his arm. The music teacher was splendidly attired in a dress of dark blue brocaded velvet, old point and black satin, and she looked so impossibly beautiful that Maggie felt completely crushed. How could a simple girl like herself ever hope to compete with such elegance, wealth and refinement? As the couple passed her by, the poor girl burst into tears and bowed her head, and Anne, a sympathetic soul, rushed over to ask the gypsy what was troubling her. John instantly realised what had happened and quickly dragged Anne across Duke Street and on to his house, lest his treachery be disclosed by a mere chit of a girl.

Anne naturally thought her fiancé's behaviour was strange and for the first time she began to question his character. She then recalled the claims of that anonymous letter she had received - about John's alleged affair with a gypsy girl. Her head was spinning in turmoil and she wanted with all her heart to deny her suspicions. But she knew that hearts were unreliable in these matters and she had to find out what sort of a man she was intending to marry. She resolved to go and seek out the young Romany in the morning, so she could quiz her about the supposed infidelity.

That night, a drunken John Hunt caught up with Maggie as she stood outside a public house in the town, still selling her wares, though the hour was late. She had not eaten since that morning and was visibly drooping, but the cad grabbed her by the arm and dragged her to a secluded alley at the rear of the pub. There, amongst the rubbish and filth, he warned her that he would slit her throat if she so much as breathed a word to Anne about the affair they had had. To cut down the likelihood of her disobeying his orders, he insisted that, from now on, she should ply her trade up in the north end of the town, near to her lodging house.

Now in no doubt that her worst suspicions about John Hunt had been confirmed, Maggie felt nothing but loathing for him. As a woman scorned, she looked him straight in the eye said, "I curse you, John Hunt; I curse you and your coming marriage - and your business!" and with that, the young gypsy maiden ran off into the moonless night.

Not long afterwards, on 6 January 1839, John Hunt took Anne to a ball at the house of a fellow cotton merchant on Hope Street, and then, at around midnight, full of whisky and false affection, he walked her home in the moonlight. They were strolling through the delph of St James's Cemetery, hand in hand, when Anne suddenly stopped dead in her tracks and turned to him. With unaccustomed boldness, she asked him directly, "Have you been true to me, John, as I have been true to you since we first met?"

"Why, yes, of course, my darling, I have been true constantly!"

To emphasise his point, John released her hand and stepped back with a look of mock horror on his face.

"Then swear upon it, John Hunt!"

Anne now had tears ready to fall from her large sorrowful eyes; eyes which no longer had any innocence left in them.

"Anne, my darling, why do you cry? Has someone -" John reached out to her.

She shrank back from him, "Swear upon it that you have been faithful to me!"

At the top of his drunken voice John bellowed out across the place of the dead, "I have never been untrue to you, Anne! May the earth open up and swallow me if I am lying!"

Anne sobbed into her handkerchief, for from the tone of his voice and his lack of respect for this place of the dead, she sensed he was not telling the truth. She saw it clearly now, he was just like the last man she had loved and lost two years ago. How could she have been so naive as to allow the same thing to happen again? John Hunt's drunken features contorted into an insincere smile, and then he roared out, with his head craned back and his eyes fixed on the moon, "May the dead rise from their graves if I have ever been unfaithful to my sweetest, darlingest fiancée - spinster of the parish - the ever lovely, Anne Jones!

What took place next would go down in the annals of Liverpool's supernatural history. As Anne was still digesting this last sarcastic outburst, a hurricane-force wind gusted up from nowhere in the cemetery, simultaneously whipping off John Hunt's hat and Anne Jones's bonnet, to be lost amongst the crumbling gravestones. The mighty wind flung Anne clear across the graveyard, and then in a howling, whistling fury, it ripped up trees that had entangled their roots around rotten, water-logged coffins, and in the act of wrenching up these oaken sentinels of the cemetery, corpses and their splintering boxes were hurled into the night air.

The worm-infested body of a quite recent cholera victim, in a state of advancing decomposition, landed on John Hunt torso-first, and its skeletal arms swung around him upon impact, encircling him in a grotesque embrace. Ghastly syrupy brown-red blood spattered all over him, and the soft buttery adipose fat and loose jelly bowels of its lower abdomen stuck to his hands, as he wrestled in a frenzy to extricate himself from the corpse.

Throughout all this Anne was screaming in terror, but her cries were swamped by the roaring devil-gales. She was forced to watch as a massive granite slab was tossed into the air by the thick gnarled root of a felled oak and came hurtling back down towards John Hunt. The philanderer desperately tried to dive out of the way, but the flying gravestone grazed his shoulder and spun him round like a child's spinning top.

Under the ancient wan eye of the moon, more trees were toppled and their roots unearthed the dead on this most terrible Judgement Night. This was not the glorious resurrection promised by most world religions, but a cruel and vicious war of the wind, waged by the elements. The remains of the dearly departed, as well as the not-missed-at-all, were thrown alike into the air, catapulted by the uprooting of the trees, which the wind still knocked down like skittles. Skulls, bones, tattered burial shrouds, embalmed men, women, infants and children of all walks of life rained down upon John Hunt, in what must surely be one of the most terrible acts of vengeance ever conceived.

Anne struggled to her feet and somehow made it out of the cemetery, unable to breathe properly, because the whirlwind was sucking the oxygen from her lungs. John Hunt was blinded in one eye by tempest-driven splinters when a tree smashed against a looming marble headstone. He staggered along after Anne with a dozen skulls rolling after him, but in the noise and confusion he fell headfirst into an open grave, spraining his wrist as he landed amongst the sludge and bones. It was then that he remembered his blasphemous challenge to God - to let the earth open up and swallow him if he had been untrue to Anne. He whimpered pathetically for forgiveness now, but by the time he had climbed out of the grave, his fiancée was nowhere to be seen.

As Hunt leaned into the demonic gale on Hope Street, and tried to make his way home, blade-sharp slates rained down all around him. A passing cart, abandoned by its terrified driver, was overturned, and its horse fell down on its side. The stricken animal's legs kicked futilely in the air; its nostrils flared and the whites of its eyes were like two great saucers, but like a beetle on its back, it could not right itself and the wicked killer wind blasted on down Hope Street, cruelly dragging the unfortunate shrieking horse across the cobbles, flaying its skin to the bone in places.

Entire rooftops were blown clean off by the windstorm, and many died in the freak weather on the so-called "Night of the Big Wind", which would be remembered with dread by the townspeople for many decades to come. The destructive hurricane continued on unabated throughout the night and it did not burn itself out until the following afternoon. Houses were demolished, ships were sunk, and many people lost their lives, crushed to death as they slept in their beds by falling chimney stacks.

A traumatised John Hunt was left with only one eye, and without his beautiful fiancée, for the first thing Anne did after that apocalyptic night of the hell wind, was to break off their engagement. If ever there was an omen bringing an unequivocal message, this had to be it. Hunt also lost his cotton business, again as a direct result of that hurricane. He held many shares in stock at the North-Shore Mill, which was an important cotton factory situated on the west bank of the Leeds and Liverpool Canal, but the wind blew in every single pane of glass in the building. The high-velocity Aeolian currents then ripped off the roof, like the lid off a sardine can, and then destroyed the machinery and scattered and shredded over a thousand valuable bales of cotton across the north-end of the city.

A furious blizzard of this shredded cotton snow fell to earth over many square miles of north Liverpool, including the ruins of Kirkdale Gaol, which had sustained heavy structural damage, including a main wall that was demolished by the gales. Hunt had not been adequately insured for a loss of such magnitude and he lost everything he owned in those few short hours.

Hundreds died that night and the destruction to property was unprecedented. One of the people who survived was Maggie, the teenaged gypsy girl. She later met and married a decent young man, who unlike Hunt, proved to be faithful and loving and she went to live with him in Chester. One of the last sights she beheld before she left Liverpool for good, was John Hunt - not the wealthy cotton merchant she had once known, but a man reduced to penury, walking the streets in filthy shabby clothes, begging for money. Maggie must have been satisfied that her curse had worked to perfection on its intended target, though unfortunately it had also wreaked so much havoc, death and destruction on the innocent throughout the whole city.

THE BOWRING PARK CHARIOTEER

The subject of the following story is an apparition which I am unable to identify. Many people have encountered it over the years, although I still haven't a clue whose ghost it is. In the 1930s, the 6A tram ran from Bowring Park to the Pier Head, and this was the tram which two twenty-one-year-old lads, Teddy and Bert, boarded to take them to a ball on Edge Lane. The ball continued until one in the morning, and when Teddy kissed his sweetheart from Edge Hill goodnight, he and Bert had to set off home on foot, as there were no trams running at that hour. The homeward journey of over three miles was not too arduous, since it was a warm night and they had the light of the moon to show the way, and they were both feeling cheery from the wine they had consumed at the ball.

As the men reached the green open spaces of Bowring Park, they intended to go their separate ways, as Teddy lived in Huyton, and Bert lived near Page Moss, but as they were saying goodnight to one another, they heard what seemed to be the distant sound of a galloping horse. They halted in their tracks and strained their ears, and realised that the horse was heading in their direction, because the strangely echoing sound of its hooves was steadily increasing in volume. What the two men saw next sobered them up in a flash and impressed an indelible memory on their minds.

Approaching them was the spectral figure of a woman, with long hair that fluttered and flowed in the breeze as she rode a horse-drawn chariot. The phantom charioteer crossed the moonlit field at high speed, coming within thirty feet of Ted and Bert, before vanishing into the night air. The rattle of the chariot wheels and the thunder of galloping hooves quickly diminished, seconds after the alarming vision faded.

Bert was so terrified that he refused to go home alone in the direction of Page Moss, because that was the direction in which the striking apparition seemed to have been headed. He therefore stayed at Teddy's home, and throughout the rest of that night, the two men hardly spoke a word. Both of them had a chilling, albeit irrational conviction that the phantom charioteer had been some harbinger of death and disaster.

A week later, Bert's mother died in her sleep for no apparent reason.

Not long after that, Teddy started work at Cronton Colliery, and in a freak accident, he lost four of his fingers after getting his sleeve snagged in machinery at the plant there. Both men believed the supernatural encounter at Bowring Park had been a warning of death and misfortune.

As Teddy was recovering at home from his accident, a neighbour happened to mention that several people in the Huyton area had recently seen the ghost of the long-haired woman driving a chariot at breakneck speed over Bowring Park. Neither Teddy nor Bert had mentioned a word to anyone about the apparition, so that ruled out a practical joke.

There were to be many more sightings of the female charioteer during the hours of darkness.

At nine o'clock on the Thursday night of Halloween, 1974, two twelve-year-old girls were crossing a field at Bowring Park, on their way home from a duck-apple party at a friend's house, when they heard the thunderous sound of a galloping horse's hooves. They stopped in their tracks and soon saw a horse come hurtling out of the darkness, the chariot it pulled narrowly missing them as it flew past, the wheels throwing up dirt and stones. Both girls clearly saw the woman holding the reins of the horse, apparently oblivious to their presence. In a repeat of her previous appearances, the phantom charioteer crossed the field at high speed, then vanished into the darkness, and the girls ran all the way home in a state of terror.

It would seem that sightings of the magnificent ghostly charioteer of Bowring Park date back to the nineteenth century, but who she is remains a mystery.

A few years ago, what seems to have been the same ghost was seen further afield - near Speke. At the time of the sighting, the M57 was being extended and the excavations uncovered a previously unknown Roman hunting lodge, so it was conjectured that the spectral charioteer probably dated back to Roman times.

THE ELVI

The following story was related to me by Richie Abbacot, who lived in Mossley Hill many years ago. I interviewed him many times during research into his claims, and discovered there had indeed been a tramp named Trajan, who frequented Sefton Park in the 1960s. I was very dubious about his story at first, but have since discovered from readers and also from the locals of Sefton Park that the Palm House has been mysteriously illuminated in the wee small hours on many occasions, dating way back to the 1930s.

In a glade in Sefton Park, sat a tramp before a small fire which was encircled by carmine-hot stones. The man of the streets, who called himself Trajan in order to obliterate the memories of his old name and former life, had driven a Y-shaped branch into the ground and laid a long thick branch across the vertical forked branch. The diagonal overhanging branch was driven into the ground, and from its other end dangled an old lavatory chain which was tied to the handle of a blackened handle-less cooking pot. The fire boiled this pot of stew, and its unusual but appetising aroma drifted some distance. A full moon hung over the park on this Saturday night of 2 July 1966, and Trajan saw a figure watching him. The watcher was trying to hide but the moonlight gave him away, throwing the snooper's shadow into the open. 'I've only got one spoon,' Trajan shouted to the figure, 'but you can drink from my cup. I can see you there.'

A 19-year-old stepped out from the oak. He had a Beatle haircut and a 'gunslinger' moustache, and cut a fine figure in his deckchair-stripes blazer, sangria-coloured dungarees trousers and buckled boots. Facially the youth resembled Manfred Mann's Paul Jones. This boy's name was Richie Abbacot, and he sat down with Trajan and rambled on about the blazing row he'd had with his girlfriend Jean, and how she'd kicked him out of her Lark Lane flat. Now he had nowhere to live. As Richie voiced his woes, the crystalline Palm House in the distance glinted in the moonlight.

'Why you here?' Abbacot asked in his lazy way of speaking. Trajan said he had decided to leave the rat race to live the nomadic life. That was it. 'I put a rose to my ear, and it whispered a message that changed my life,' said Trajan in all seriousness, and he gazed up at the reddish star Antares, the rival of Mars, twinkling in the south. 'Are you on drugs?' asked poker-faced Abbacot. The wanderer shook his head twice. Abbacot wanted to know what this message from the rose was. 'It said: "be *you* before it's too late" '

'Is it okay if I sleep here tonight?' Abbacot asked, 'I was going to sleep in the tram shelter in the Penny Lane roundabout otherwise.'

'I'm not sure,' said Trajan, 'this is a special night.' Abbacot asked him why it was so special, and the tramp came back with a far-fetched-sounding reply: 'The Elvi and their kin celebrate in this park tonight. They may take you – just snatch you away to their world.'

Abbacot decided the vagrant had some psychiatric issues, and just nodded. So it was the roundabout shelter tonight then, he thought. He enjoyed the thick meaty soup with Trajan, and just after midnight, the tramp gave him some rum. Abbacot started to sing a hit from that year, *Pied Piper* by Crispian St Peters - when suddenly, the Palm House lit up with a ghostly blue light. 'What's that?' Abbacot's eyes bent towards the unearthly radiance. 'I told you, ' said Trajan, 'the Elvi – the elves, and the Red Caps and the Wendigo – and the faeries of course – all going to see Pan.'

'This I gorra see,' Abbacot got to his feet, and like a moth to the flame, found himself drawn to the beautiful multi-faceted gem of the Palm House, sparkling from within now as if it contained a forest of Christmas tree-lights – and what beautiful faint music floated on the night air from the domed greenhouse. 'No!' screamed the tramp.

A vast circle of spellbound foxes surrounded the Palm House, each of them gazing with their chestnut-brown eyes up at the radiant panes. These sensitive creatures, dismissed by us know-nothings as lowly scavengers, knew that something unearthly was at large in the great conservatory tonight, as did the tawny owls of the park, with their golden aureolin saucer eyes fixated on the crystalline Victorian structure. And to the glowing Palm House went Richie Abbacot, trancelike, sleepwalking, as if he was in a blissful dream, mesmerised by the iridescent colours and that beautiful music of pipe and harp-string. People who had died and been resuscitated had reported hearing this beguiling music at the gates of death...

'No! Come back!' Trajan the vagrant seized Abbacot by the shoulders and roughly turned him around. In a low gruff voice through gritted teeth, he warned: 'If you go in there you will never be seen or heard from again!'

'It's beautiful though, let me go in...' said Abbacot with a silly dreamy smile. Trajan dragged him away, and when Abbacot tried to break free, the tramp slapped him hard across the face, and the teenager fell to the ground. He snapped out of the spell. From the shadow of an immense oak, Trajan explained that the Palm House, completed back in 1896, had been erected on the site of an ancient circle of stones known to occultists as the House of the Zodiac. The circle was possibly linked to what are now known (wrongly) as the Calder Stones. The House of the Zodiac was some gateway to another world, far away in time, but somehow dimensionally close.

'And how do you know all this?' Abbacot asked the tramp.

The vagrant cast a tearful eye at the moon, then said: 'A long time ago, a girl I loved dearly vanished in this park. It was reported in the newspapers and the police thought she had been murdered at first because terrible screams had been heard in the park that night.

My beloved fiancée Catherine was taken that night by the Elvi.

'How did they take her? Where were you?' Abbacot wanted to know, and Trajan immediately told him. 'She wanted to know the "Secret that No Woman Must Ever Know" – a powerful esoteric secret passed down by the Elvi to their male successors. The secret allows the Elvi males to have dominion over the feminine aspect of every part of nature – including human females. Marie Antoinette, Cleopatra, Catherine the Great, Nefertiti, Helen of Troy, Eva Peron, and many of the prominent history-making women of the ages were mere puppets to the ones who knew the Secret. My Catherine heard me talk about it, and so she read my secret notes, and she learned that the Secret was uttered at a July Sabbat held at the House of the Zodiac, and she sneaked out one night and tried to eavesdrop here – but was drawn in by the rites; by the music and the colours.'

'Is Catherine still alive, wherever she is now?' Abbacot asked, and Trajan nodded, and wiped his tears with his cuff. 'And do you know the Secret?' the young man asked, with great intrigue. Trajan nodded 'Don't ask me to tell you,' he told Abbacot, 'you're young and vain and the Secret would destroy you and so many women. I had intended to go to the Elvi tonight, but now you'll probably follow.'

'I won't. Tell me the Secret, please, Mr Trajan – It'll get me back with Jean,' said Abbacot, and never saw the punch coming. He awoke shortly afterwards, bound to a tree. His head ached. By the time he was freed it was morning, and Abbacot never saw the tramp again.

DUKE'S STREET'S WEEPING WIDOW

The Weeping Widow of Duke Street was one of the most feared apparitions in Liverpool from Edwardian times to the 1930s. Around the outbreak of World War Two, the Widow went into retirement for a while, but returned with a vengeance in the 1970s, and she continues to be seen to this day. She is always seen in the vicinity of the so-called "Black Church" – the Great George Street Congregational Church – known today as the Blackie, because the building was, for many years, black as coal with a century's layer of soot and grime. The ebony temple looked strikingly sinister in those days, until it was sand-blasted clean in the 1980s – but the Blackie – now a very respectful Culture Centre - still has something of a paranormal reputation. Several years ago a young lady named Claire, who was an editor with a local publishing house in Liverpool, told me how, one afternoon, she had been walking up Berry Street, when she suddenly noticed a woman in an old-fashioned black ankle-length dress and a huge bonnet, gazing over at her from the steps of the Blackie. The outdated woman's face was pale, and she seemed to be aware that Claire was looking at her, even from a distance of a hundred yards or more. Claire crossed over the road which took her to the corner of Duke Street – and when she looked back towards the former chapel, she saw that the woman in black was gone. I told Claire that she was lucky, as many people had seen this apparition over the years, and most of them had afterwards heard of bad news after seeing her – but only if they saw her wearing her funereal veil. Claire was sure the woman had not worn a veil, and luckily, the young editor did not received bad news – but she never walked anywhere near the Blackie after that day. Paul Murphy was not so lucky. In 2003, he left a restaurant in nearby China Town one evening around 8.30pm. It was a drizzly November evening, and as Paul walked through the grand ornate Chinese Arch, he happened to glance to his right – and there she was – facing him, a woman in the stark black clothes of another age, with a huge hat on her head and a dark veil upon her face. She seemed quite tall – about 5 ft 8 or 9 – and she looked very solid for a ghost. Paul felt the hairs on the back of his neck stand up, and when he later gave me an account of his encounter, I saw goosebumps rise on his forearm – the sure sign that a witness is telling the truth. Paul had a flat on Catharine Street, and usually walked straight up Upper Duke Street, but he was so spooked by the baleful attention he was receiving from the woman in black, he hurried off toward his left – towards Berry Street, and went the long way home. Paul called into the Philharmonic pub on Hope Street and had a single whiskey to steady his nerves. He was glad to see an old college friend named Chris in the pub, and he told him about the woman in the antiquated clothes and black veil on the steps of the Blackie. The mention of this woman seemed to strike a chord with Chris, and he said, 'She's supposed to be bad luck. Are you sure she had a veil on?'

'What do you mean – bad luck?' Paul asked, feeling cold inside despite the whiskey.

'Ah, it's all bloody nonsense,' Chris said, back-pedalling – realising he shouldn't have told his friend about the ominous figure.

The next day, Paul's father paid a visit. He had not spoken to his son for years because of some family matter, and so Paul was very surprised to receive a visit from him – but he wondered where his mother was. 'Where's mum?' Paul asked, and his father's eyes seemed watery and so sorrowful. He reached out his arms and hugged his son, and began to sob. 'She's dead; she's dead,' he said, and his words were hardly intelligible because he was crying so heavily.

'She's what, dad? Dad! What did you say?' Paul pushed him away and looked into his father's tear-soaked face.

Paul's father took a deep breath and said: 'She said he had pains in her chest. I told her it was wind. She's dead.'

Paul's mother had died from heart failure. She had been a vegetarian and exercised regularly. She never smoked or drank. It was a big shock to everyone who had known the health-conscious woman. Not long afterwards, Paul Murphy recalled the veiled figure standing outside the Blackie. Had it been a grim coincidence? Had some student been playing a pathetic prank, dressed up as an old-fashioned woman, just to scare passers-by? Very unlikely, Paul reasoned, and like Claire, he never went anywhere near the Blackie again.

Further back in time, in 1978, a courting couple from Toxteth – Elaine and Bobby, made the mistake of kissing in the shadows of the Blackie one moonlit August night. The parents of the teenagers were dead against the lovers seeing one another, but Bobby and Elaine used to meet at the Rodney Youth Centre, and then go to the chippy or sometimes to one of the cinemas on Lime Street before heading back to Toxteth. On this humid night, the young lovers embraced on Duke Street, and as Bobby kissed his girlfriend's neck, she let out a yelp – but not with pleasure. 'Bobby, who's that?' Elaine broke away from her boyfriend, and he turned to see who she was talking about. A woman in black stood there, in a high-collared jacket and a dress that went down to the pavement. The moonlight shone from behind her, revealing the silhouette of her face against the fine black lace veil that she wore. She was crying, and making a spine-chilling low-pitched wailing sound. Elaine held onto Bobby, and she could feel his arm trembling. 'What do you want?' Bobby asked, and all of a sudden the woman in black let out an ear-piercing scream and flew towards the couple as if she was on wheels. Her legs did not move beneath that long black dress. The couple fled down Duke Street, and Elaine became so weak with fear she collapsed, Bobby had to carry her, by way of a long circuitous route that took in Nelson Street, to her home on Windsor Street. Elaine's brothers were going to batter Bobby, because they thought he had somehow been responsible for their sister's fainting fit, but luckily a friend of Elaine's mother said she herself had seen the woman in black near the old former church many years ago, and it always meant someone was going to die. Three days later, Bobby's brother was killed in a car crash in Kent.

A DANCE WITH DEATH

In the summer of 1885, a small slender woman with a pale childish face visited Liverpool. She was twenty-nine-year-old Elizabeth Berry of Oldham, and she had come to the city to visit a relative who lived on Duke Street.

After the visit, Elizabeth journeyed across the Mersey on the ferry to see a cousin over at New Brighton, and ended up staying at the seaside resort for three days. On the last day of her visit, Elizabeth entered the tent of the expensive and controversial fortune-teller, Madame Rosamund, who had intrigued her since the day she arrived. Rosamund, who claimed to be of Romany descent, broke the golden rule of fortune telling: never reveal the details of a forthcoming death to a client.

"You have had many deaths in your life -

Elizabeth," said Rosamund in a strange-sounding low voice, as she peered knowingly into the dark glassy depths of a purple-tinted crystal ball.

"Yes, yes, I have," Elizabeth replied, then queried: "But how do you know my name?"

"Your husband gone ... your son gone ..." Madame Rosamund whispered.

A shiver of apprehension shot down Elizabeth's spine. What the fortune-teller said was true. Four years ago, Elizabeth's invalid husband, Thomas, had died suddenly, and just over a year later, their son had also passed away. At the time of his death he had been sleeping in a damp bed in Blackpool. Elizabeth had received the sum of seventy pounds from an insurance policy when her husband died, and five pounds for the death of her son.

"Oh! The shadow is reaching out now for your daughter ..." said Rosamund enigmatically, looking at her terrified client from under her jet-black lashes.

Rosamund's large dark eyes widened and probed deeper into the very nucleus of the crystal sphere. Elizabeth felt faint at the shocking news, but there was another terrible revelation still to come. Oblivious to Elizabeth's evident distress, Rosamund continued to reel off what lay in store for the young widow in the future.

"You will dance with a tall dark stranger, and he will drop you and take your life. His eyes are brown - they twinkle like the stars - and he will captivate you, but he will surely kill you. His eyes will be full of tears when he sees what he has done. You will then go to the terrible place of darkness, wailing and the gnashing of teeth."

Trembling, Elizabeth stood up, and backed away from the sinister fortune teller. The unrepentant Madame Rosamund covered the crystal ball with a dark green velvet cloth and gently shook her head, "I only read the future, my dear, warts and all."

Some time later, Elizabeth was invited to a ball in Oldham by her local butcher, thirty-five-year-old Tom Whittaker. Elizabeth politely declined the invitation, concerned lest Whittaker should turn out to be the tall dark man with the twinkling brown eyes who would kill her. He was certainly tall and dark-eyed, and Elizabeth had often winced at the way the young butcher would hack the blood-drained carcasses with his enormous meat cleaver. She shuddered at the recollection. No! She would rather stay at home with her knitting, thank you very much!

A month after that, old Mr Hargreaves, the counter clerk from the local post office, invited the pretty young widow to a soiree at the local church hall. Mr Hargreaves was bald and blue-eyed, so there was no way he could be the brown-eyed killer foretold by the fortune-teller, and she accepted his invitation, thinking it would make a pleasant, if rather unexciting, change.

So Elizabeth Berry walked hand in hand with a man old enough to be her father into a church hall one hot July night in 1885. The two of them joined in the dancing until, at one point in the evening, Mr Hargreaves sat down to rest his weary legs, leaving Elizabeth on the periphery of the dance floor, still eager to join in the dancing. She made a very pretty picture, with her black curly hair tied up with a silk crimson bow, and her ivory white dress prettily adorned with pearls and pink roses. Her round face was childish, and being powdered and flushed from all the dancing, she didn't look a day over sixteen.

She did not have to wait long before a tall man with hair as black and curly as Elizabeth's own approached her. He invited her to dance, but she shook her head and cast her eyes down, nervously. Death had arrived.

"Oh, come now, don't be such a wallflower," teased the man in a deep rich voice, betraying an American accent.

Without waiting for a reply, the tall dark stranger grabbed her hand and Elizabeth felt dizzy and faint. She almost fell towards him. Her heart was palpitating. She was a helpless doll in his muscular arms, and he waltzed wildly with her across the dance floor. Everything was swirling. The chandelier swam by overhead, and the other couples spun past like mad dervishes. The American's cologne was masculine and as overpowering as he himself was. The heady aroma stifled her, yet Elizabeth Berry had never felt more alive in all of her twenty-nine years.

When the musicians stopped playing and the waltz ended, Elizabeth and the American were out of breath, and both were obviously filled with lust for one another. Growing increasingly agitated, Mr Hargreaves had been watching all these goings on from the sidelines and at the earliest opportunity he grabbed Elizabeth's arm, upon which the American, a Texan whose name was Brett, said, "Sir, may I compliment you? Your daughter is truly the finest English Rose I have set eyes upon since coming to this country."

Hargreaves's ample cheeks puffed with fury, and in no uncertain terms, he told Brett that he was not Elizabeth's father, but a good friend. Two other men who had been eyeing Elizabeth Berry with lecherous desire, seized their opportunity and they confronted the American and accused him of insulting a senior citizen of Oldham. A serious fight ensued, and Hargreaves and another man bundled Elizabeth Berry out of the church hall and took her home. At her gate, Hargreaves made a pass at Elizabeth, but she laughingly told him that she was not interested in him in a physical way, merely as a friend. When Hargreaves heard the bare, unpalatable truth, he surprised her by bursting into tears, then sucking his thumb!

That night, Elizabeth lay awake in her bed, thinking constantly of Brett's wide manly shoulders, his sleek black hair, and those dark penetrating brown eyes. She was so totally smitten that she convinced herself that Madame Rosamund had lied to her - the handsome American couldn't possibly do her any harm.

The summer mellowed as the weeks passed, and in the late August of 1885, a young local policeman named Bob Oakley invited Elizabeth to another ball, this time in Manchester. The ball had been organised by the Manchester Police Force, and most of the people attending the occasion were either policemen, ex-policemen, or their relatives. Young Oakley never danced once with Elizabeth Berry, as he didn't get a chance. She had created quite a stir, and the hot-blooded police constables crowded about her and queued up to take her in their arms and sweep her across the dance floor.

Of all the men who waylaid her that evening, only one caught the eye and heart of Elizabeth, and his name was James. He was tall, with hair as black as coal, and eyes of smouldering lignite brown. They flashed with emotion as James twirled her effortlessly around the dance floor. Elizabeth sat at a table with James and found him to be the most perfect, courteous, gallant and handsome man she had ever set eyes upon. She told him about her bereavements, and how she hoped to rebuild a life for herself and her daughter and become a nurse at the Oldham Workhouse, but when Elizabeth tried to discover if James was a policeman, he steered the conversation away in another direction. All Elizabeth was able to ascertain from the conversation was that James was a bachelor. Anyway, whatever his occupation, she argued to herself, he was obviously a kind and caring man. Yet again, although James matched perfectly Rosamund's description of Elizabeth's future killer, her emotions were powerful enough to blot out the fortune teller's awful predictions.

Then came a most curious coincidence. James learned that Elizabeth's surname was the same as his - Berry. If they married, James mused, Elizabeth would still retain her original surname. All this talk of marriage gave Elizabeth the courage to hint that perhaps they should keep in touch, but James Berry sighed and told her that his work would be taking him to another town, faraway, in the morning. After that, he was needed in another part of the country, and such was the itinerant nature of his job, that he was rarely in one place for more than a day at a time.

That night, James guided Elizabeth out on to a balcony, as every other couple savoured the last waltz. They clung to each other and kissed passionately by the light of the full moon, as the last strains of the music filled their ears. James said he knew in his soul that he would meet Elizabeth again one day, and when that day came, he would give up his work and marry her. They both cried on the balcony beneath the moon and stars. But, within half an hour, James was travelling east, and Elizabeth was travelling west back to Oldham.

Elizabeth Berry worked for a while as a nurse at the Oldham Workhouse, but she did not really enjoy the work, and inwardly believed that she deserved a better station in life. Her annual salary was just twenty-five pounds, and that was not nearly enough to pay for good clothes and a decent lifestyle. Elizabeth had a strange dual personality, and she would be kindness itself to the patients one day, and cruel and heartless to them the next. There were also strange rumours circulating about the daughter Elizabeth Berry hardly mentioned. This was eleven-year-old Edith Annie Berry, whom she had placed in the care of an aunt.

In January 1887, Elizabeth invited the child back into her life, but unfortunately, the girl fell gravely ill within days of the reunion. Elizabeth Berry's neighbours, who had no doubt already decided that she was a bit of a flighty piece, because of all her admirers, whispered that the widow was cursed, but others attributed Edith Annie's illness to a rather more sinister cause. After all, it was widely known that Edith's mother had recently taken out an insurance policy on her daughter, and stood to receive ten pounds compensation if the girl should die. This was true - however, Elizabeth Berry had also taken out a second policy that would pay out one hundred pounds to either Edith or her mother, depending on who lived the longer.

Little Edith Annie died in agony at five o'clock in the morning on the day after she had fallen ill. Given that Elizabeth Berry had now lost a husband, a son and a daughter to mysterious illnesses, and had received insurance payouts in each case, foul play was suspected. A Dr Patterson and several other doctors performed a post-mortem on Edith Annie - and discovered a powerful poison - possibly sulphuric acid - both in her stomach and in samples of her vomit.

Several people who had known Elizabeth came forward and expressed their belief that she had even murdered her own mother with poison, as she had died in similar circumstances. So Elizabeth's mother was duly exhumed - and poison was indeed found in her stomach. Other former friends added to the case for the prosecution, claiming that Elizabeth not only smoked opium, but was an immoral flirt who read sensational lurid novels. All Elizabeth Berry could say in her defence was that if, as the prosecution claimed, she had poisoned her mother, husband and children, then she must have been insane at the time.

However, her pleas of insanity went unheeded and she was tried, found guilty and sentenced to death for the murder of her mother by poisoning. A second case -that she had murdered Edith Annie - was not brought before the courts. The date set for her execution was Monday, 14 March 1887, and the place was Kirkdale Prison.

That fateful day soon arrived, and hundreds of Liverpudlians who had eagerly read the lurid accounts of the dreadful poisonings, braved the snow and icy winds as they gathered at the foot of the prison walls. Immediately prior to the execution, the hangman visited Elizabeth in her cell. She looked up as he entered and realised at once that it was James Berry, the man she had danced with two years before. When they saw one another, they stood motionless, both of them in shock. The prison warders glanced back and forth between Elizabeth and James, until one of them said, "Have you met before?"

James Berry nodded, and asked if he could spend a few private moments alone with the condemned woman.

"Of course," said the senior warder. "Knock when you want us to collect her."

The hangman and the murderess embraced in the cold dark cell, and both faintly sobbed. Madame Rosamund's prophecy had come to pass: You will dance with a tall dark stranger, and he will drop you and take your life. His eyes are brown, they twinkle like the stars, and he will captivate you, but he will surely kill you. His eyes will be full of tears when he sees what he has done...

James assured Elizabeth that her death would be quick and painless. He would make sure of that in the positioning of the knot around her beautiful, delicate neck.

Outside in the prison yard, warders were sprinkling sand over the snowy path to the gallows, to make sure that Elizabeth would not slip. Meanwhile, in the cell, the hangman was saying, "I never forgot you in those two years, Elizabeth. No woman has eyes as beautiful as yours. No woman on this earth has touched my heart the way that you did that moonlit summer night."

The hands of the prison clock ticked relentlessly on,

and soon the warders grew impatient. They knocked on the cell door and asked James Berry if he was ready. In a choked voice, he replied that he was. The chaplain accompanied Elizabeth and the warders and the executioner to the gallows. James Berry climbed up first and readied himself for the dreadful task that lay ahead. He glanced down and saw that Elizabeth had fainted. Two warders carried her up to the scaffold, and she was positioned over the trapdoor - or 'the drop', as it was known.

As James Berry pinioned her feet together and adjusted the straps, Elizabeth regained consciousness, and gasped in horror as the heavy noose was adjusted around her neck.

"May the Lord have mercy upon me," she whispered. "Lord receive my spirit."

The white hood was gently placed over her head, and she kissed the hangman's hand as he pulled the cloth over her soft face. The chaplain prayed in a low muttering voice, and James Berry closed his eyes as he threw the lever which drew the bolt. In an instant, the trapdoor sprang open and Elizabeth Berry plunged into eternity.

James Berry would later voluntarily retire from his grisly occupation and openly condemned capital punishment as an obscene abomination. People often asked him why he had abandoned and attacked his own profession in such a way, and Berry would always refuse to give a satisfactory explanation, but I'm sure that Elizabeth's death was the sole reason.

WHO KILLED JULIA WALLACE?

William Herbert Wallace was born to lower-middle-class parents at Millom in Cumbria on 29 August 1878. His first job was as a draper's assistant in Barrow, but having an ambitious mind, he found the occupation boring, and longed for grander things in life than a future in the fabrics industry. He dreamt of an exciting and more fulfilling life abroad, such as the one his younger brother Joseph led in Shanghai, working as a printer for the British Government. By the autumn of 1903, 25-year-old William Wallace left England's shores for Calcutta, where he had landed a job at the outfitters Whiteway and Laidlaw. This 'career move' was a disaster. The climate was unbearably hot and the hours were long with low pay and virtually no prospect for promotion. Wallace's troublesome left kidney was also bothering him again. He decided to put in for a transfer to the Shanghai branch of Whiteway and Laidlaw, and his application was accepted, but agonising pains in his faulty kidney caused him nothing but grief, and he was advised by doctors to return to England for renal treatment. In the winter of 1907, he resigned from the overseas outfitters and sailed home to England. Within weeks of his return, he was sent by his doctor to Guy's Hospital in London to have his left kidney removed immediately.

Wallace was an avid reader of the classics, and one of his favourite books was the *Meditations,* written by the ancient Stoic philosopher Marcus Aurelius. Wallace strongly identified with Stoicism, which advocates freedom from passions and desires, and he adopted the Stoic creed, which is: Don't expect too much out of life, but strive to improve it by discipline and hard work.

Wallace later became a Liberal Party election agent in Yorkshire, where he met a pretty dark-haired woman named Julia Dennis. On 24 March 1914, after a courtship lasting three years, thirty-six-year old William Herbert Wallace married Julia, and he seems to have been under the impression that she was just a year older than him, but she was not thirty-seven at all; she was in fact, fifty-two years of age. She had lied about her age. The age difference was probably of no consequence anyway to two people in love, but William would have been unaware that his new wife was probably beyond child-bearing age. On the 28 April each year, William would celebrate his wife's birthday, unaware that he was marking a birthdate that was almost sixteen years behind the real one. The outbreak of the First World War put paid to Wallace's job as an agent for the Liberal Party as politics took a backseat to one of the greatest conflicts in the history of the planet. William Wallace never saw active duty in WWI, possibly because of the precarious state of his health after the removal of his kidney; he continued to have problems with the remaining kidney until it would one day fail with fatal consequences when he was in his early fifties.

Less than a year after the wedding, Mr and Mrs Wallace moved to Liverpool, where William had, through the influence of his father, landed a job with the Prudential Assurance Company as an insurance collection agent for the Clubmoor area of the city. Before retirement, William's father Benjamin had himself worked for the Prudential, or "the Pru" as it was nicknamed in those times. The Wallaces lived at 26 Pennsylvania Road in the Clubmoor district, but moved out after just four months to live in a red-brick terraced house of 29 Wolverton Street, a rather dreary-looking cul-de-sac in the Anfield area. The couple rent the house for fourteen shillings and three pence per week, and from this period onwards, William Herbert Wallace lives in a clockwork world. He settles into routines ruled by the clock. He dabbles in chemistry, and has converted a back room in his house into a small laboratory. He also plays the violin as a hobby, but isn't very good at it. Julia plays the piano in the parlour and without a doubt she is the better musician. This musical leisure time in the parlour is allotted a set amount of minutes rather than hours. For sixteen years, Wallace held the same job without promotion, and throughout this period the couple led a content, but rather humdrum life of routines that were governed by the clock; breakfast time, lunchtime, worktime (for Wallace, but Julia stayed at home), leisure time, teatime, suppertime, bedtime. Almost every week, William would play chess at the Liverpool Central Chess Club, which met at Cottles Café, 24B North John Street, in the city centre. On the wintry Monday night of 19 January 1931, William Wallace left his terraced Anfield home and rode a tram to the city centre, where he was due to play a game of chess at Cottles Café. At home, his wife Julia was recovering from a bad cold.

At 7.15 p.m. that Monday evening, a man entered a telephone box on Breck Road, just 400 yards from Wolverton Street. He lifted the receiver and asked the operator to connect him to Bank 3581, the number of the café where Wallace was to play chess. There was a technical hitch, so the operator recorded the number of the caller's telephone box: Anfield 1627.

At 7.20 p.m., the phone rang at the chess club and waitress Gladys Harley answered. A man's voice asked: 'Is that the Central Chess Club?'

Miss Harley said it was. The caller asked for a 'Mr Wallace', and Harley beckoned the club captain Samuel Beattie to come to the phone. Beattie, a cotton broker's manager, had known Wallace for eight years, and suspected that the caller wanted to discuss insurance business with his friend.

Beattie cleared his throat with a cough and spoke into the receiver: 'Samuel Beattie, club captain here. May I help you?'

'Is Mr Wallace there?' the caller enquired.

Beattie said he wasn't, then suggested the caller should ring up later when Wallace was due in.

'Oh no, I can't. I'm too busy,' said the caller, 'I have my girl's twenty-first birthday on, and I want to do something for her in the way of his business. I want to see him particularly. Will you ask him to call round to my place tomorrow at seven-thirty?'

Beattie asked the caller for his name and address. The answer he received was: 'The name's Qualtrough. R. M. Qualtrough.' And the address given was 25 Menlove Gardens East, Mossley Hill.

At 7.45 p.m., William Wallace came into the chess club. Beattie passed on the message from Mr Qualtrough, a man Wallace had never heard of. The prospect of earning a 20 per cent commission on an annuity for Qualtrough's daughter was soon looking irresistible to Wallace.

On the following evening at 6.45 p.m., Wallace took two tram journeys to Menlove Avenue. He could find a Menlove Gardens North, South and West, but no Menlove Gardens *East*. He made several enquiries in Mossley Hill, but the locals told him the address he was looking for did not exist – there was no Menlove Gardens East. Wallace returned to Wolverton Street, and found that the front and back doors of his home were locked against him.

He decided to try the back door once again. It took him 30 seconds to reach the back door from the front of his house. He met his neighbours, John and Florence Johnston as he came down the alleyway. Wallace told them how the doors of his home where locked against him. Mr Johnston said: 'You've tried the back door?'

Wallace said he had but it had been locked. Johnston said: 'That's funny, try it again, and we'll wait. If you can't manage to get it open, I'll see if my key fits it.'

Wallace tried the back door again - and this time the handle turned and the door opened. The insurance collector rushed into the house. Not long afterwards he found his wife Julia lying dead in the front parlour. She'd been horrifically bludgeoned to death.

Wallace called in the Johnstons, the neighbours he had met as he was coming down the alleyway to try his back door again. John and Florence Johnston would later tell the police that they had been leaving their backyard on their way to see their daughter in Townsend Avenue, West Derby, when Wallace had bumped into them.

'Oh, you poor darling,' Flo Johnston said, as she knelt beside her dead neighbour and felt her wrist for a pulse. John Johnston stood in the parlour doorway. 'Is she cold?' he asked. It was an insensitive question. Florence nodded to his question, and Mr Johnston said: 'Don't disturb anything love, I'm going for the police.'

Mr Wallace asked his neighbour to call upon a doctor as well. Mr Johnston said: 'Any particular doctor Mr Wallace?'

Wallace grumpily replied: 'The nearest one!'

Johnston didn't go off immediately. He lingered around the kitchen, where the murderer had evidently wrenched off the door of a cabinet containing photographic equipment. The homicidal intruder had also rifled a small cash box that had usually contained the insurance man's takings. Four pounds had been stolen, and the murderous burglar had taken the trouble to replace the cashbox on the top shelf. After Wallace had examined the box, Mr Johnston said: 'You'd better see if everything's all right upstairs before

I go for the police.'

Wallace rushed upstairs, leaving the Johnstons in the kitchen. He returned a few minutes later and said there were five pounds in a jar in the spare bedroom which hadn't been stolen. Mr Johnston then asked: 'Was the light on in the [front] kitchen when you got back?'

'No, ' Wallace said, 'I put it on, and the one in the parlour.'

A few minutes later, Johnston went to Dr Dunlop's surgery on Lower Breck Road, but Dunlop told him this was a job for a police surgeon. Johnston therefore went to Anfield Road bridewell and told a PC Saunders about the murder.

Back at the Wallace's kitchen, Mrs Johnston suggested brewing a pot of tea. Wallace sobbed. 'Well, we'll have a fire!' Mrs Johnston shouted, and put woodchips and coal on the kitchen hob fire.

About ten minutes later, PC Fred Williams arrived at the house in Wolverton Street by bicycle. He quizzed Wallace and the Johnstons, and several detectives turned up shortly afterwards. Wallace told them how he had last seen his wife alive at a quarter to seven, but at 9.50 p.m., the insurance man's story was apparently blown apart by Professor MacFall. The police pathologist analysed the blood clots around Julia Wallace's head, then calmly announced that the woman had been dead since about six o'clock, perhaps before.

To the police, this damning estimation given by MacFall meant William Wallace couldn't have last seen Julia alive at a quarter to seven. Now, let us go forward nine years in time for a moment.

On the night of the 19th June 1940, a fierce aerial battle raged over East Anglia as a force of British aircraft met a fleet of Nazi bombers. The losses on both sides were severe. One casualty was a Blenheim night fighter, piloted by a 23-year-old Liverpool man, Sergeant Alan Croxton Close. The gunner parachuted to earth, but Sergeant Close bravely remained at the controls of his plane as it went down in flames. He aimed his injured craft away from the village at King's Lynn and saved many lives through sacrificing his own. It wasn't the first time Alan had saved someone's life. Nine years before, in 1931, Alan Close had saved the life of William Herbert Wallace.

On the night of his wife's murder, the case against William Wallace looked very bleak. He claimed he had last seen his wife alive at 6.45 p.m. when he embarked on the fruitless journey to meet a client named Qualtrough in Mossley Hill. However, a bungling forensic 'expert' - Professor MacFall, a man who had a history of opium addiction, had calculated that Julia Wallace had been dead at 6 p.m., possibly before, which meant that Wallace was lying. Shortly after 10 p.m. that traumatic evening, Detective Superintendent Hubert Moore - Head of CID - turned up at Wallace's home in a drunken state. When MacFall told Moore how long Julia had been dead, the CID chief quizzed Mr Wallace in the kitchen. In his mind, Moore believed Wallace was the killer. I have seen the official notes and marginalia that Moore made in his notebook, and without a doubt, he thought Wallace had murdered his wife and had tried to make it look as if a burglar had killed her. What Moore didn't know was that Professor MacFall had grossly miscalculated

Julia Wallace's time of death. MacFall had not bothered to take the temperature of the body or the parlour. Instead he thought the blood clots around Julia Wallace's head 'looked quite old'.

Moore lifted the emptied cash box down from the top shelf in the kitchen and remarked, 'You know, I cannot for the life of me understand why a thief would go to all that trouble of putting the lid back on the box and placing it back where he'd found it.' When Moore later discovered that the call to Wallace's chess club had been made from a call box on Breck Road, he was ecstatic. It had to be Wallace. That phone box was a mere 400 yards from his home.

Wallace was subsequently arrested, charged with his wife's murder, and put on trial. His only hope of salvation came from the testimony of the 14-year-old milk boy - Alan Croxton Close. It transpired that he had delivered a can of milk to Julia Wallace on the night of her murder – at a quarter to seven. Julia had talked to Alan about his cough when he called. What's more, James Allison, a second youngster delivering the *Liverpool Echo* to the house next door to the Wallaces distinctly remembered Alan chatting to Mrs Wallace on her doorstep around 6.40 p.m.

When Detective Superintendent Moore heard about Alan Close's testimony, it cut him to the bone. All the same, Wallace was arrested, and later put on trial for the murder of his wife. During the summing up by Justice Wright, one juror was sound asleep. The Judge tried to direct the jury to return a Not Guilty verdict. The jury retired, talked mostly about the perks they'd enjoyed as jury members, then returned with a verdict of Guilty. The court and Justice Wright were stunned by the verdict. The death sentence was read, and Wallace was taken to Walton Gaol in a Black Mariah. The insurance agent appealed against the sentence, and the unbelievable happened. The Court of Appeal quashed the conviction that had condemned Wallace, which was unprecedented. There is no doubt that the testimony of Alan Close was highly instrumental in saving Wallace from the hangman's noose. However, William Wallace's troubles were far from over.

In order to get to Menlove Gardens on the night of his wife's murder, William Wallace would have had to have left home no later than 6.49pm, yet milk boy Alan Close had spoken to Julia Wallace at 6.45 p.m., so if we are to believe that Mr Wallace killed his wife, he would literally have had about four minutes to bludgeon her to death - whilst wearing nothing but a mackintosh. We would then have to accept that Mr Wallace – who was a heavy smoker with one kidney (which was afflicted with a chronic renal condition) could take a bath, get dressed, fake a break-in, dump the murder weapon (which was never found) bolt the front door, lock the back one, then sprint all the way to the tram stop.

This scenario, is of course, absurd, and the Court of Criminal Appeal thought so, which is why Wallace's death sentence was quashed. Unfortunately, the people of Liverpool and beyond believed that Wallace had killed his wife, and when the insurance agent was given back his old job at the Prudential, colleagues he had known for years treated him like a convicted criminal. Customers also refused to answer the door when he called, and people turned their backs on him in the street. They could not accept that Wallace was an innocent man who had found himself at the centre of a living nightmare.

If William Wallace didn't kill Julia, who did? A 32-year-old man named Ian Forbes of Crown Street, Edge Hill gave himself up at Prescot Street police station on 14 May 1931 and admitted he had killed Julia Wallace. He was a methylated spirits drinker who was later found to be schizophrenic, and had been nowhere near Anfield on the murder night. Then a James Gilmore, also aged 32, confessed to the murder. He was later admitted to Rainhill Mental Hospital. There were many more false confessions from an assortment of dreamers and cranks. One such fantasist was Richard Gordon Parry, a 22-year-old amateur actor who had once worked for the Prudential insurance company with Mr Wallace. It has been alleged by countless authors and theorists that Parry was Qualtrough, and that he had sent Wallace on a wild goose chase just to get him out the house so he could kill Julia and frame her husband. In fact, Parry had not been in the Wallace's house for two years. A dubious rumour claimed that Parry had worn an oilskin coat, gauntlets and wellington boots as he clubbed Julia, but the forensic investigation established that there were no distinctive blood trails created by blood dripping off a waterproof surface on the parlour carpet. Parry travelled in a car yet no car was seen anywhere in the Wallace's neighbourhood on the night of the killing.

All the books and theories concerning the Julia Wallace murder do not reference the following curious fact. The police thought the circumstances surrounding the killing of Julia Wallace had an eerie parallel with a burglary that had taken place weeks before and just four doors away from the Wallace's home in December 1930. Samuel Shotton, a retired postman, had returned from holiday with his wife Clara to find their house at 19 Wolverton Street burgled, yet there had been no forced entry, even though the perpetrator of the crime had needlessly tossed pillows and blankets from the bed up in the Shottons' spare room - creating the impression that the burglar was a disorganised soul who had been rummaging about for money and valuables. The person who had burgled Samuel and Clara Shotton's home in Wolverton Street had known exactly where the couple kept their savings, and he had known that the couple were away on holiday, almost as if he had inside knowledge, and what's more, he had even gone to the trouble of replacing the lid on the box that had contained the savings. Now, up in the Wallaces spare room on the night of the murder, the pillows and blankets were found in disarray, even though Julia Wallace's expensive mink coat and jewellery were found untouched in a drawer in that spare room. It seemed as if a duplicate key had been used to gain access to Wallace's home on this occasion as well. It's worth noting that there had been a similar series of burglaries at the beginning of 1930 in Wolverton Street and some of the surrounding streets, and a 'skeleton key' was used in each robbery. Who had such a duplicate key? John Sharpe Johnston, the next-door neighbour of William Wallace did. That is why he said: "Try my key" when Wallace had bumped into him in the alleyway on the night of the murder. Wallace had told Mr Johnston that his back kitchen door had been locked when he tried it thirty seconds before, yet when he retried that door-handle – at the suggestion of Mr Johnston - he was baffled to find that someone had just unlocked it. I believe that person was John Sharpe Johnston. I believe he killed Julia Wallace, and being a next-door neighbour, "Qualtrough" was able to leave the scene of the crime in seconds to walk eighteen feet down the backyard of the murder house into his own backyard. This explains why Qualtrough went to ground so fast after killing Julia Wallace, and why he was never seen running or hurrying away from the scene of the crime by one single witness in the area.

With this hypothesis in mind, let us revisit the night of the murder. Wallace, upon his return from the fruitless quest for the fictitious Qualtrough at the non-existent Menlove Gardens East, goes to the front door of his home, only to find that it is locked. He goes to the back of the house via the alleyway to find the backyard door unbolted, which is odd, because Julia always bolts that door when her husband is out. Wallace walks up the yard, tries the back kitchen door; and he finds that it is locked. He returns to the front door; and it is still locked. He then takes just thirty seconds to walk to the back of the house to try his back kitchen door once again, and Mr and Mrs Johnston happen to emerge from their backyard door with perfect timing. John Sharpe Johnston has just unlocked the back kitchen door and walked just a few feet to his own backyard door where he and his wife wait to intercept Wallace. John Johnston had just washed and has changed his clothes. So has his wife Florence, for they both admitted to this at the ensuing court trial. Their excuse is that they washed and dressed because they were about to visit their daughter in West Derby — and were ready to embark on the tram journey at 8.45pm. Phyllis, the daughter of the Johnstons however, admitted she was not expecting her parents to call that night, and when they did call, it was usually between 6pm and 7pm. John Sharpe Johnston and his wife were not in the habit of calling upon their daughter or anyone else at such a late hour as almost 9pm, because Mr Johnston had to be up early to travel on an arduous route by tram and ferry boat to Cammell Laird shipyard on Wirral, and was often in bed by eleven at the latest and up at 4am. The behaviour of the Johnstons speaks volumes on the night of the murder. Reading through the official files and the court transcripts of the Wallace case, the neighbours of the Wallaces act somewhat out of character from the moment they meet William Wallace in the alleyway. Wallace tells them he can't get into his house, and enters his backyard to try the back kitchen door he had tried less than a minute ago, and John Johnston, standing in the doorway of the backyard with his wife, tells Wallace to try the back kitchen door again. 'Try it again and we'll wait here,' Mr Johnston says, 'If you can't manage to get it open I'll see if my key fits it.'

And as if by magic, Wallace turns the handle of the back kitchen door and it opens effortlessly. John Johnston's suggestion to try his key to open the door of his neighbour's back kitchen leads us to one of those little-known facts surrounding this classic case which I unearthed. In 1929, the Wallaces discovered to their horror that some of the keys to the houses in Wolverton Street fitted their own doors. On one occasion, a drunken neighbour, Mr Samuel

Cadwallader, from 33 Wolverton Street, used his key to enter the Wallace's house one night as the couple were in bed. Julia screamed hysterically and the inebriated Mr Cadwallader apologised for his unintentional entrance into the house, which he mistakenly believed to be Number 33. Not long after this, Mr Cadwallader passed away, so we can discount him as a suspect, but he was a friend of John Sharpe Johnston, and its reasonable to assume that Johnston would have been aware of the security vulnerability of the locks on the doors of Wolverton Street. Wallace mentioned this security issue to the police after the murder, and admitted he had not bothered to have his locks changed because he trusted his neighbours. Wolverton Street residents Samuel and Clara Shotton, who had their house burgled just before the Christmas of 1930, were also very trusting towards their neighbours - and had actually informed the Johnstons to keep an eye on their home while they were away. The police never regarded the Johnstons as suspects because the pathologist John Edward Whitley McFall had mistakenly estimated the time of Julia Wallace's death, pointing the finger of suspicion at William Wallace. The insurance agent's version of events for the night of the brutal murder simply didn't add up if Julia was dead before he had left the house. If the police had checked the Johnstons out they would have uncovered a couple of curious postcards in the sideboard of the Wallaces' neighbours that came to light in the 1940s. These postcards are of interest because they completely contradict the testimony of the Johnstons when Edward Hemmerde KC, Counsel for the prosecution, asked the couple at the trial at St

George's Hall, if they knew the Wallaces well. John Sharpe Johnston said he hadn't even known Mrs Wallace's first name was Julia, and Hemmerde then asked the Johnstons how many times they had been in the home of the Wallaces in the ten years they had lived next door to them. Just three times, Florence Johnston had told Hemmerde. 'What? Just three times in ten years?' said an apparently surprised Hemmerde. Florence and John maintained that they had sat in the parlour of the Wallaces three times in ten years, and, Florence was careful to add, they had not been in any other part of the house, such as the kitchen where the rifled cash box had been kept. The Johnstons created the impression that the Wallaces were virtually strangers to them. The Johnstons never explained two postcards sent to them by Julia Wallace while she holidayed with her husband in Anglesey, postmarked 23 July 1926 and 6 July 1928. The 1926 postcard, addressed to Mrs Johnston, reads, 'This is a lovely place, and we have such a nice place to stay...best Wishes to All' – and it is signed 'J. Wallace.'

The second postcard, sent to Mrs Johnston from Julia from Port Padrig, Cemaes Bay, Anglesey, in 1928, is more interesting. It contains an apology from Julia for not leaving Florence Johnston any money to buy food for Puss, the Wallaces cat, and Julia promises she will pay Florence the money she owes her as soon as she returns from Anglesey. It turns out that the Johnstons were also entrusted with keys to open and close curtains at the home of the Wallaces each day (to create the impression someone was in the house and discourage burglars) and to collect mail during the fortnight's holiday. It is not beyond the bounds of probability to suggest that the Johnstons mooched about in Number 29 Wolverton Street while the Wallaces were on holiday, and perhaps found the fabled nest egg that Wallace was said to keep somewhere in the house. Wallace was a known pennypincher who lived on less than four pounds per week, and his miserliness was something of a running joke to those few people who knew him. What was Wallace doing with the money he was saving?

Back to the night of the murder; when William Wallace entered his home via the back kitchen door, John Johnston and his wife Florence, stood in the backyard and after a minute or so they heard Mr Wallace calling his wife's name twice, then saw the light in the middle bedroom's upstairs window flare up. Then the Johnstons saw the light of a match being struck by Wallace in the window of the smaller upstairs room which the insurance agent used as a laboratory where he taught himself chemistry as a hobby.

Less than two minutes later, Wallace came out of the back kitchen into the backyard looking very distressed. 'Come and see!' Wallace cried out, 'She has been killed!'

'What is it?' Johnston asked, ' Has she fallen downstairs?'

The Johnstons follow Mr Wallace into the house via the back kitchen, then into the front kitchen, out into the hallway, and into the front parlour, where the Johnstons see Julia Wallace on the rug with her brains pouring out, and Florence Johnston says, 'Oh you poor darling,' then feels for a pulse. Her husband John, standing in the doorway of the parlour, asks in a rather callous manner, "Is she cold?" At this point, the killer could still be lurking in the dark house, but the Johnstons are very laid back. 'Would you like a cup of tea Mr Wallace?' Florence asks, then makes a fire at the hob in the front kitchen as Wallace sobs. John Johnston sees the aftermath of the burglary in the kitchen. Wallace shows him the cashbox and says he thinks four pounds has been taken, and then he points to a cabinet that had had its door wrenched off by the burglar. It had contained nothing but photographic equipment. Johnston then says to Mr Wallace: 'You'd better see if everything's all right upstairs before I go for the police and a doctor.'

But hadn't Mr Johnston already seen Wallace go upstairs when he stood in the back yard of Number 29 with his wife a few minutes ago? He had seen Wallace move with a lighted match from the middle bedroom window to the laboratory window. Given the horrific circumstances an understandably confused Wallace goes upstairs anyway, and leaves the Johnstons alone downstairs for a few minutes.

Mr Wallace then returns and says 'Everything's all right up there. There's five pounds in a jar they haven't taken.'

Johnston still lingers around the front kitchen for a while, then leaves his wife in the murder house as he goes, rather pointlessly, for a doctor (who tells Johnston to go straight to the police station on Anfield Road, as Mrs Wallace is obviously beyond medical help). The Johnstons had achieved their mission of getting back into the house to see if they had left any incriminating evidence from their botched burglary attempt. What was the evidence they had left? Well, police found a number of matchsticks next to the corpse of Julia Wallace, and believed that for some reason, the killer had struck a match to survey the fatal injuries he had inflicted upon his victim. The lingering killer had evidently dropped each match when it had burnt down and then struck another one. The first person to remark upon these matches was Florence Johnston, and she also asked Mr Wallace if the box of matches on the table by the parlour window were his or Mrs Wallace's – as the insurance man was still reeling in shock as he knelt by the body of his murdered wife. Wallace is so bewildered and disoriented by the nightmarish situation, he says the matches may be his, but he isn't sure. Why is Florence so fixated with such a trivial matter of matches when her next-door neighbour has just been bludgeoned to death and is lying on the floor with her brains oozing out of her smashed skull? Still, Florence persists, querying the ownership of the box of matches and says they must belong to Mr Wallace. Are they in fact matches belonging to the Johnstons, left behind when they fled from the murder house? Are they the matches John or Florence struck after they came back into the house to see if Mrs Wallace was dead? Florence picks up the box of matches, planting her fingerprints on them before a witness.

In 1955, Fred Williams, the former policeman who had been the first to arrive at the scene of the murder at Wolverton Street, was being treated for influenza in Broadgreen Hospital when he recognised one of the consultants in the ward as Dr Robert Coope, a man who had investigated the crime scene of the Julia Wallace murder 24 years before. To Dr Coope, the retired policeman told Dr Coope he had something to tell him that had been playing on his mind for too many years. Williams was seriously ill, and had difficulty breathing, but managed to tell the doctor that he believed he knew who had killed Julia Wallace. He started by saying that Mr Wallace was innocent. Williams had only interviewed three people: Mr Wallace – and the Johnstons. Dr Coope was extremely busy that day and promised he'd come back to see the ex-policeman in the morning to hear his views on the old murder case, but Williams sadly died from influenza soon after making his intriguing comments, so we'll never know what he had to say.

The police could not work out why no blood splashes were found either outside the parlour in the hallway or on the living room door. It was as if some person had been standing between Julia Wallace and the door as she was battered to death. Could it be that Florence Johnston was standing between Julia and the doorway as her husband battered the woman's brains out?

In April 2001, I appeared on a programme on BBC Radio Merseyside about local crimes and appealed for people who had known the Johnstons to get in touch with me. A seriously ill man named Stan who had known John Johnston got in touch with the local criminologist Keith Andrews. Stan said Johnston had died in January 1960 of senile dementia at an old folks home on Westminster Road. I have checked this information and found it to be true. Stan said that days before Johnston died, he confessed to killing Julia Wallace. He admitted it was he who had made the Breck Road telephone call to the chess club to get Wallace out the house. Florence had Julia's cat 'Puss' and was supposed to lure Julia next door to get it. Julia's cat had been missing for days. But John Johnston had surmised that Julia had gone to Menlove Gardens with her husband when he saw them go out the backyard together, because Julia had on a mackintosh. Julia had in fact been walking down the alleyway looking for Puss, and Johnston didn't see her return. The Johnstons waited for a while, then slipped into the Wallace's house via the back kitchen door, which John unlocked with his key. He went in search of the insurance man's monthly takings and a nest egg he believed to believed to be upstairs. That nest egg, if it ever existed, was nowhere to be seen, and there were no monthly takings because Wallace had been off work with a bad cold and unable to collect the usual amount of money for that month.

Disappointed with the meagre cash they found, John and Florence decided to try the front parlour. As they entered they got the shock of their lives when the flu-stricken Julia Wallace rose from her couch with the mackintosh over her. She wasn't supposed to be there. 'Mr Johnston!' Julia probably shouted, alarmed and then puzzled as to why her neighbours were in her house. John decided to hit her with the jemmy he'd used to smash open the cabinet in the kitchen. He had to kill her, because she now knew the identity of the man who was burgling the neighbourhood. The only fingerprints that would be found at the murder scene belonged to Mr Wallace, the sloppy detectives and police – and the Johnstons. On the following day, the Johnstons suddenly moved out of Wolverton Street and went to live with their daughter at 358 Townsend Avenue. Florence was subsequently treated for shingles and had treatment for what was then known as 'bad nerves'. Years afterwards, in the 1950s the Johnstons moved to 13 Braybrooke Road in West Derby. One day, a neighbour stopped at the garden gate of the Johnstons to chat to Florence, and in the course of the conversation, the topic turned to the subject of the Wallace Murder. Florence Johnston said something about the world-famous case, and suddenly, her husband John Johnston, who had been standing in the hallway, obviously eavesdropping on his talkative wife and the neighbour, came marching down the path. He dragged Florence into the house, and, according to the neighbour, when she next saw Florence, the woman sported two enormous black eyes. Not long after that, an ambulance called at the Johnstons. Florence was dead. According to Mr Johnston, his wife had awakened in the night complaining of pains in her upper arms. 'Go back to sleep love,' Mr Johnston had told her, 'you'll be all right.'

The next day he found her dead in bed. She'd died from an embolism.

Raymond Chandler, the writer of crime fiction, took a great interest in the Wallace murder case, and finding no solution, he remarked that the murder could never be solved. I believe he was wrong. I believe that the one person who suspected the Johnstons of being Qualtrough was Edward Hemmerde KC, ironically the very man chosen to be Kings Counsel for the Prosecution. Hemmerde examined and re-examined the Johnstons, questioning them about the times they had visited the household of the Wallaces: 'You say you knew the Wallaces as neighbours?'

'Yes,' Florence Johnston replied.

'Had you ever been in their house?' Hemmerde queried.

'Yes,' said a barely audible Florence Johnston.

'How often?' asked Hemmerde.

'About three times,' said Mrs Johnston.

'In ten years you have been in *three* times?' Hemmerde emphasised the 'three'.

'Yes,' answered Florence Johnston, 'in the front room only, where the body lay; the sitting room.'

'Were they both there on those three occasions? The two of them?' asked Hemmerde.

'No, only Mrs Wallace,' Mrs Johnston replied.

Hemmerde told the court that Qualtrough had to be two people, as there was no single vantage point in the area of Wolverton Street where Qualtrough could position himself to ascertain whether or not William Wallace had left his home by the back or front door on the night he went on what would turn out to be a hopeless quest for the non-existent address. Hemmerde suggested that if Qualtrough was two people, one could watch the front of Mr Wallace's house and the other could keep watch on the alleyway, and therefore be wholly sure that Mr Wallace had taken the bait and gone in search of the make-believe Menlove Gardens East.

Qualtrough was obviously acquainted with the layout of Menlove Gardens to know that there was a Menlove Gardens North, a Menlove Gardens South, and a Menlove Gardens West, but no Menlove Gardens East. John Sharpe Johnston worked at the Cammell Laird ship-building yard in Birkenhead, and one of his close associates there was one Dan Roberts, a shipping clerk, who lived at 30 Menlove Gardens West. Mr Johnston had visited Roberts at his Mossley Hill home on many occasions – but those visits suddenly ceased after the murder of Julia Wallace. The Johnstons were well acquainted with the domestic routines of the Wallaces. The partition wall separating their houses was so thin, the Johnstons admitted in court that they knew when Amy Wallace – William's loud sister-in-law – was visiting, because they could hear her voice, and yet the Johnstons never heard the intruder smashing the cabinet in the Wallace's front kitchen, and never heard Julia being struck on the skull eleven times or the sound of her body falling to the floor. Nor did they hear anybody knock at the doors of the house – and yet, the Johnstons told the court that they clearly heard Wallace knocking on the front and back doors of his home when he couldn't gain entry on the night of the murder. In 1931, Cammell Laird, John Johnston's employer, made only one vessel, as the knock-on effects of the Great Depression, which had started in the United States with the Wall Street Crash of 1929, reached Britain with devastating results, especially for the northern industrial cities. The 1930s (up until World War Two) saw the longest ever recession of the twentieth century. The outlook was bleak, money was hard to come by, and the crime rate soared as a result. I believe the murder of Julia Wallace was not a premeditated murder but the result of a robbery attempt that went horrifically wrong. I think the blunt weapon that killed Julia was the jemmy bar John Sharpe Johnston used to wrench the door off the cabinet in the front kitchen, and when he found himself confronted with Mrs

Wallace in the parlour, he probably lashed out as she tried to escape from him, as all of the eleven blows were concentrated on the back of her head, and the first one probably killed her. Had Mrs Wallace been allowed to live, she'd have reported her neighbour to the police, and Mr Johnston wouldn't have just been sentenced to jail for a number of years, he would have lost any hopes for future employment as well, and faced everlasting disgrace.

It would be terribly arrogant of me to claim that I had solved the Julia Wallace murder case. In all probability, we will never know the truth of the matter, but I do believe that John Sharpe Johnston should be seriously considered as a suspect in future studies of this classic cold case.

ARAMINTA

Before it closed its doors for good in the approaching shadow of the gargantuan Grosvenor Paradise Project, which built the vast ultramodern shopping complex known as Liverpool One, I was a regular visitor to a veritable magpie's nest called Quiggins, a vast store of old books and Victorian and Edwardian antiques tucked away in an old cobbled lane in the backstreets of Liverpool. Early in 2006, I happened to be browsing in a flea market section of Quiggins when I found a scuffed leather-bound book with mildewed end pages, containing old yellowed news clippings and handwritten notes from Victorian times. The theme of the book was Lancashire vampires, and the author is anonymous. The chronicle of Lancashire vampires mentions a 'bloodsucking specimen of the Lost Race of Homo Sapiens' that perpetrated a number of outrages around the time of the first siege of Liverpool in 1643, during the power struggles between Charles I and Parliament. The vampiric man was said to have bitten the necks of a number of women in the town, and was duly captured and transported in chains to Liverpool Castle (which stood where Derby Square is now situated). Alas, the weird-looking man somehow managed to slip from his shackles during the journey, and vanished into the night.

Flipping the pages forward we come to an account of a Victorian vampire hunt, distilled from five cuttings from the *Liverpool Mercury* newspaper, which starts in the autumn of 1894 at Windermere Terrace, near Prince's Park, Toxteth. A widow, referred to as a Mrs Penny, awoke in the dead of night, unable to move, as something bit into her neck and back. The widow felt blood being drawn and fainted. The next morning she remembered the terrifying incident and wondered if it was a nightmare, until she saw bloodstains on her sheets and pillow. She touched her neck, and felt wounds and clotted blood there. A doctor was summoned and saw four puncture marks, but was at a loss to explain them. His best conjecture was that a sadistic intruder had stabbed Mrs Penny in the neck and back, but the widow said she had felt lips against her skin and had felt the blood being sucked out of her body before she blacked out.

The mystery deepened on the following evening when screams where heard from the nearby Convent of the Faithful Companions of Jesus. Someone had tried to attack one of the nuns after climbing through a window and had fled through a second floor window after the nun had let out a scream. The police put more constables on the beat in the neighbourhood of the sinister attacks, but the blood-sucking assailant then struck in another part of the city.

The police believed the culprit to be a maniac, and never dreamt that the assailant at large was something that had been reported for thousands of years in every culture upon this earth – a vampire. Extra policemen were put on the beat around the Prince's Park area, but the thing which craved blood struck in another part of the city on the night of Sunday 14 October. A full moon hung high in the sky that night, and at one in the morning, a jaundiced fog drifted in from the Mersey. At around 1.15 am, Mr Edward Blair, a cricket bat manufacturer of 79A Duke Street, was awakened by the sounds of women screaming somewhere nearby. He ran to his window and opened it in time to catch a glimpse of an amorphous black shape flying eastwards at treetop level along Upper Duke Street towards Canning Street, before it was lost to sight in the swirling fog. Minutes after witnessing this frightening spectacle, PC Tom Norris came up Duke Street on his beat and investigated the source of the screams he had heard from as far away as Hanover Street. The hysterical women were the Davies sisters and their cousin Hannah Griffiths at 177 Duke Street. Hannah told the policeman an incredible tale to the young policeman that was backed up by the testimony of the Davies sisters. At midnight Hannah had awakened out of breath, and had therefore opened her window to let in the crisp night air, but by one o'clock the fog was infiltrating the room, so Hannah got up to close the window – and in a corner of the bedroom she was startled to see a woman with a pale ghastly face, large dark staring eyes, long pitch-black hair, clad in a strange black robe that ran to the floor. Hannah screamed, and turned to run for the door, but the sinister female intruder darted across the room and seized Hannah in a vice-like embrace. She threw her on the bed, bit into her neck, and was starting to draw blood when the Davies sisters burst into the room, alerted by Hannah's screams. The sisters screamed in horror at the sight of the thing that was pinning their cousin to the bed. One of the sisters clubbed the eerie assailant on the head with a candlestick but she didn't flinch. Hannah was trying her utmost to push the woman in black off her but the wiry female wouldn't budge. Elizabeth Davies, sensing the thing on top of her cousin was evil, rushed to fetch her bedside Bible from her room, and she returned holding the Holy Book before her. 'In the name of Our Lord, depart!' she screamed, and the fiend looked up to reveal its horrifying face. It's features twisted, and blood dripped from its contorted mouth before it flitted away from the bed – and dived out of the window. A doctor treated Hannah's neck wound – two neat puncture marks – but was unable to explain what had inflicted the injury. The strange case was passed into the hands of sergeants William Foster and Irwin McGhee, based at Lark Lane police station. Foster believed a demented female attacker was to blame for the assault on Hannah Griffiths, but Irwin McGhee was a devout Catholic and an avid student of the supernatural, and he believed a vampiress was at large. No two men so unlike one another in character had ever been forced to collaborate before, yet Foster and McGhee were required to work together in an effort to unravel the bizarre mystery that had been haunting night-time

Liverpool that autumn in 1894.

'A vampire is behind all this,' said Irwin McGhee, sitting at his desk at Lark Lane police station, reading an old leather-bound volume by Dom Calmet, an 18th century authority on vampirism.

Foster's sceptical reply was: 'You know as well as I do McGhee, that Hannah Griffiths was lying; no one can jump out a second floor window without sustaining injury and run off. She was lying because a man friend inflicted those injuries, but what a cock and bull story to tell to cloak the truth, and you believe it all.'

'Then what about the nuns? Were they lying as well?' McGhee queried. On the desk he had a crucifix, a rosary and small phial of holy water.

Foster took a swig of whiskey from his hip flask. 'At the risk of insulting your Catholic mentality, nuns are only human like the rest of us, and when they heard about the blood-sucking maniac a few doors away they had to get in on the act, it stands to reason.'

'How would it profit them? Wake up man,' McGhee glared at his colleague. 'Something is taking place that is beyond your everyday understanding, and unless you start taking this case seriously, you may as well go home.'

After a thoughtful pause, Foster said 'Very well. What do you have there?'

McGhee explained the nature of the vampire, its history, and even local legends of the ancient sanguinarians. McGhee had studied the supernatural since he was sixteen, and he had heard some very eerie tales of vampires in Liverpool from his Irish grandfather. 'At a cemetery in Everton there is said to be a female vampire,' said McGhee solemnly. 'I have seen the cover of her tomb disturbed periodically, and I think she is behind these recent attacks.'

Midnight found Foster and McGhee at the Everton graveyard in a thick fog – at the very tomb of the suspected vampire. McGhee waited with an iron spike and a hammer as the muscular Foster bravely lifted the loose slab and slid it across the tomb. A lantern was raised to reveal a disintegrated coffin from which a skeletal hand protruded. The coffin lid was slowly lifted by Foster. The head of the skeleton had been severed and lay almost at a right angle to the spinal stump of the neck. There was also a clean hole in the breastplate of the female corpse – where she had been impaled by an occultist – or perhaps even a priest - many years ago. The decapitation was another safeguard to stop the corpse being possessed by a vampire spirit. The slab was respectfully replaced, and McGhee made the sign of the cross and muttered "Rest in peace. Amen."

The sergeants returned from their fruitless 'vampire hunt' at the Everton Cemetery and reached the station at 80 Lark Lane just after one in the morning. PC Blackburn dutifully brought the sergeants two hot mugs of cocoa and them told them a curious thing. A drunken man had come into the police station at half-past eleven, asking to see someone about the peculiar goings-on at Duke Street. The man said he had been sent by Edward Blair, one of the witnesses to the recent strange incident. The man had given his name as Edwin Thompson, but had been so heavily intoxicated, PC Blackburn had put him in the holding cells to sleep off his alcoholic stupor. Foster and

McGhee hurried to the cells where the shabby-looking inebriate was stretched out snoring on a bench. Shortly after he was roused, he squinted at the sergeants, and gave his full particulars, which came as something of a shock, because he turned out to be an eccentric gentleman of considerable wealth who lived at 20 Canning Street. He told the policemen a remarkable tale. For the past month he had observed a 'phantasm' entering and leaving the house diagonally opposite his own after dark. That house – number 23 - was the residence of a rich gentleman named George Lawson, and night after night, Mr Thompson, his brother, and several servants had watched the eerie comings and goings of a shadowy, gaseous form that floated through the air and entered the roof of Lawson's home. Sergeant Foster didn't know what to make of the weird account, but his colleague McGhee believed Thompson had seen the vampire responsible for the series of nocturnal attacks in the city. On the following morning, Foster and McGhee paid a visit to George Lawson and informed him that burglars had been seen on his roof, trying the skylight, and during the house call, he seemed very nervous, as if he was hiding something. That night, Foster and McGhee sat in a room at Edwin Thompson's house, keeping watch on Lawson's Georgian residence across the street. Just after midnight, both policemen saw what appeared to be a wisp of dark smoke drifting up from the slates of the roof. The vapour expanded steadily and rose up from the rooftop, leaving a faint misty trail in its wake. William Foster strained his eyes as he watched the apparition slant upwards into the night sky, heading north. It was soon lost to sight. The two sergeants looked at one another, stuck for words for a moment. Minutes later, a quarter of a mile away, in Abercromby Square a widowed woman in her fifties named Magdalene Gee was startled out of her sleep when the veranda doors of her bedroom burst open. Before her eyes a dark mist rapidly condensed into the form of a woman in black. The stranger's face was deathly pale, contrasted by staring, jet-black eyes. She hovered silently towards Magdalene, and the widow, sensing an aura of intense evil about the terrifying phantom, grasped the crucifix hanging from the chain around her neck with a trembling hand, then held it towards the supernatural intruder. The demonic female backed away, made an unearthly hissing sound, and bared long pointed teeth – then once again became a body of dark vapour which drifted out the window into the night air. Magdalene let out a shriek and ran out of the bedroom, and her screams alerted PC Fred Mattinson, passing by the house on his beat. At half-past twelve, Foster and McGhee witnessed the smoky form return to 23 Canning Street via its roof. The news of the sinister Abercromby visitation reached Lark Lane via the Dale Street Detective Office on the following morning. It was time for Foster and McGhee to pay Mr Lawson another visit. They called upon the millionaire just after 4pm as the purple shade of the October dusk was reaching over the western skies of the city.

Once again, the sergeants used the pretence of roof burglars being at large to explain their visit, but Mr Lawson was a canny man, and although he granted the policemen access to inspect the attic for signs of attempted entry, he had an idea what the visit was really about – the vampiric attacks on the women of Liverpool Lawson offered the sergeants a sherry, engaged in small talk, and seemed only too glad when it was time for them to leave. On the following morning at 11pm, Foster and McGhee called at the home of Edwin Thompson, the well-to-do but perpetually intoxicated gentleman who lived across the street from Lawson. A butler ushered them into the sitting room, and almost a quarter of an hour elapsed before Thompson appeared. He stood swaying before the fire and McGhee asked him if he had seen any unusual guests visiting Lawson's home of late. Thompson leaned on the mantelpiece for support, spent a moment in agonised contemplation, then said that a woman in odd funereal black clothes had arrived at Lawson's house one Sunday several months ago. He had never seen her before and what's more, he had never seen her leave the residence. All of a sudden, Thompson pointed to the window and shouted, 'By Jove! There! There she is!'

The sergeants ran to the window. A carriage had pulled up at the house of Lawson, and the millionaire and a strangely dressed woman in black – with her face covered by a dark veil – were descending the steps. Foster and McGhee flew out of the sitting room and were on the street in seconds. They hailed a hansom cab and instructed the driver to follow the carriage trundling down Canning Street. The pursuit stretched to the Pier Head, where, it transpired, Lawson and the woman intended to board a ship bound for Ireland. Foster and McGhee confronted Lawson, expecting him to threaten them with harassment, but instead, he became melancholic, and told them a bizarre story.

The woman with him was his lover, and she was pregnant with his child. Her name was Araminta, and she had been driven out of Hungary because she was the last of a line of vampires that had lived in the country since the days when it was a part of Transylvania. Araminta despised being a vampire, and no man she had loved had ever accepted her for what she was - until she had met Lawson. Now the couple wanted to settle in Ireland for a while before going on to America.

As George Lawson gave this eerie account, Sergeant Foster gazed at the pale ghostly face of Araminta faintly visible through her veil - and he was disturbed to see black tears drip from her eyes as she silently wept. The police sergeant reached for his service revolver, but McGhee seized his hand and said, 'No William!'

'We can't let them go somewhere else where this thing will suck the blood out of other innocent people!' said Foster. His fear was driving him on to shoot the woman. He pushed McGhee away and aimed the gun at the woman in black, who stood there calmly, resigned to her fate. Lawson threw himself into the firing line of the revolver, and tried to throw a punch at Foster, but missed.

McGhee shouted 'No!' as Araminta suddenly climbed over the safety chain on the Landing Stage and jumped into the freezing October river.

Foster stepped over the safety chain and fired the revolver repeatedly into the waters, then McGhee pushed him aside and dived into the waves to save the woman – but only managed to recover her bullet-ridden clothes. Not a trace of Araminta's body was to be found. Lawson stood staring into the Mersey, sobbing. Araminta was never heard from again. Had the self-tormented vampiress committed suicide, or had she simply made an escape? We will probably never know – unless Araminta returns one day. You may find the aforementioned tale far-fetched, but it actually took place – although whether Araminta was a real vampiress or simply someone with delusions is unknown. The great French philosopher Jean-Jacques Rousseau, writing during the Age of Reason and Enlightenment, once stated: 'If ever there was in the world a warranted and proven history, it is that of vampires. Nothing is lacking; official reports, testimonials of persons of standing, of surgeons, of clergymen, of judges; the judicial evidence is all-embracing.'

THE MAN OF THE STREETS

A couple of years ago I had a fascinating conversation with a reader named Frank who had thoroughly researched his family tree and discovered a rather depraved black sheep in the process. The perverse ancestor in question was a cousin of Frank's grandfather, and as the sickening but fascinating story was told to me on the condition that Frank's ancestor should remain anonymous, I shall henceforth refer to him, not by his real name, but by the alias of Albert.

Throughout the late 1880s to the late 1890s, Albert worked as a mortuary attendant at the various morgues of Liverpool, and in 1891, Albert was employed at two morgues. That year, Albert was instructed to remove the clothes and undergarments from the corpse of a 23-year-old female named Catherine Laurie. Catherine had died at the Southern Hospital with a plethora of severe burn marks and other wounds on her body.

Neighbours said Catherine had been heard to cry out "Murder! Bring a police officer!" and "He is killing me by degrees!" and this latter exclamation was said to be in relation to the woman's husband, who was said to be a very cruel and habitual drunk. Albert, the mortuary attendant, stayed beyond his normal hours with the corpse of Mrs Laurie, and a subordinate of Albert, a lad who had what we would now call severe learning difficulties, left the mortuary around 9pm, but then returned about fifteen minutes later because he left a scarf behind. This young man caught Albert practising necrophilia with the dead woman. He was attempting to 'make love' to the corpse of Mrs Laurie. Albert allegedly paid his assistant to remain quiet, but the lad is thought to have said something to the chief coroner Clarke Aspinall. Aspinall grilled Albert about the serious allegations and the mortuary assistant vehemently denied them, suggesting that the 'half-witted accuser' (as he called him) had himself shown such necrophile tendencies in the past. The young assistant to Albert was therefore dismissed from the job.

Not long after this, at the morgue at brougham Terrace (where births, marriages and deaths were registered for many years) Albert was left alone with the corpse of an unusually tall woman in her thirties who had committed suicide after being jilted by her lover (who was a married army captain). On this occasion. The coroner turned up unexpectedly at the morgue, an hour earlier than he was due, and in the course of the post mortem, discovered, after a cursory examination, that the woman had had a' recent sexual connexion' - even though she had been pronounced dead by a doctor three and a half hours ago. The coroner immediately turned to Albert and asked him if he had 'been interfering' with the corpse, and the mortuary attendant ran to a stone sink and threw up with fear. The coroner asked him again if he had committed a sexual act with the body and Albert said he felt nauseous at the audacity of the accusation, and reminded the coroner that he was a man in his fifties, and a respectable church-going pillar of the local community. The coroner apologised, and asked Albert if anyone else had been in the morgue recently. By a sheer coincidence, a window had been broken at the morgue sometime earlier – probably by mischievous stone-throwing street urchins – but Albert claimed that the window in question had been half opened when he came into the morgue a few hours earlier. The coroner said he would report the matter to the police, but Albert said if news of the sexual connexion with the corpse would only serve to upset relatives of the dead woman. The coroner agreed. Albert however, began to keep a secret diary of his disgusting crimes from this moment on, and he recounted past incidents, including the peculiar but intoxicating affections he had felt towards an auntie who had been laid out in her open coffin at a wake off Scotland Road when he was a young man. The shocking and obscene details of that incident could never be put into print.

Around the end of the 1890s, a woman was decapitated at a factory outside of Liverpool, and her body was brought to a makeshift morgue on the outskirts where Albert was presented with another stomach-churning opportunity. In his diary, Albert said he felt a thrill just looking at the headless cadaver of the shapely woman who was about 25 years of age when she met her violent horrific end. 'Three sweet times,' Albert scrawled in his diary, but then something bizarre began to happen to the degraded corpse-lover: he began to see the headless woman everywhere. He was on an omnibus travelling up Bold Street one rainy afternoon as thunder rolled in the low grey skies, when he saw a woman sitting opposite, dressed in the height of fashion with a dark Ulster coat, a long dark green ankle-length dress – but she had no head. A man in a bowler sat next to her whistling a tune as he adjusted the ends of his curled-up moustache. Albert screamed out and stood on many feet as he blundered his way blindly off the bus. In the pouring rain he ran to Church Street, continually looking back at the omnibus, which was barely visible through the sheets of heavy rain as it trundled up Bold Street. An actinic eyeball-searing lightning flash lit up Church Street, as if God was taking a photograph of the metropolis, and Albert ran wildly through the crowds of men with straw boaters dripping with rain and their ladies with their shiny black wet brollies. As the ladies laughed and screamed at the lightning, Albert sought sanctuary from what he imagined (in his guilty mind) to be God's thunderbolts. He dashed under the awnings of the shops - the great flapping canvas covers emblazoned with adverts. The necrophiliac scanned the crowds; there was no sign of that vengeful headless corpse. Albert raced across the cobbled road of Church Street, narrowly missing the hulking trams, horse-drawn goods wagons laden with stacked crates and jam-packed sacks, as well as the damned cyclists, the ruthlessly-driven hansom cabs, and of course, other pedestrians hurrying through the sky-born deluge. Before he even reached his intended destination: Bunney's, the greatest emporium in the north of England – he saw *her*, waiting there, wearing that same long Ulster and the grass-green dress that went down to her black ankle boots. Now he could see the vivid red stump of the neck! How could this be a hallucination? He could even see the rain trickling down the slender pale neck from the red disc of raw exposed muscle and flesh.

Albert turned and ran into the grounds of St Peter's Church, and here he started crying. He prayed out loud to God, begged for forgiveness, and even promised Him he'd castrate himself. He looked around at the heavy rainfall battering the clumps of flowers set beautifully in the gardens of the church. The three dark green slatted benches along the path were empty and glistening in the downpour. There was a blinding flash, followed seconds later by a roll of thunder that sounded like the Crack of Doom. There was the usual chorus of screams and on this occasion a little girl passing the church screamed and burst into tears as her mother dragged her along. The headless woman was standing by the nearest bench, with her arms open – reaching out for Albert. On this occasion he heard a vile gurgling noise, as if air from the dead woman's lungs was being piped up through the severed windpipe. No matter where Albert went, he was pursued by his accursed one-day stand, and even when he went home to his wife, Albert would look in terror through the windows and see the headless harasser on the other side of the street. In the dead of night he would startle his wife with his screams as he suffered nightmare after nightmare of the headless corpse with its wheezing, bubbling severed throat as it tried to assault him in the way he had assaulted it, as part of some twisted retribution. Of course, no one else could see the thing stalking Albert, and his wife became so fraught with the constant bizarre and nerve-shattering behaviour of her unhinged husband, she soon left him. Albert then believed the only temporary haven from the horror was to take to the streets, to mingle with the bustling crowds, where there should be safety in numbers. Many people in late Victorian Liverpool probably saw this man of the streets who wandered wide-eyed and restlessly back and forth through the multitudes of the city's thoroughfares and assumed that the acute anxiety etched on Albert's face was the by product of too much alcohol. Albert is thought to have ended his days in an asylum, where the headless phantasm of a guilt-ridden mind probably continued to pursue him, perhaps even unto some vague vestiges of consciousness beyond bodily death when the brain is sometimes known to continue, even during the autopsy. The diary of the necrophiliac was discovered, hidden away as a hot taboo-riddled work, until it found its way to an antiquarian bookseller. A Liverpool man named Frank, bearing a rather unusual surname, spotted the dog-eared diary in the antique bookshop one Sunday and realised he had the missing piece of a dark genealogical jigsaw puzzle. The great uncle no one liked to mention when he was a child was now revealed to have been a corrupt, thoroughly amoral reprobate.

And it is strange how, as I set down this unsavoury tale of such a sickening nature, a report came on the radio in my study which I can only describe as an act of sickening synchronicity. The report said that a copy of a shocking booklet, first published in post-Edwardian times (sometime after 1910) had been found among the papers of its author George Murray Levick, a biologist and British Antarctic explorer who died in 1956. Levick was a biologist and medical officer with Captain Robert Scott's ill-fated Terra Nova Expedition at the South Pole, and he spent an entire austral summer (1911-12) among a rookery of Adelie penguins, observing their courting, mating and chick-rearing behaviour. However, what Levick recorded struck him as so shocking (at least to his Edwardian values) he felt compelled to write down his observations in Greek. Levick was upset when he saw the male Adelie penguins mating with dead females, and when he returned to England, he was very reluctant to publish his observations for fear of offending Edwardian sensibilities among his peers. One hundred booklets detailing what were originally looked upon as depraved acts of necrophilia were circulated amongst a select group of scientists, but a few of these publications were finally made public in 2012. Today, wildlife experts and biologists know an awful lot more than their counterparts of a hundred years ago, and they know that the penguins were not committing necrophilia in the same context as humans who practise that form of sex. The Adelie penguins saw the female penguins (some of whom had been dead for months) frozen in a certain position and assumed they were ready to mate.

THE SUMMER OF THE LEPRECHAUN

All of the old legends and tales of folklore from every part of this planet say there is a secret commonwealth of mystical beings who live alongside us. These beings, referred to as elves, devils, leprechauns, lutins, the Feadh-Ree, fairies, boggarts, trows and other legendary names, are said to be grouped into various species, and for most of the time, we are as aware of them as we are aware of the grotesque monsters of the microscopic world who munch our flakes of dead skin. Dust mites would be terrifying alien creatures if they lived on our scale of size, but until the invention of optical and electron microscopes, no one suspected their existence or could have imagined how unsightly they looked. Could there be creatures around you as you read these words that are presently unknown to modern science? Our eyes see only a small narrow slit of the total electromagnetic spectrum which contains all of the radiations of the universe. Red, orange, yellow, green, blue, indigo and violet, and all of the shades between those colours is all we can perceive with our eyes. We are blind to infra-red, ultraviolet and countless other invisible 'colours'. To see the craters of the Moon we had to invent the telescope for our feeble eyes, and to see our own blood corpuscles we had to devise the microscope, because our eyes have fixed lenses like a cheap throwaway camera. Our ears also have their limitations, depending on our age. Human hearing differs vastly from the acute hearing abilities of a dog or a cat, and a human being's listening range is determined not only by age, but hereditary factors as well. Sense of smell, once highly important to man for survival in prehistoric times, is now swamped by chemicals from deodorants, aftershaves, perfumes, air-fresheners and so on. Our senses of vision and hearing are restricted, and our sense of smell has been made redundant almost, and even our survival instincts are being progressively eliminated by the society mankind has created. We are protected from danger and violence by armies and the police, whereas in ancient times we had to look after ourselves, and all we had were primitive weapons and instincts. We could smell animals such as sabre-toothed tigers and bears laying in wait for us, or spot them laying low in the undergrowth or the shadows of a cave, but now our senses in the modern world are so dulled we can step off a sidewalk into the path of a red double-decker bus we didn't notice. It's the same with our food and drink, which is analysed, processed, irradiated, filtered and treated with antibiotics and all kinds of artificial additives. We are then, cocooned from the reality our ancestors lived in. The ancients were fitter than us, and ate wholesome food. Their water was not filtered or tampered with; their wines contained no chemicals such as copper sulphate - just the produce of the grape. Their minds were sharper than ours, as can be seen by the engineering feats of Stonehenge and the pyramids. The ancients claimed to have a Third Eye, located traditionally in the brain just behind the centre of the forehead. This eye perceived mystical impressions too subtle for our coarser senses to register, and was regarded as the seat of intuition and heightened instincts. If we compare this to our patterns of consciousness today, we will admit to being in a state of trance most of the time as we watch television, the screen of our mobile phones or a computer monitor as we surf the Internet. It's as if our hi-tech, sanitized world, television, film and computers have turned us all into zombies who are entangled in self-woven nets of daydreams. Across the world, attention spans are shrinking, drug and alcohol abuse is on the rise, and mindless TV channels and idiotic violent videogames are proliferating to feed robotic stupefied minds. As a race, we have never been as out of touch with reality in our history. Long ago, when we worked in harmony with nature living off the land, sowing and reaping by the seasons, and using our instincts, we inhabited a whole different reality from our existence today. There was an unquestioning belief in the existence of a supernatural race of beings. There was a symbiotic, balanced relationship between us and them. Their lands were never to be touched by human hands or developed, and their 'fairy paths' were to be kept clear from obstructions of any kind. Occasionally, mischievous members of the fairy race purloined or borrowed items from humans and sometimes even stole livestock, but on the whole they kept to themselves. They sometimes imparted remedies and miracle cures to humans and even melodious songs and catchy tunes, but the fairies mostly kept well away from man, woman and child. They gradually became very wary of mortals because of humanity's propensity for greed and battle. The ancient fairies were regarded by man with some suspicion, as no one could be sure of their origins. Some maintained that the little people were fallen angels, or perhaps something God had created in the past which was never mentioned in the Bible. There was even once a theory that fairies were members of a small aboriginal race of Eskimos who had strayed into the northern extremities of Scotland! However, most of the legends across Western Europe stated that the fairies had been driven underground into caves and mounds by warrior bands of invading Celts. In Britain and Ireland they mostly inhabited the western parts of the isles, with colonies in the outer isles of Scotland, the Isle of Man, Cornwall, Wales, Cheshire, Lancashire and Cumbria. Later invaders to our islands almost spelt extinction for the fairies, and when Christianity reached these shores, over-zealous friars, exorcists of the church and 'limetours' swept across the land, blessing barns, fields, woods, streams and the remotest farmhouse. The new religion, brought here by St Augustine, the first Archbishop of Canterbury, in 597 A.D., led to the establishment of a monastery at Kent, and although King Aethelbert welcomed the missionaries cautiously, he allowed them to preach and was even baptized by them himself in the end.

The 'old religion' however, did not die easily. At night, before roaring log fires, the old storytellers related enchanted tales of witches, ghosts, elves, fairies and trolls. The children would listen in wonder to the colourful stories of supernatural beings no one was allowed to talk about anymore, because the new church had forbidden people to discuss anything paranormal. And yet, from Douglas to Liverpool, from County Clare to Derbyshire, from Anglesey to Alderley Edge, from Cornwall to Clitheroe, fireside tales of the fairy folk were very popular late at night.

In the Twentieth century, a long period of rational scepticism, the little people made an unlikely comeback - at a time when a new mystery was capturing the imagination of the human race: the flying saucer phenomenon. In the summer of 1964, there was a wave of UFO sightings across the UK and parts of Western Europe, and there were many reports of classic flying saucer-type craft seen in the airspace over the North West of England. There has long been an undeserved association with flying saucers and little green men, so when alleged encounters with elf-like beings were reported in Britain that summer, in places such as the Isle of Man, Lancashire, North Wales, Cheshire and Cumbria, some ufologists connected the reports of 'leprechauns' with the saucers, and hypothesized that the little people visiting from another planet were being mistaken for the fairies of old. Locally, on 1 July 1964, a leprechaun mania broke out across Liverpool when a group of schoolchildren told bemused parents and teachers that they had seen little green-skinned people wearing white hats in Jubilee Park, Jubilee Drive, in Kensington. The children's tales were naturally dismissed as immature imaginings - until adults also reported seeing strange things around Jubilee Drive. This took place in the back garden of a Mrs Williams at her house on Edge Lane on the Wednesday afternoon of 1 July, 1964. Pensioner Mrs Williams and her 67-year-old neighbour Mrs Jones sat at a tea table they'd prepared in the sunny, secluded garden. Mrs Williams brought the hissing kettle from the kitchen and poured it into teapot on the table. Muffins and biscuits were laid on as usual, and the honey in a jar had been made from Mrs Jones's own bees. It was a typical English afternoon tea on a glorious sunny day, but when the women started to talk at the table, they found their conversation increasingly drowned out by the unusually loud chattering of magpies in the shrubberies at the bottom of the garden. Then Mrs Williams recoiled in shock, because something surreal and a little frightening stepped out from the stark shadows and into the bright sunlight. A figure, about two feet in height or less, with pale yellow-green skin stood there. He wore a small white helmet, very similar to the safety headgear worn by modern cyclists, and was clad in a one-piece suit which had reflective texture of plastic. The face looked human, but childish, and it was much smaller than a normal face. The diminutive visitor also looked male, but he didn't stay there long. Mrs Williams saw him too, but let out a squeal of surprise, and at this, the little being turned and fled into the shrubs. The women were too scared to go and see how the entity had gained entry into the garden, and the next morning Mrs Jones brought her nephew and his Alsatian dog to the bottom of Mrs William's garden - and there was a small opening in the fence were a rotten strip of wood had been broken. The nephew repaired the fence. He and his aunt noticed that the German shepherd dog was very uneasy while it was in the garden, and seemed to be able to see something they couldn't.

That day, Mrs Jones was reading the *Liverpool Echo*, when she received quite a surprise. On page five of the newspaper, a small column, entitled 'Leprechauns Go Bowling In The Park' stated:

Thousands of children joined in a big hunt in Liverpool last night for - leprechauns. They invaded Jubilee Park in Jubilee drive, hunted among the shrubberies, tore up some small plants and turf, scaled surrounding walls, and searched empty houses.

The Great Leprechaun Hunt all started after someone had reported seeing "little green men in white hats throwing stones and tiny clods of earth at one another on the bowling green the previous night.

That story buzzed through all the schools in the area, and when the schools closed yesterday afternoon, the youngsters swarmed to the park .

It was all too much for Irish parks constable James Nolan. "I don't believe in leprechauns myself," he said.

He called in the city police. Police in cars and on motorcycles arrived. They cleared the hundreds of youngsters from the bowling greens - the reported playground of the wee folk - closed the gate, and stood guard.

But beyond the bowling green gates the youngsters milled, tiny tots to 14-year-olds. They crammed the top of the covered reservoir for a better view of the bowling green. Tolerant bobbies wandered about trying to get the youngsters on the move. But the kids would not believe that there were no little green men. It was not until after 10pm that the park was cleared.

How the story started was not known, but last night was the second night running of the leprechaun hunt.

And how did those little brownies who help the Irish housewife with her chores come to arrive in Liverpool? Maybe they flew from old Ireland. A woman resident in Crosby last night reported seeing "strange objects glistening in the sky, whizzing over the river to the city from the Irish Sea."

Mrs Jones took the newspaper to her neighbour, and Mrs Williams was thunderstruck by the peculiar report. Mrs Jones was a religious woman, and regarded the reports of the 'leprechauns' as something sinister. A friend of hers who attended the local church of St Cyprian claimed that a vicar had warned her about the things 'masquerading as fairies' for they were of the devil, and out to undermine Christianity. Mrs Williams was a little more progressive in her way of thinking and disagreed with the vicar's views. She believed that the leprechauns had something to do with the recent spate of flying saucer sightings across the country.

As the leprechaun mania grew in intensity throughout Liverpool, legions of children stormed the parks of the city. The little people were seen in Abercromby Park, in Stanley Park, in Newsham Park, and in Sefton Park, where a 13-year-old girl said she even grabbed one little man but he slithered from her grasp and fled laughing. Around this time, over two hundred children also invaded the sanctum of St Chad's in Kirkby to tell the Canon John Lawton of the little people they'd seen locally. In one field near Kirkby, the elfin figures were seen dancing in the moonlight one night, and on the following day a type of corn circle was found at the scene. Weeks after that incident there were sightings of 'trolls' outside St Mary's Church in Northwood. Alas, when that exciting summer of the leprechaun ended the little visitors from elsewhere made themselves scarce - but will they return one day?

THE OLD SWAN MASS GRAVE

One of the greatest and enduring mysteries in Liverpool's history started to unfold in the autumn of 1973, when a gang of workmen set about clearing land to build a two-storey Roman Catholic primary school between St Oswald's Street and Montague Road, in Old Swan. The £450,000 St Oswald's Primary School would be built on scrubland near to the church, and Father Patrick James McCartney did warn the workmen that they were likely to come across 'a few graves' during their excavations, but no one at that point knew about the sinister, macabre secret which would soon be brought to light. An unmarked coffin was unearthed, then another one, but the foreman, Thomas Breen, told his men to carry on, and the coffins were solemnly put aside with the utmost respect. However, the workmen soon discovered that in an area 40 yards square, there were coffins piled sixteen high, arranged in a cube. This cube was sketched by a local art student living in the Old Swan area at the time, and is reproduced on the cover of this book. Building work was immediately suspended, and the Clerk of Works had a look at the unusual find. It was a mass grave, and the total number of coffins discovered totalled 3,561. The mystery then deepened, because there were no records of any mass burial in the registers of St Oswald's Church. This seemed to indicate that the 3,561 bodies had been stacked in the ground prior to 1840 – the year when registration of burials became compulsory.

Local and national historians were naturally intrigued by the Old Swan mass grave, and some theorised that the dead were plague and cholera victims, but people who had died of such diseases were usually put in quicklime without coffins. Furthermore, the dates of the plagues and cholera outbreaks in Liverpool and the numbers of the victims, as well as the time window within which they were buried, simply did not tally with the facts regarding the mass burial at Old Swan. Some historians even thought the answer to the baffling mass burial had something to do with the Benedictine Fathers who built a church near to the huge grave in the 18th century.

Before the historians could examine the mysterious coffins, the Home Office ordered Liverpool City Council to cordon off the mass grave with a 10-foot-high security fence. Officials in Whitehall subsequently gave instructions to cremate the unknown dead and to deposit the remains at Anfield Cemetery. The workmen then had to wait 18 months before the building of the school could commence, and in the meantime, the media was warned off when reporters tried to discover what had been found off St Oswald's Street. The news leaked out that investigators had deduced that the 3,561 bodies had all been buried at the same time, which meant it certainly had not been a plague pit or a pauper's grave. What then, is the truth behind the mystery of the Old Swan mass grave?

In 1995, several historians contacted Whitehall, hoping to discover why the Home Office had given orders to cremate the unknown dead of Old Swan, and a spokesman said he couldn't trace any records of the incident. The files relating to the mysterious mass grave had apparently been destroyed. The puzzle then, of how 3,561 bodies came to be buried off St Oswald's Street, remains unsolved. Victims of plague and cholera were dumped in pits often filled with quicklime, but the thousands of bodies found at Old Swan were not only placed in coffins, they had been buried in groups according to their age, which suggests all of the internments took place simultaneously. This means there are two possibilities, both of them controversial. Were over 3,000 people massacred at Old Swan at some time in the 1840s? If we suppose there had been some uprising, and that the authorities had dealt with the revolt by massacring the dissenters, would they have afterwards buried the victims in coffins? Thousands of poor people were disembowelled and hanged by the authorities in England during the Peasant's Revolt of 1382, but news of the massacre could not be contained, and soon spread across the country. Although Old Swan was a peaceful rural suburb when the bodies were buried there en masse, news of any rebellion and subsequent carnage would surely have been impossible to contain.

The only clue that seems to provide a solution to this mystery lies in several curious reports from council workmen who claimed that a few of the coffins did indeed bear name-plates. If these reports are true, then this could point to an intriguing possibility never considered before; that the coffins were moved from another graveyard and reburied at Old Swan. In 1838, the foundation stone to St George's Hall was laid. At that time, the site excavated for the hall's foundations lay adjacent to St John's Church. The grand building to be erected was extremely important, as it would house the Assize Courts as well as huge hall of unprecedented proportions. However, for the work to proceed, many of the 82,491 coffins in St John's Churchyard had to be removed to make space. The army of builders and civil engineers working on the St George's Hall project also suggested that the unsightly St John's Church itself should be demolished, as it would prove to be an eyesore next to a monumental building worthy of ancient Greece. An infirmary and a lunatic asylum had already been levelled to make way for the hall, but now there was the problem of the church graveyard to contend with, and some local historians now believe that this state of affairs - first proposed by myself - could have led to the origin of the Old Swan Mass grave. I happen to disagree though, for I have given my own hypothesis much thought.

The way the coffins were neatly laid out at Old Swan smacks of military involvement. All of the bodies had decent intact teeth – meaning they were young when they died – and were placed in particular sections, according to their age groups, and the coffins were perfectly aligned. Around the time frame in which the bodies were deposited at Old Swan – around 1838 to 1848 – one major building project was underway in Liverpool: St George's Hall. An infirmary and lunatic asylum were promptly demolished to clear the vast space needed for the grand building, and some local historians believe that many thousands of the 82,491 graves were moved from St John's churchyard, which partially overlapped the building site. Who moved these graves, and where were they moved to? Well, the old maps tell the tale, for on a map of Liverpool in the early 1840s we see a huge barracks standing next to the building site cleared for St George's Hall. It's no stretch of the imagination to envisage the authorities secretly enlisting the regiment stationed at these barracks to transport the coffins exhumed from St John's churchyard to a new burial site. The assignment would be carried out in strict secrecy because of the delicate nature of exhumation and reburial. In 1868, for example, 2,000 coffins were removed from the graveyard of St Peter's Church – on Church Street - and re-interred at Anfield Cemetery. The coffins at Old Swan had been buried simultaneously, in perfect alignment, and this would have required some manpower and organisation to achieve. To an army of trained military men with spades, the task would have been completed within days. The early railway, which ran from Lime Street to the Liverpool suburbs, could have been used to secretly transport the coffins – under the cover of night - to the burial site in the rural open spaces of early 19th century Old Swan. This is all theory of course, and I personally believe that the solution to the Old Swan mass grave lies in another direction. Thomas Breen, the foreman who oversaw the removal of the bodies in the mass grave, is now in his seventies and lives in Woolton, and he vividly recalls that there were no infants among the dead, which does pose a problem to the theory about the bodies of Old Swan being transplanted from an existing churchyard. Surely there would be infants among the dead? Mr Breen also remarked that the coffin wood was almost impossible to burn and a lot of it was buried on the site of the school. Perhaps if some of this wood could be recovered today, there may be some traces of DNA material to be had, however slight. Mr Breen told me how, at one point during the gruesome excavation, a perfectly preserved young woman with reddish hair, dressed in a white garment, slid out of a damaged coffin and landed in the rain-soaked mud with a sickening thud. Within minutes her pretty face and youthful body started to disintegrate as the atmosphere set in. When the rain worsened at one point, a young grave-digger found himself sinking into a quagmire with the bodies sliding out of their decaying coffins. The excavation pit became waterlogged and the whole scene was reminiscent of a scene from the film *Poltergeist*, with coffins opening and corpses floating in the water.

As I stated earlier, the Home Office has suspiciously 'lost' the files referring to the Old Swan mass graves burial site, so it may be some time before we learn the truth about this enduring mystery. However, I proposed a very controversial theory several years ago in one of my newspaper columns. Here is an extract to convey the gist of the theory:

In 1840, registration of all burials became mandatory, so most historians have assumed the Old Swan mass grave must date back to a time before that. I, however, believe no registration of burial was kept for very sinister reasons. In Mulberry Street, not far from the Cambridge Pub in the city centre, there is a plaque on a wall which reads: *Near this place, in 1847, some 2,600 destitute Irish Famine migrants were buried in unmarked pauper's graves. They had died in extreme poverty in the parish of Liverpool, so ending their flight from the Great Hunger (1845-52).*

I believe that this plaque, which most people pass without even reading, throws light on one of the greatest cover-ups in British history; an Irish holocaust in fact. Could there be some sinister reason why the Home Office ordered the remains of 3,561 people unearthed at Old Swan to be incinerated immediately? Could the bodies found in the graves be victims of a chilling mass murder committed by soldiers in the summer of 1848, when hundreds of thousands of starving immigrants from Ireland arrived in Liverpool? In July 1848 there was a great influx of 296,231 immigrants from Ireland, and most of them were disease-ridden and starving, but not because of the so-called "Potato Famine". The British Government of the day had sent "Food-Removal Regiments" to Ireland to take meat, grain and dairy products from the farmers at gunpoint, and all of the food was put into the holds of ships bound for England.

The Irish people did not die from a lack of potatoes, but from the regiment's removal of Ireland's meat, dairy products, vegetables, grains and fruit. Enough of these foods were siphoned from Ireland to feed 18 million English people. Surely the Irish Famine was the result of the potato blight? That's what my history teacher told me at school all those years ago. *Phytophthora Infestans*, the official cause of the potato blight, spread from America to Europe in 1844, and then to England, and from there it reached Ireland. Only Ireland suffered a famine at this time. England didn't, nor did the United States or any country on the Continent. Ireland starved because of the Food Removal Regiments, not because of the potato blight. I am now venturing into the realms of 'informed speculation' but it is an historical fact that in the summer of 1848, over 2,000 armed soldiers from London encamped at Everton, with orders to deal with the Irish 'insurgents'.

As well as those soldiers, 20,000 special constables were sworn in and the police were augmented with 500 extra officers, as well as 800 members of the Cheshire Yeomanry joined their forces.

Three warships also arrived in the Mersey and dropped anchor. Not long afterwards the 'containment squads' moved in on the diseased and starving immigrants, removed their children, then herded the Irish men and women to a containment camp in a field on the outskirts of Liverpool.

I believe that these people were then systematically shot, and buried in unmarked coffins. The children of the dead were either sent to orphanages, the

Workhouse or transported to Canada and Australia - and that is why no children were found among the 3,561 bodies in that mass grave at Old Swan. I have been told by students of Irish history that other mass graves have been found in other parts of England, including one in Islington, London, and there are many in Ireland too. I may be way off the mark, but I'm not alone in my opinions, and there are many academics who believe there is more to the so-called Great Hunger than meets the eye. Perhaps when the truth comes out, 3,561 souls will rest.

Not long after I had put forward this conjecture, a certain local historian in Liverpool said my theory was nonsense, but then I found material in several Victorian newspapers, including the *Illustrated London News* which strengthened my theory. I presented these articles to the historian in question and he has since apologised for calling my theory nonsense and now subscribes to it. One of the articles in the *Illustrated London News* - dated 2 August 1848 – gives an in-depth report on the military encampment at Everton and other areas of Liverpool, and here's an extract from that article:

There are more reasons than one why an encampment is formed at Liverpool. Troops are drawn hither, because it is the nearest port of embarkation to Ireland at which vessels of transport may be instantly found, if an emergency arises.

Liverpool holds within it a dense population, many of them Irish. Where there are most Irish the population is most dense; where it is most dense it is within the easiest reach of the mightiest mischief - the firing of the warehouses and docks. It is said, and the magistrates here in Liverpool believe the saying, as do the principal commercial men of all shades of politics, that there is now no doubt that a conspiracy existed last week...the head conspirators giving directions from Ireland - to burn the warehouses and docks of Liverpool, and by so doing appall the empire of Britain. This is a second and conclusive reason, for accumulating a military force here.

The Camp described within the article consisted initially of the 46th Regiment of Infantry, and was later augmented by a battery of artillery and the 81st Infantry. These troops were sent to Everton to 'deal' with any sympathizers of the recent rebellions against the British over in occupied Ireland. Is it possible that the military over-reacted to some perceived threat among the Irish immigrants and ended up resorting to nothing short of an atrocity at Everton? And was this massacre covered up by burying the victims en masse in the peculiar grave at Old Swan? We may know more some day.

SUMMON THE BERSERKER

From the late 1990s up to 2005, a larger than life, yet modest, middle-aged man known only as O'Neil, was a fairly regular visitor to The Swan Inn on Wood Street. Without a doubt, he practised magic. Not the mechanical sleight-of-hand street-magic variety, but the type we associate with the great Merlin in that lost Arthurian age, though of a far lesser magnitude. He was conversant with spirits and was very scathing of show business mediums and charlatans, and he would only enlist the help of the dead when it was an absolute necessity, because he had learned at an early age that the true medium risks his sanity by knowing too much about his and everyone else's future.

O'Neil did not take drugs, but he was fond of his drink; perhaps it served to dull his keen but ultimately troublesome psychic senses. If you visited the Swan Inn during the time period to which I am referring, you would probably have seen O'Neil but wouldn't have given him a second glance. You would have seen a man with straggly mousy-grey hair in a scuffed leather biker's jacket and faded jeans, Doc Martens and a world-worn face, pulling on a roll-up of Golden Virginia tobacco. At heart, he was a very inoffensive man, but because he chose never to lie in life, he upset many people when he gave them straight answers, and this happened one December night at the Swan, in 2005.

Liverpool, being a maritime city, is prone to heavy fogs, and in November 2005 the mother of all fogs enshrouded the whole of the North West. Flights in and out of John Lennon Airport were cancelled because of it. It spread as far as Manchester and Blackpool and caused transport chaos and fatalities on the roads, and unlike the usual fogs, this one stuck around for days. When O'Neil came into the Swan Inn that night for his usual Guinness, and perhaps a short or two, wisps of the fog snaked in behind him. He took his place in his usual corner seat with his drink, and then in came his young friend, Harlan, talking about astrology and palm-reading. O'Neil laughed and remarked that around thirty million people in Britain followed the advice of "newspaper horoscope prophets" and that there must be some turmoil going on in the heavens when two football teams meet on the pitch, because we would have twenty-two star-signs in conflict, plus the referee and linesman's star-signs battling it out.

"Then what about palms?" Harlan asked O'Neil, studying his own young soft work-shy hands.

"Now there's an very interesting subject ..." O'Neil was saying, when there came sniggers from a neighbouring table.

Two huge bikers sat there, clad in black motorcycle leather jackets, black tee shirts, Kevlar-panelled jeans, Harley Davidson Interstate zip boots, and Nazi tattoos. They were both smirking at O'Neil.

O'Neil did his best to ignore them, and had just taken Harlan's palm in order to study it, when the bikers came over to the table and sat themselves down by the mystic and his young friend.

"Read our future, mate," ordered the tallest and broadest of the two trouble-causers, and he thrust out a rough-palmed hand and laughed, "if we have any future that is."

O'Neil looked at the biker's hand for a few moments, then with a serious voice asked, "Are you sure you want to know?"

"Don't give me that shit," said the biker, using his aggression to try and cover up his nervousness. "You can see nothing ... no one can ... and you're filling this lad's head here with rubbish. You're just an old charlatan. Admit it!"

The biker's associate giggled, and under his breath he muttered, 'He's an old dickhead'.

"Very well, I'll start with *your* past," said O'Neil, looking quite ruffled by the uncalled-for insults.

"Sure, go ahead!"

The outspoken biker shoved his palm right under O'Neil's nose. The Liverpool shaman took hold of that palm, placed it on the table, and bluntly said, "You've lost so many women over the years because you're a violent man. You hit women."

The biker blinked rapidly and said nothing but it was obvious to the two onlookers that O'Neil had touched a delicate nerve.

"Oh, come on, who hasn't struck a woman?" said the biker, but behind the bravado and the smile his eyes looked distressed.

"And you stole from your mother on her deathbed."

After dropping this bombshell, O'Neil looked up from the palm to the biker's face with uncharacteristic contempt. Harlan had never seen such a look of disgust in his friend's face before.

The biker withdrew his palm and felt for the hunting knife which he kept in a sheath sewn into the inside of his jacket. He let loose a string of shockingly obscene expletives, at which a gothic-looking woman entering the Swan Inn shouted over, "Hey, there's no need for that language!"

The other biker grabbed hold of his friend's hand and stopped him from pulling out the knife destined for O'Neil's heart. "Don't man!" he pleaded, "No!"

The once-sceptical hard-knock who had had his shameful past so publicly revealed by O'Neil's chiromancy, stood up and shrieked, "I'll be waiting out there for you!" He then threw the glass of Guinness in the mystic's face and swaggered out of the pub, repeating his threats.

Later that night, Harlan cagily ventured out into the fog - and soon spotted the burly biker waiting in a dark warehouse doorway, but there was no sign of his friend. Harlan rushed back into the pub and warned O'Neil to go to his home - wherever that was - via Hanover Street, but O'Neil somehow knew that the biker's friend would be waiting there; he could sense them both waiting.

"The other one has a machete, and he's used it before," was O'Neil's chilling remark.

"Then call the police. What are you waiting for?" Harlan urged his old friend.

"I'll call on a much higher authority to protect me, but it'll probably cause even more bloodshed," was O'Neil's mysterious response.

"What do you mean?" asked Harlan, intrigued but

still worried.

"I need your help, Harlan," said O'Neil, rolling yet another cigarette. "We need to call him ..." he added.

"Call who for heaven's sake?" said Harlan, getting frustrated. "Stop talking in riddles. Can't you see this is really serious?"

"I need to call my guardian ... a berserker," said O'Neil, whilst calmly licking the Rizla paper and sealing his cigarette. Then he chillingly revealed how this guardian had, many years ago, knocked at his door in order to show him the severed head of a man who had raped the girl he loved.

Harlan went cold. He was speechless. He had never once had reason to doubt the incredible things his friend had told him, for it was a fact that O'Neil never lied - but surely he didn't have the power to conjure up one of the most feared warriors of history?

"Norse Occultism," said O'Neil, and went over to the female Goth who had scolded the foul-mouthed biker, and asked to borrow her makeup mirror. At first she thought he was joking, but he pleaded for it and promised to return it very shortly. She delved into her handbag and located it, then handed it to him with a sarcastic lop-sided smile.

O'Neil took it back to the table and then rooted through his own pockets for his trusty Swiss Army knife. "I need blood," he quipped.

"Last orders," shouted the barman.

O'Neil inflicted a small wound on his thumb, and then squeezed a few droplets on to the mirror.

"Vali, God of revenge," he intoned. "By my own blood I beseech thee to dispatch my guardian in the reign of Nott, Goddess of this night ..."

"Hey, mate, what're you doing to my mirror?" the gothic lady shouted over, drawing people's attention to the weird ritual. "That's not blood, is it?" she asked, wide-eyed, with a look of disgust. She'd seen some sights in the Swan over the years, but nothing as bizarre as this.

O'Neil ignored the Goth's questions. His eyes bulged and his muscles tensed as he proceeded to speak in an unknown language, and he frothed slightly at the mouth. Harlan was visibly trembling, because he could literally feel the buzz of electrical tension in the air. Silence descended on the Swan Inn - all eyes were on O'Neil. Suddenly, he fainted and slumped forwards on to the table, scattering ashtrays and spilling drinks, which made people assume that he was drunk. The clientele supped the last of their drinks and started to leave, and as they did so O'Neil regained consciousness. The first thing he did was to look into Harlan's eyes and with great solemnity declare, "He's here. I saw him."

O'Neil and Harlan were the last customers to leave the pub. They stepped out into a literal void of ghostly all-enveloping fog. The lamps of Wood Street were greatly diffused like distant nebulae, and passers-by appeared as insubstantial as the faint shadows of ghosts and spectres.

All of a sudden, the muffled silence of the fog was pierced by echoing screams. Not just the screams of women, but of men too, and not the usual screams of high-jinks fuelled by drink and drugs, but screams from witnesses to some shocking horror. O'Neil froze in his tracks, and Harlan halted too and looked back at him. The disturbance was coming from the Slater

Street intersection. O'Neil beckoned Harlan to follow him down Colquitt Street, but as they sneaked along the street, close to a wall, they heard the thundering steps of something striding by, and Harlan glimpsed a tall stocky phantasm walking along. It was as pale as a watermark in the fog, yet he could clearly make out a pair of horns on the stranger's head! He also carried a sword and circular shield.

That was enough. Harlan dashed after O'Neil, and they walked and walked until they reached Chinatown. O'Neil advised his friend to go straight home, and Harlan reluctantly obeyed. He walked for miles through that unending fog until he finally reached his home on Hawarden Avenue, off Smithdown Road, where he told his older brother all about the night's strange events. His brother looked at him condescendingly and said it was time he grew up.

Out of curiosity, on the following morning, Harlan rode the Number 86 bus into town and inspected Wood Street, looking for evidence of the berserker. He found splashes of clotted blood near Concert Street, and streaks of blood on the kerb near Hanover Street. He also heard strange stories about the berserker from his friends in the Krazyhouse club. Moshers, skater-punks, metalheads and Goths told him that "a drugged-up psycho", dressed like a Viking, had almost slaughtered two bikers, but the victims had run for their lives and escaped. The accounts varied slightly, but Harlan knew the truth of the matter and kept quiet.

At around this time, I also heard about a severed index finger being found on Wood Street, but whether there was a connection with this story, I am not sure.

As far as I know, the violent bikers never returned to the Swan Inn, and O'Neil is now believed to be living quietly in Wales.

A genuine practitioner of magic has a great knowledge of grimoires - a comprehensive collections of spells and invocations which can be used for enlisting the help of demons. The demon Agares, for example, is conjured up to cause earthquakes, amongst other things, and the demon Behemoth (mentioned in the Bible's Book of Job) is concerned with food, drink and feasting, while Astaroth, the Prince-demon of Hell, will truthfully answer any questions about people or events, past present or future.

I know many people who mock magical rites, yet will mutter "Bless you" when someone sneezes. The celebration of a twenty-first birthday, the blessing of the Christian Eucharist, or even the rite of passage known as bar mitzvah - are all ceremonial observances - the performance of rites. Magical rituals are indistinguishable from many of the everyday things we do that seem, on the face of it, irrational. We throw a pinch of salt over our shoulder for good luck, cross our fingers in hope, avoid walking under ladders and so on. Call such things superstition, if you like, or are they a subconscious harking back to the days when the practice of magic was widespread?

VOICES

One busy morning a few years ago in Liverpool's Lime Street Station, a man in his early twenties called Simon, was standing among the swarming crowds of rail travellers and commuters, with his hands cupped over his ears. He might as well have been invisible, because most people rushed past him as if he wasn't there, and those that did notice the scruffily dressed young man with the uncombed hair and stubbly face soon hurried around him and away from him. For the past 5 years, Simon had been suffering from a form of schizophrenia. He had been a heavy cannabis smoker, and one day at his bedsit on Lark Lane, he was awakened by a room mate. 'Come on Simon, get up mate, you're late for college.' He said.

Simon yawned and opened his eyes and looked

around. There was no one there.

He heard laughter.

This scared the young loafer, and he looked around nervously then asked, 'Who's there?'

'Me,' said a voice from nowhere.

'Where are you?' Simon queried.

'In your head mate, in your noggin,' said the voice. And everywhere Simon went, so did the voice, night and day. Simon was so frightened he eventually went to see a psychiatrist, and was told he was schizophrenic. The condition might have been caused by smoking to much marijuana. So he gave the weed up, but the voices stayed with him. Simon's social life was destroyed by the endless chattering in his head. A girl he had dated for a year abandoned him because the voices even distracted him as he tried to make love. They would laugh, and jeer, and come out with obscenities. One day Simon was almost beaten to death when he went to a cinema on Edge Lane. The voices started arguing among themselves until he couldn't hear the film and so he told them to shut up, and two skinheads thought Simon was telling them to be quiet and they jumped him outside and kicked him across the car park.

And now, 5 years on, he was homeless, and he slumped into a corner in Lime Street Station and pleaded for the voices to go away as the normal sane people got on with their lives and went to work. Then all of a sudden, a new voice was heard among the usual accents of the invisible persecuters. The voice got stronger and stronger until it actually drowned out the evil voices. A man's well spoken voice said, 'Simon, I can help you.'

'Go away, leave me alone!' Simon said.

'No Simon you must listen to me please, I can save you!' said the voice.

'How can *you* save me?' Simon asked. People passing by sneered at the man sitting on the floor of the station, talking to himself.

'Look over there at that woman, quickly!' the voice urged him.

'Where?' Simon took his hands from his ears and looked about.

'Walking towards the escalator, the blonde woman, do you see her?' the voice sounded heartbroken.

Simon saw the woman, heading for the escalator lading to the underground. She was about forty years of age. 'Yeah I see her so what?'

'She was my wife,' the voice told him, 'I was married to her for fifteen years. Then I died. Stomach cancer.'

'Why are you telling me this?' Simon asked. He thought it might be one of the bad voices playing a trick.

'I want you to give her a message,' the voice said.

'It's too late now she's gone down to the underground,' Simon told him.

'Well, she comes back tonight after work. Then you can give her the message.' The voice said and Simon sensed deep sad emotions from the voice.

'If I give her the message, how will you help me?' Simon was more curious to know.

The voice said: 'I know how the other spirits get into your mind, and I know how to close the way in. They want to drive you to suicide because they want to try and get you to join them.'

'You don't even exist, you're all in my mind, I'm

schizophrenic, that's all.' Simon cupped his hands round his ears again, and then two policemen moved him on out of the station into Lime Street. But the new voice stuck with him.

The voice spoke from his left side, saying: 'Simon, please believe me, my name is Frank Hughes, I died in, let me see, when was it? Three years ago. There's no time here so it's confusing. Anyway, when five o'clock comes I want you to go to my wife – her name is Hannah – and I want you to tell her something.'

A bus on Lime Street sounded its horn and a woman screamed. A man grabbed Simon by the arm and pulled him onto the pavement in the nick of time. Simon had been so distracted he'd drifted blindly into the road.

He swore and cursed the new voice, but it somehow calmed him down and told him to go into a red telephone box, which Simon did. It was quieter in there and the voice said, "when you see my wife say, 'Hannah Hughes, your husband Frank still loves you, but you have to move on. He wants you to be happy, go to David, he loves you so much.' "

Simon borrowed a pen and a piece of paper from a student and wrote down the words the spirit of Frank Hughes told him. Then the voice said, 'Simon, the other spirits are very angry, and they're forcing their way back in, but hold on, and don't let them distract you. When I come back they'll never bother you again.'

And sure enough all the same old malevolent, evil, sinister voices came back with a vengeance. 'Throw away that paper now, pretty please,' said a childish voice. 'I'll kill you in your sleep Simon, unless you tear up that paper!' said another invisible speaker.

Simon wandered around the town, into cafés, through St John's Gardens, and at a quarter to five he arrived back at Lime Street Station, where he was moved on twice by the police. He returned just after five o'clock, and his heart skipped a beat when he saw the blonde woman. He looked at the paper, and tried to read the words, but the voices in his head sounded like the roaring crowd at a football match. He cursed at them and read the scrap of paper, then started to follow the blonde woman. He shouted: 'Hannah!'

She glanced back, but when she saw Simon, and the state of his appearance, she hurried on.

'Hannah! Hannah Hughes!' shouted the down and out.

This time she slowed down and halted, and looked at Simon.

He hurried to her, and scanned the piece of paper, then said: 'Hannah Hughes, your husband Frank still loves you, but you have to move on. He wants you to be happy, so go to David, he loves you so much.'

Hannah was speechless. 'How do you know my name? Who are you?' she asked Simon.

Simon was suddenly overcome with the strangest sensation he had ever experienced. All of the voices stopped as if someone had thrown a switch in his head. He felt spasms in his mouth, and a creeping numbness in his tongue as if it had been injected with cocaine. Something was taking him over. His mouth and tongue moved and he spoke in a voice that wasn't his. He said, 'Hannah it's me, I love you. I missed you so much.'

Hannah was engrossed yet obviously a bit scared.

Simon was talking now and yet he didn't know what he was saying. And he found himself all choked up with sadness with his arms around Hannah. Then he found himself kissing her. She pushed him back and screamed, and ran away into the crowds. He fell on the floor, with tears in his eyes, yet they didn't feel like his tears. Two policemen arrived on the scene and restrained the vagrant, yet he couldn't hear what they were saying. All he could feel was terrible sorrow, and the feeling of lost love. The voice of Frank Hughes said, 'Simon, thank you for letting me hold my wife for a moment, thanks for letting me kiss her, thanks for letting me tell her how much I missed her. All that released love has sent those evil voices scurrying away. They'll never come back, I promise they won't.'

And the voice faded away. And as Simon was led to a police van, he started to laugh, because the voices had all gone. They never did come back, and Simon is now living a peaceful life in Chester.

STRANGE BIRD OF PASSAGE

Flinders Street is no more, but back in the late nineteenth century it was a busy Kirkdale thoroughfare that ran from Commercial Road to Stanley Road, and in the year 1897, a rather suspicious-looking gentleman called at one of the lodging houses on this street. He was of middling size, and he wore a long full-length tweed-wool frock coat and a black slouch hat, and he carried an old scuffed oversized portmanteau case.

The lodging house, at Number 79 Flinders Street, was run by a world-weary Irish Liverpool man named Joe Turner, and from the moment he set eyes on the lodger, he thought there was something sinister about him. The stranger signed his name in the lodging house register as Mr Jones, but people in the area believed he was a Lithuanian, as he had been heard speaking in that language by Mr Isaacs, a local Russian-born grocer. Jones had a long prominent aquiline nose, a small bald head with tufts of hair above the ears, and a striking stoop, as if he'd been accustomed to crouching in his occupation and he'd stuck like that. Perhaps he was a clerk or a writer.

Mr Jones demanded, and was given, the attic lodgings as advertised in the window, and paid for a fortnight's stay in advance. Joe Turner's nine-year-old nephew, Paddy, lugged the new lodger's heavy oblong-shaped portmanteau up the six flights of stairs - and received only a nod and a smile from Jones in return. Then the door was slammed in his face.

Very strange things happened in the city that week, and only young Paddy had the brains and the intuition to connect them to the mysterious Mr Jones, but nobody was prepared to listen to his conclusions.

One late afternoon, an enormous black bird, resembling a raven, but with an estimated wingspan of some twelve feet, was seen in flight over the Huskisson Branch Dock. Stevedores and merchants, who shared a suspicious nature with their seafaring counterparts, regarded the bird as a bad omen. One sea captain, who had recently returned from San Francisco, believed the creature to be an imported Californian condor - a giant South American bird with a nine-foot wingspan, although it was known that such birds had a bald yellow head, and the ominous bird wheeling above them had a black head.

Everyone on the quayside, and people on the waterfront's Regent Road, stood spellbound, watching the giant bird as it circled above them and occasionally plunged down to the banks of the river. It flew towards the east, and cast a gargantuan shadow over Stanley Park, where it was seen to dive and seize something. Some witnesses claimed that it was a small child, but the general consensus was that a dog had been picked up by the talons of the enormous bird. The rumours of the giant bird swept the city, and most intelligent people dismissed the weird story as superstitious nonsense.

However, two days later, at 5.30am, Mr Jones crept from his room carrying a hessian sack and went down into the backyard to empty its contents into the dustbin. Paddy was awakened by the creaking of the stairs and peeped out of his bedroom window. He saw him carefully covering the refuse with newspapers and instantly became suspicious, so he later went down to have a look in the bin. What he saw chilled him to his marrow. Under the crumpled papers he found several fish heads - as well as the skeletal remains of a small dog...

"You're talking daft now, Paddy," landlord Joe Turner told his nine-year-old nephew when the lad told him what he'd seen and claimed that Mr Jones, the new lodger up in the garret, had dumped the remains after his 'giant bird' had eaten the flesh.

"And where exactly would he be keeping this giant bird?" Joe asked young Paddy, whilst lighting his pipe.

"In Mr Jones's big case, of course, Uncle Joe!" the child replied. "That'll be why it was so heavy."

Joe smirked and patronisingly patted the child's head, but the conversation with his nephew had turned his mind to his enigmatic new lodger. He leaned on the mantelpiece in the front parlour, thinking about Mr Jones, and how he always went out to eat - and never even came down for breakfast. Perhaps he had to eat kosher food, or was on some other special diet, the landlord reasoned. Out of curiosity he went into the backyard and examined the dustbin - and to his utter horror he found the six fish heads and the stinking carcass of an animal, just as Paddy had described. On closer examination he saw that the animal was a young mongrel dog. Joe recoiled with a handkerchief to his mouth. Of course, he did not believe for one minute that any bird had eaten that dog, but perhaps some 'heathen' from Lithuania, where dogs were perhaps considered to be a delicacy...

Whatever the explanation, Joe wanted to get to the bottom of the grisly remains and so he climbed the sixty steps up to the garret to have words with Mr Jones but there was no answer when he knocked and when he tried the handle, he found that the door was locked from the inside.

"I know you're in there, Mr Jones!" shouted the landlord through the keyhole. "So you might as well come out now."

This finally elicited a response; the lodger shouted something back in his foreign tongue and threw an object at the door. This was not the reaction that Joe Turner was expecting. He had had some very strange lodgers in his time, but this fellow was in a class of his own! He went back down to the parlour and apologised to his nephew for doubting his story. Paddy looked up from cleaning out the ashes from the fireplace.

"I told you he was creepy, didn't I, Uncle Joe," he said, wide-eyed, kneeling on the newspapers which he'd spread across the hearth rug. "It must be a pretty big bird to pick a dog up and eat it like that," said the boy, lost in morbid contemplation.

"Listen, son," said Joe. "I'm telling you once and for all, no bird ate that dog,'" and he shook his head dismissively. "It's that lunatic upstairs who ate that dog. They've obviously got very peculiar tastes in food where he comes from. They'll eat anything"

"Uncle, where is Lithuania?" Paddy inquired.

His uncle, who hadn't got the faintest idea where it was, simulated a long coughing fit after puffing on his pipe, in order to evade the question. Eventually he stopped and said, by way of diversion. "Mind you don't get any of that ash on that rug."

"You know I'm always careful, Uncle."

Uncle Joe then warned his nephew not to go anywhere near the Lithuanian, saying that he could get into real trouble by poking his nose into things he didn't understand. But Paddy was not to be fobbed off. He was now even more convinced that their strange lodger was up to no good and he intended to discover exactly what was going on.

That evening, as Uncle Joe was snoring under a newspaper slumped in his fireside armchair, Paddy crept back upstairs to the garret, and peeped through the keyhole of Mr Jones's room. The room was bathed in the reddish gold light of a setting sun, and the garret window was wide open. At first, Paddy couldn't see or hear anything and thought he may have gone out. But then he nearly jumped out of his skin when he suddenly heard the lodger crying out. He uttered a succession of unfamiliar words and then made a dreadful inhuman rattling sound which seemed to resonate from deep down in the back of his throat, as if he were choking. There then followed a tense period of silence during which Paddy scarcely dared breathe, terrified lest he should be discovered by the creepy lodger.

What he saw next froze him to the very depths of his soul with fear. A giant black bird waddled into view, blocking out the sun's dying rays," and Paddy blinked through the keyhole in total disbelief. Its great claws rasped on the floorboards as the six foot tall bird struggled to manoeuvre itself in the cramped surroundings. The freaky creature had a man's head, but with the incongruous addition of a huge beak at the front - and a startlingly bald head. It had the head of Mr Jones! Somehow that bird was Mr Jones! By some sort of devilry the lodger had metamorphosed into this grotesque hybrid with feathers and fur covering his round chest from the neck down. Mr Jones's hands had been transformed into the talons of a bird, and he was now perched at the open window, ready to fly off.

Paddy couldn't suppress a small gasp of fright as the bird flexed its enormous wings, and it was alerted immediately. It cocked its mighty head to one side, all its senses primed. Then it turned its head through one hundred and eighty degrees and the lens of its huge domed eye zoomed right into Paddy's eye at the keyhole. In a flash it hopped down off its perch and flew in a frenzy of fur and feathers at the door, its great beak smashing repeatedly through the wooden panels, as if they were matchwood...

Paddy's terrified screams echoed down the stairways of the house where they reached the ears of the slumbering Joe Turner. He woke up with a start and fought his way from under the newspaper before flying out of the front parlour to the foot of the stairs. He looked up the stairs to the source of the screams and heard his nephew's footfalls clattering towards him.

"Whatever's wrong, Paddy?" he asked, as the lad reached the first floor landing and he began to climb the stairs towards him, but Paddy came hurtling straight past his uncle and bolted into the parlour, where he disappeared under a table. Joe crouched down beneath the table and could plainly see that the child was trembling uncontrollably from head to foot.

"Paddy, what's wrong with you?" he asked, sternly. "I can't help you if you won't tell me what's wrong. You've not been up to see that foreign chap again, have you?"

As the boy's breathing gradually slowed, he managed to give a garbled account of his encounter with Mr Jones and of his incredible metamorphosis into the huge bird, and he quivered when he described how the unholy creature had gone for him and smashed great holes in the door. Joe had heard enough. He marched straight over to the sideboard, pulled out an old biscuit tin, lifted the lid, and took out a loaded revolver, then set off to confront whatever it was up there in the garret. He could see where something had torn jagged holes in the attic door, just as Paddy had described, but peeping through them, Joe could see no signs of either the Lithuanian lodger, or of any giant bird. Holding the revolver out in front of him, he unlocked the door with his master key and cautiously entered the room. The garret windows were still wide open, and a brisk breeze from the river had chilled the room. Joe closed the windows and lit the gas mantle. He jumped when he heard the floorboard creak outside the door, but it was just young Paddy. He had conjured up enough courage to come out from under the table and was now determined to help his uncle fight that grotesque bird of terror.

"Go back downstairs, Paddy," his uncle told him, as his eyes took in the lodger's shirt, waistcoat, trousers and long-Johns lying on the bed.

Paddy stayed put, wiping tears from his reddened eyes.

"But, Uncle I ..." he began, when the room suddenly darkened as something hovered outside the windows. It started to thump against the window panes, startling them both. Joe raised the revolver and aimed it straight at the casements, which were now bulging inwards, threatening to give way at any moment. He backed away towards the doorway, where Paddy was crying again. Then with a sudden roar, the windows burst open, and shards of glass and splintered frame showered the garret. Joe Turner froze with fear. An enormous black bird with a vaguely human beaked head squeezed through the window and entered the room - with something writhing frantically in its mouth.

The tip of each extended wing touched the walls on either side of the room - a span of at least fifteen feet. The unfortunate cat - for that was what it was -which was trapped in the monster's beak, was torn to shreds by two great claw-like hands, and the bird was so engrossed in its feeding frenzy that it didn't notice Joe Turner, and, mute with terror, he stepped behind the damaged door and closed it over. He took several deep breaths and then opened the door again and aimed the revolver straight at the bird. Its head twisted to face him and it let out a blood-curdling squawk as the landlord discharged six shots into it in quick succession. The bird screeched horribly and lunged at him, but Joe turned and ran, pushing Paddy ahead of him as he did so.

Uncle and nephew tumbled down the stairs with the nightmarish bird from Hell waddling obscenely after them. When Paddy picked himself up on the next landing, he saw his uncle groaning and clutching his knee. Halfway up the stairs lay the stunned bird with a glazed look in its eyes. Joe Turner scrambled painfully to his feet and cautiously approached the bird to have a closer look - upon which the bird suddenly became animated and batted him with its wing and raised its head, emitting a high-pitched cry which must have been heard for miles around. Joe was sent crashing through the banister and rails and fell on to the next flight of stairs in a senseless heap. The giant bird then seemed to summon all of its remaining strength and it slowly raised itself up. Having done so, it then steadily began to hobble down the stairs towards Paddy...

Paddy screamed out to his uncle, who was lying motionless among the splintered handrail and balusters on the descending flight of stairs. "Help me! Help me!" he yelled. The grotesque wounded bird hopped awkwardly down the stairs, limping and tilting its head to look at him side-on with its domed red-iris eyes. The boy decided to take a chance, and racing past it, picked up a length of the broken baluster and started taking swipes at the creature, aiming at its head. The bird shrieked like a stuck pig and desperately tried to extend its wings to shield itself from the blows raining down on its bald head. But so enormous was the bird, that it was hemmed in between the wall and the stairway rail and couldn't manoeuvre itself properly in the tight space. Paddy couldn't believe it when, unable to defend itself, he saw it slowly turn and limp back up to the garret, leaving him sobbing over his injured uncle.

Joe Turner soon regained consciousness, but before he and Paddy had a chance to discuss what to do next, they heard a knock at the front door. Joe groggily staggered downstairs with his nephew and opened the door to find an old man wearing a long black coat and a homburg hat. The man introduced himself as a Mr Steiner, and said that he'd observed the giant bird flying to and from the garret, and what's more, he claimed that he knew precisely who the 'bird-man' was. Most astonishing of all, he also claimed that he could kill him. There was something open and honest about the old foreign-sounding man, despite his wild claims, so, somewhat apprehensively, Joe decided to admit him into the house. Perhaps he really could help rid them of the avian menace.

Having accepted the drink that he was offered, the stranger proceeded to tell Joe and Paddy a very unsettling story.

In broken English, Steiner told how, in the twelfth century, a snowstorm, almost unprecedented in its severity, had almost buried a Lithuanian village near Vilnius. The fallen snow quickly turned to ice and refused to thaw for months, and during the long freeze, the villagers were unable to get out to look for food. After having eaten all their winter preserves and grain as well as every animal within the confines of the village, the villagers were staring starvation in the face. They were almost ready to resort to cannibalism, when a strange gigantic bird suddenly landed in their midst. It had been seen around the region for many years and was said to be the embodiment of an evil magician who had been transformed into a bird a hundred years before, as punishment for inflicting terrible atrocities on the people of the region.

Now, to the starving villagers the bird meant only one thing: food. It was soon shot and stoned and then lassoed. However, the bird did not finish up in the communal cooking pot. Instead, a prominent local family used brute force to claim the creature as their own, and it was promptly roasted on their spit, filling the whole village with delicious aromas, which nearly drove the famished villagers mad. A holy man warned the family against consuming the bird's flesh, predicting that they would all be cursed as a result and in time would themselves change into such a bird. The ravenous family listened impatiently to his warnings but ate the bird anyway.

The snows eventually thawed and spring arrived. Most of the villagers had survived the great hunger, but the people of the castle were not so lucky, and they slowly began to turn into giant birds; birds with an unholy appetite for human flesh. They fed off the hapless villagers for many years despite them trying everything to defend themselves. Eventually it was discovered that the creatures could be killed by using silver-tipped arrows and so the cull began. But some of the giant birds escaped, and underwent a secondary metamorphosis, becoming human again for a while.

Mr Jones was the last descendant of this cursed clan. Steiner had followed him all the way to Liverpool - and was now ready to kill him and so put an end to the curse. The old man produced a gun. explaining that it had silver-tipped bullets in its chamber. He then climbed up to the garret, accompanied by Joe Turner and Paddy.

They found Jones still partially transformed into the devil bird. Without hesitation, Steiner shot him three times through the heart. The tormented feathered figure toppled backwards out of the garret window, but somehow managed to cling to the window frame with its claws. Steiner held out his hand, and a gnarled clawed hand weakly grasped his palm. The old man then pulled the partially transformed creature back into the room, where it collapsed on the floor and died. Before their eyes the corpse slowly changed fully back into a man again, before disintegrating into a pile of grey dust.

Until his death in the late 1950s, Paddy Turner told anyone who would listen about this strange incident, and swore that it had really happened. Who knows? Perhaps Shakespeare was right; maybe there really are more things in heaven and earth than are dreamt of in our philosophy.

CAN YOU KEEP A SECRET?

One rainy mid-week evening in 2007, a 40-year-old Clubmoor man named Stephen was staggering down Bold Street with the lapels of his jacket turned up in an effort to keep the biting wintry wind at bay, and his head was bowed at the icy rain that was slanting towards him. Stephen had just had a row with his girlfriend in the Newington pub on Renshaw Street, and had stormed out into this inclement weather. Upon reaching the bottom of Bold Street, Stephen halted at the steps of the Lyceum, then decided o go inside to a drinking and eating establishment with the rather corny title of Prohibition. Stephen paid for a glass of Stella, and stood at the bar, wondering if his girlfriend Kellie was looking for him. She'd probably go to O'Neill's bar, and then when she saw he wasn't there, she'd probably try Flanagan's Apple or Labinsky's...

An old man's voice interrupted Stephen's train of thought. 'You look as if you've got the whole worries of the world on your shoulders.'

Stephen almost smiled. He was not in a mood to talk to anyone, especially this relic in his sixties with a tribal tattoo on his forearm and a Status Quo tee shirt. Stephen felt old enough now that he was forty, and this old geezer only made him feel older. Kellie had only just turned twenty-two years of age, and this age difference had been the source of this evening's argument with her – well, the age difference and the knife. She wore a pair of Aldo platforms which made her tower over Stephen, who was just 5 feet 5 inches tall. Kellie was 5 feet 7 inches in her bare feet, and the Aldo shoes added another four inches. 'You hate me looking down at you, don't you?' she had told Stephen in the Newington, in front of all her young mates as well. 'You hate me being taller, younger; hate me being everything!' she had said, and her friend Emma had started giggling. Then she told everyone Stephen carried a knife because he was beaten up by a gang once and had never gotten over it. 'It's not even a big knife,' Kellie had laughed, 'it's a teeny one like his thingy!' And Kellie's mates burst into laughter, so Stephen smashed his pint to the floor and left the pub.

'These birds today leave nothing to the imagination, do they?' the old man reflected on the revealing outfit of a 19-year-old drinker standing less than six feet away. 'Skirt right up past her arse – she powders four cheeks in the bog I bet,' the oldster said, gritting his dentures, eyeing the blonde who had that clear brightness of living youth in her eyes; something that no artificial eye make-up could ever mimic.

'Do you mind?' Stephen raised his voice, and then left the bar room shaking his head. A drop of rain, dangling from a hair on Stephen's head was shaken loose by the judder, and landed in the drink of a shaven-headed young man who was drinking at a table with his girlfriend. He glared up at Stephen.

'Sorry mate,' Stephen apologised, and shuffled out the room and into Prohibition's large impressive dining area. This was set well apart from the noisy bar room, in a beautiful circular room which once housed the Lyceum's library and newspaper reading room, all those decades ago in the age of the hansom cab.

Stephen felt such a failure sitting alone amongst all of the couples in the Prohibition restaurant, but he pushed his depressive thoughts of being temporarily single from his mind by studying the long tall laminated menu. He decided to try the 'Mexican Platter' and a glass of rosé. While Stephen waited for his platter to arrive, he felt the urge to urinate, and asked a waitress where the toilet was. 'Upstairs, through that door up there,' she pointed to a balcony about thirty feet in the air, and Stephen couldn't help but think that it was a ridiculous place to have a toilet, and he walked to the staircase which eventually took him up to the balcony, and then he had to find the door to the toilet. The first door opened into a tiny room full of mops and buckets. Then he found the toilet, peed in the urinal, washed his hands, held them under the dryer – and spotted something in his reflection. By the hard unflattering illumination of the neon light over the washbowl, he saw the crow's feet radiating from the tail of each eye – and that clump of grey hairs just above his right sideburn. He plucked them out, along with the healthy dark brown ones, and swore at them. To age-conscious Stephen the hairs were frosty little reminders of mortality; aide memoires from the Grim Reaper who will come to all in his own time. 'You are turning into a right morbid bastard, Ste,' Stephen told his reflected face.

'Can you keep a secret?' said a voice behind Stephen which startled him and caused him to break wind. He coughed in an attempt to cover the embarrassment and turned around. A very pale-faced young man of about 21 perhaps, with coal-black hair, centre-parted, was emerging from the toilet cubicle. He stood there with the cubicle door ajar, smiling, and then he stepped out to reveal his odd dark-green velvet suit, white shirt and royal-blue satin tie.

'Have I got what?' Stephen tried to flick the uprooted grey hairs from his fingers but their roots adhered to them.

'I said, "Can you keep a secret?" Can you?' said the young man in green. His clear eyes sparkled and there was not a single line or blemish or any minor imperfection on his face.

'Depends what the secret is doesn't it?' Stephen walked towards the toilet door, thinking the youth was unbalanced or on drugs.

'Go ahead,' said the young man, gesturing with his immaculately-manicured fingers for Stephen to go out the toilet ahead of him.

Stephen pulled the door open and walked out into the corridor, which was quiet and rather secluded, as the bustling dining area was far below on the ground floor behind a door. Stephen's feet began to quietly tread the plush carpet of the corridor when the man in green velvet shouted after him: 'You don't have to be old!'

Stephen halted and turned – his curiosity aroused. 'What?'

The young well-groomed man halted at a red regency-styled door, and nodded at its panels. He said: 'Come in here and I'll show you a secret, and if you promise not to tell, I have plans for you that you never dreamed in your wildest hallucinations.'

Half of Stephen's mind swore and said, *'No Ste, this is shady – creepy – go downstairs now!'* And the other half of Stephen's conscience said, *'I'm curious! Go with him! You'll be okay; if he tried anything you'd just have to punch his lights out, he's a gimp.'*

And the latter half of Stephen's mind swayed him. He watched the man in the green suit open the door and step into a darkened room. Stephen went to the doorway, and his nostrils were immediately assailed by the sweet scent of joss sticks – and the fragrance quickly brought back memories of certain new age shops in the old Quiggins building on School Lane.

'Come in and close the door,' said the man in green, standing about twelve feet inside of a room dimly lit by a purple light.

'Is this a club?' Stephen found himself asking, and he felt as if he was becoming high on the overwhelming aromatic incense.

'Come through here, come on,' the youth beckoned him as he walked towards an archway. Stephen followed him, and felt as if every step he was taking was in some dream, for reality seemed to be evaporating. At the end of the archway there was an immense vault, and it looked too big to be contained by the Lyceum, and this spatial anomaly made Stephen feel a bit uneasy. In this huge room, everything was weakly lit by a crimson light, and Stephen couldn't believe his eyes. Some fifty or more naked young men were kissing one another, and frolicking about on the thick elaborately patterned carpet that covered the floor of the vault. A few of the hedonistic strangers were drinking and smoking, but as Stephen got over the initial shock of the orgy, he realised that all of the naked men were in their early twenties.

The young man in the green velvet suit who had led Stephen into this Bacchanalian hideaway began to take off his clothes, and he advised Stephen to do the same. 'If you want to be twenty-one again, take off your clothes now before the master arrives!' he urged the forty-year-old outsider.

'You can go and f-' Stephen was saying when a loud deep horn sounded, and the whole vault shook. two tall dark doors, some twenty feet in height, slowly swung open, and there stood the stuff nightmares are made of. A tall monstrosity of a giant man, about twenty feet in height, stood there, with dark-green shiny scales covering his arms and legs. His stomach was huge and pear-shaped, and his black glistening phallus was like an elephant trunk. Two curling horns were set upon the scaled being's head, and a pair of animal eyes stared from a long stretched face with a hook nose. All of the men ran to the giant and bowed their heads at his feet.

Stephen turned and ran to the archway, but a naked youth blocked his way and stood there, smiling.

'Get out of my way!' Stephen screamed, and he

heard the creature bellow with deep bone-shaking laughter.

The nude man refused to move, and so Stephen reached into his coat and felt the knife in his leather scabbard. He withdrew it, and then lunged forward. The naked young man tried to grab the knife with both hands but Stephen lashed out and stabbed one of the youth's hands. The young disciple grimaced, but still tried to stop Stephen from leaving. Stephen came out with a stream of swear words, and then he thrust the blade of the knife into the face of the youth, bursting one of his eyes. The next thing Stephen knew, he was running for his life under the archway. He ran through the purple gloom of the outer room, and quickly found the door that had admitted him to this nightmare. He opened it, ran out into the hallway, and when he reached the dining area, he saw a friend named Sean who he hadn't seen in years, and he told him about the club upstairs with the naked men and their weird demonic idol. Sean smiled and said, 'Well I don't fancy going up there then.'

'I'm not kidding, mate come and see!' Stephen told him, wild-eyed, and out of breath. Then he realised he had blood from the stabbed disciple on his hands, and he showed the red stains to Sean, who seemed a bit afraid. 'See?' Stephen said, thrusting his blood-stained fingers at his friend's face, 'that's his blood; the fellah who tried to stop me!'

'Hey, can you keep the noise down please?' said an irritated man seated at a table with his wife and children.

'Sorry mate,' Stephen said, and he took Sean by the arm and led him to the stairway.

'I believe you, I believe you!' Sean said, feeling embarrassed by the looks he and his old friend were attracting from the diners in the restaurant.

'No you don't, but I'll show you!' Stephen said, and almost dragged his friend up the stairs.

When the two men had reached the corridor where the regency-styled door had led Stephen to the wild gathering of promiscuity and God knows what else – there was a sweet smell in the air. But that was all that remained of that strange den of unrestrained sexual activity and demonic worship. The door which led to the vault was never found. Stephen left the Lyceum and wandered about in the rain, trying to make sense of what had happened. He had wanted to be young again when he pulled out those grey hairs as he stood before the toilet mirror – and then that young man in green velvet had appeared. Was he some agent of the Devil who could give youth back to the vain in return for their very souls? I told Stephen that I had heard of similar 'clubs' to the one he almost joined. Some are said to exist in close proximity to the more extreme hedonistic dens of the city centre, and when the victim is at his or her lowest ebb, when drugs and drink have lowered the power to make rational decisions, the agent provocateur of the Devil springs into action.

To this day, Stephen shudders whenever he even passes the old Lyceum building.

HILTY

Occasionally a story comes my way on which I cannot throw any light whatsoever. Such tales seem to defy all explanation, and despite my many years spent studying the paranormal, I am at a loss to rationalise them. The following story certainly falls into this category. Perhaps you can fathom it out?

It all started when eleven-year-old John Murphy and his six-year-old sister Mary visited their Aunty Frances, an oddball of a woman with peculiar behaviour patterns, who lived off Heyworth Street, in Everton. The only reason they were paying the visit was in the hope of getting a few bob for sweets, because Frances, as barmy as she was, was a generous person whenever she had money, especially to her nephews and nieces.

On this particular windy Saturday afternoon in March 1965, Frances left her eight-month-old baby, Jim, in his cot in the parlour and then said she was just popping out to have a word with Mrs Winneral, who lived about thirty yards down the road. She wouldn't be long she said, and warned little "Meddlesome Mary" not to disturb the baby's sleep. "I'll be back soon, Carrot Cake," she then said to John, insensitive to the fact that he hated that nickname, referring as it did to his mop of bright red hair.

Mary had brought her little plastic baby doll Miranda with her to the house, and she tried to shove it into the cot, on top of little Jim, who was fast asleep.

"Stop that, Mary," John warned her. "You'll wake the baby and then Aunt Frances won't get us any sweets."

"I won't!" shouted Mary, standing on a chair so she could get a proper view of Jim.

"Be quiet will you? She told you not to wake the baby," and John snatched the doll off his little sister.

"Give me that back - now!" shrieked Mary, her nostrils flared and her little eyes bulging with annoyance.

Just then a tiny mongrel dog ran into the house. It sounds like a far-fetched cliché to our ears in these times of sky-high crime rates, but in those days, you really could leave your front door open, and sometimes - on rare occasions -cats or dogs would stroll into your home off the street. This scruffy little canine specimen had a loveable face with large expressive eyes. Mary fell in love with him right away and picked him up and began to fuss over him, but he barked in protest and sprang from her over-enthusiastic rib-cracking embrace and scampered into the kitchen, where he began sniffing the air as the meaty aroma from a pan of stew simmering on the stove reached his nostrils.

John used a fork to skewer a piece of partly-boiled stewing steak from the pan, then blew on it until it was lukewarm. The dog sat on its hind legs in a begging posture, whining in anticipation of the treat he was about to receive. Mary giggled and asked if she could feed the dog the morsel. "No you can't," replied John, and he dropped the piece of meat for the dog, whose little jaw opened with perfect timing and caught the food mid-air. The animal had very muddy paws and Mary suggested they should wash him, so John fetched a washtub from the yard and put it down on the kitchen floor. He filled a copper kettle to full capacity and put it on the gas ring and then found some newspaper, and tore a strip off to screw up into a taper. He used the flame under the pan of stew to light the other gas ring and put the kettle on it.

Somewhere along the line, John put the washtub on the ancient gas cooker and took the pan of stew off the boil to give himself more room to directly boil the water in the washtub. Mary stood on a stool, with a ladle in her hand, scooping water from a running tap into the washtub. Two fierce rings of flame licked the underside of the galvanised tub. The plan was to dunk the dog in the warm tub and give him a good wash, but the furry little scavenger, suspecting something of the sort, had escaped back the way he had come.

Meanwhile, Aunty Frances was still busy gossiping with Mrs Winneral and the two women had recently been joined by gossiper extraordinaire, Mrs Huggins. Now Frances Murphy was a little afraid to leave, in case Mrs Winneral and Mrs Huggins started talking about her the minute her back was turned. Left to his own devices, John decided to go and have a mooch around upstairs in the bedrooms, and when he came down just five minutes later, he found Mary hysterical, and in tears. "A man took the baby!" she screamed, and pointed down the hall, towards the kitchen. There were ominous boiling and bubbling sounds coming from the kitchen, and steam had settled on the vestibule door's pane of glass and was even trickling down the walls. John felt butterflies in his stomach. "Where did this man go?" he cried.

"In - the - kitchen!" Mary managed to tell him between convulsive sobs. She was so distressed she almost made herself sick.

John walked into the kitchen and his heart sank when he saw that the door leading to the backyard was standing ajar. The water he and Mary had left in the bathtub was now boiling furiously, and in it lay a baby bobbing about in the bubbling reddish water. John turned around and ran past Mary, heading for the front parlour. The cot was empty, just as she had said. His heart somersaulted. The baby had been boiled alive by a madman.

Mary tried to grab at John as he ran out of the house, but he was too quick. She watched him run down the street and vanish around a corner. "John!" the little girl screamed, "Come back, John," and she rubbed her red swollen eyes of stinging tears with the sleeves of her jersey.

John fled down Heyworth Street, and almost tripped over the old arthritic dog that was always to be found sitting on the pavement outside the premises of Fletchers the Butchers. An elderly man who knew John's father came out of Bolams the Barbers, wiping the nape of his neck with a handkerchief. He could see that the lad looked terrified, and tried to stop him to ask what the matter was but John dodged him and ran blindly across the road. A hackney cab sounded its horn after screeching to a halt, missing the running boy by inches.

John Murphy aimlessly wandered the grey streets of Liverpool, trying to drive that sickening image of the boiling baby from his mind. Why was he even on the run? He had not been responsible, but he was terrified of facing the formidable Aunt Frances. She was unpredictable at the best of times, so who knows how she might react on finding that her baby had been boiled alive? She had left the baby in his care, after all. What would she do when she found little Jim all red raw, and as soggy as an over-cooked cauliflower? She would have found out by now, John reflected with a tear being blown across his cheek by the fierce March wind. Another depressing thought then entered his troubled mind; what if the police did not believe Mary's story about the intruder putting Jim in the tub? Then they would think that he had done it, and how could John disprove it?

Downcast and in deep thought, he passed a pub called the Clock Inn, on William Henry Street, as a thick dark cloud killed what little sunlight remained of the dying day. As he was passing an alleyway, a grubby hand shot out and grabbed him by the collar, and for one nasty moment, John thought it was a policeman's hand. "Come 'ere, you!" said a young gruff voice. The voice belonged to a thickset lad, a little older perhaps than John, and a little taller than him too. He looked tough with his shaved head, and a pair of wonky NHS spectacles balanced on his nose, with a plaster covering one of the lenses.

"Get off," John tried to remove the rough's hand from his collar but the bespectacled bully clenched his other hand and made a fist at the runaway. "You're coming with me, carrot-top," the skinhead announced, and he dragged John down the alleyway.

"My mum's only just round the corner," fibbed

John, but the tough guy with the lazy eye knew he was lying and told him to shut up.

"I want yer to do somethin' for me, and then maybe yer can go." The delinquent, whose name was Jack, let go of John's collar at the other end of the alleyway and pointed to some unattended roadworks nearby. "Get them lanterns for me - both of them. If yer don't, and yer run away, I'll come after yer and batter yer."

John looked at the two unlit red paraffin-fuelled danger lights situated next to a hole in the road. "Alright, I'll get them. And then do you promise I can go?" he asked in a quavering voice.

"Hurry up!" the young tyrant ordered, and pushed John out into the street. John sneaked up to the tall striped tent that a watchman would usually sit in at night. He peeped from behind it at two women who were chatting about fifty yards away. When he was sure they were not watching him, he walked out from behind the tent as nonchalantly as he could and picked the lamps up by their U-shaped handle strips, and then walked back to the instigator of the theft, who was peeping out from the alleyway.

"That's it!" said the young yob, and was pushing John back down the alleyway until suddenly he started tugging on the back of his coat. "Hang on," he said, and pushed open the old flaking door to one of the backyards and shoved him inside. His tormentor followed and bolted the door after them both. They crossed a small yard full of tall purple-headed weeds sprouting from the cracks in the uneven paving. A few loose bricks from the half-collapsed neighbouring wall lay scattered here and there.

The strong-armed child opened what had once been

the door to a back kitchen in an old derelict house on William Henry Street. Most of the windows were barricaded with sheets of corrugated iron, and the houses on each side were also empty, and scheduled for demolition in the near future. In the immediate space inside the kitchen, the unknown hard-knock took out a lighter and lit the wicks of the newly acquired roadworks lamps. He then closed the door behind himself and John, and gravely issued a set of curious instructions, whilst keeping a very serious expression on his face that seemed in advance of his age. "Stay right behind me, and do exactly as I say."

He walked forward holding aloft the two lamps, which only gave off a feeble red light, through the kitchen, and into a long dark passageway. There must have been over a hundred square razor blades embedded in the walls on each side of that narrow passageway and John Murphy stared in fear at those walls, wondering what sort of maniac would do such a dangerous thing as planting blades in them.

"There's a wire 'ere, step over it carefully," instructed the weird hoodlum. A thin but highly dangerous length of piano wire, sharp as cheese-cutter wire, had been strung – wall to wall - across their path at calf level. Both children stepped over it with the utmost care and then, about four feet down the razor-walled passageway, there was another thin piano wire strung horizontally from wall to wall at neck level. They both had to duck to avoid it. Anyone running into this wire would risk serious injury, if not partial decapitation.

At last they reached a huge room with a bunch of candles burning on a dusty old table. The place was filled with a strong smell of dirt, damp and decay.

"Alright, my name's Jack," said the menacing boy, placing the red lamps on the table. "What's your name?"

"John Murphy, but why have you brought me here? I want to go home." John was extremely upset, and imagined that Jack was going to kill him, or do something unspeakably evil to him.

"If I show you a secret, d'yer cross yer heart and hope to die?" asked Jack.

"Yes, I cross my heart." John traced a cross on his chest with his index and middle finger. "And then can I go?"

"If he says yer can, yer can."

"Who do you mean?" John asked, looking around nervously for his accomplice.

Instead of answering, Jack pitched another strange question at the poor lad, "Who d'yer love most in all the world?" he asked.

There was a pause as John thought about the question for a moment. The March winds outside whistled and howled through the cracks in the windows and floors of the old ruined house. "My mum," he finally replied. Jack did not acknowledge his reply but instead just pitched another strange question at him.

"If yer tell anyone about what yer see in here, yer mum'll have a really horrible death, have yer got that?" As he delivered this threat, Jack's top lip curled up with an expression of pure hatred. "Y - y - yes."

John's knees felt as if they were about to buckle under him. What was the secret Jack was going to reveal? Had he killed someone in here? Was that what the stomach-churning smell of decay was all about?

"Hilty? Are you there?" Jack suddenly enquired, seeming to address the darkness, his one visible eye swivelling as he turned, as if he were looking for something on the dilapidated walls. All John could see was peeling old wallpaper and holes in the wall where crumbling plasterboard showed through. He did notice a long thin black gap in the wall facing him, and that gap suddenly moved. In fact it turned out not to be a gap at all - it was something which struck John Murphy dumb with heart-stopping terror.

A enormously tall figure, easily over seven feet in height, stepped out from the wall. It had a pointed, teardrop-shaped head, and wore what looked like a black balaclava, through which a very sinister white face was showing. That face was almost triangular in shape, with a pointed chin. The lips of the oddly smiling mouth were jet black, and the teeth looked red, as if they had - as if they had blood on them. The eyes were ringed with heavy black borders and were pink with tiny dark pupils. The clothing this weird figure wore was close-fitting and black, and the shoes were very long and pointed. A sweet sickly smell, which seemed to be a mixture of lavender and decomposition, suddenly pervaded the room.

John felt goose pimples rising on his arms, legs and especially the back of his neck. He was so afraid he thought his pounding heart would explode out of his chest. The figure spoke in a high-pitched effeminate voice. "What have you brought me this time, Jack? Red hair is it? He must be descended from some bastard of a Dane."

The tall entity in black reached out an impossibly

long skinny arm and a black gloved hand with abnormally long fingers extended out to John's face, but the boy suddenly found himself turning away and running for the passageway.

The unearthly thing's mood changed in a flash and it let out a terrifying high-pitched shriek. Even in his panic, John remembered the piano wire and slowed down and felt for it with a trembling hand. He deftly ducked under the wire as he heard thudding footsteps closing in behind him. He ran a few more feet and then stopped and felt the air for the second piano wire with the sole of his shoe, and having located it, then hopped over it, all the time aware that Jack was hot on his heels.

Having reached the end of the lethal passageway to run across the kitchen, John pulled the door open and ran across the neglected backyard, through the tangle of weeds, to the back gate. Jack came tearing out of the kitchen doorway, but as he did so, John bent down and picked up one of the loose bricks from the crumbling wall. With both hands he hurled it with all his might at Jack's face. There was a sickening dull thud, and Jack toppled backwards and lay groaning amongst the weeds. John quickly undid the bolt of the backyard door and tore off down the alleyway.

When he got back on to William Henry Street it was deserted, and it was only then that he regained the power of speech. He screamed out for help until he thought his lungs would burst. Suddenly, one of the corrugated sheets covering one of the front windows of the empty house on the street was rammed forward by someone inside the derelict premises - someone with substantial strength, in fact. A long black arm was thrust out from the gap behind the sheet, and once again those long tapering fingers and thumb tried to grab at John Murphy. It managed to seize his coat, and the high-pitched voice inside the house emitted a string of obscene swear words as the thing cursed the escapee. John fled, abandoning his coat to the entity's clutches. He did not stop running until he was a great distance away and he was amongst people once again.

The heavens opened and he went the rest of his way home without his coat in a downpour, and when he reached his house he hammered as loudly as he could on the knocker, still nervously glancing behind himself, expecting that skinny devil in black to come haring down the road at any minute.

John's mother answered the door and after scolding her son because he had gone out "gallivanting" without telling anyone where he had vanished to, Mrs Murphy hugged him and they went into the house together, where Mary was sitting watching television and Mr Murphy was snoring in his armchair under the pages of the pink *Football Echo*, which were vibrating in a comical manner. As Mrs Murphy dried off her son in front of the fire, he rattled off his strange account of that day's extraordinary happenings, but she was only half listening and just put it down to childish prattle. However, on the following morning, when Mrs Murphy and her son went in search of his new coat, they found it torn to shreds and draped over the railings in front of the house on William Henry Street.

It transpired that the "strange man" who had taken the baby that Saturday afternoon had been Mrs Winneral's brother Desmond. He had collected the baby and taken it to its mother, Frances, on Mrs

Winneral's instructions, just so she could prolong their gossiping session. Desmond was said (in those times) to be "a bit slow". He had gone out of Aunt Frances's house through the backyard door and into the entry. The baby in the boiling bath had, of course, been Miranda, Mary's doll, which the little girl had accidentally dropped into the tub. The redness of the bubbling water was the scarlet dye running from the doll's clothes.

As you can imagine, John Murphy was mightily relieved to learn all this, but he had terrible nightmares about Hilty for years afterwards. Even though John told his mum what had happened, Jack's dire promise of Mrs Murphy suffering a horrible death never came to pass, nor did anything fatal ever happen to John for telling his mum about the uncanny figure in the 'bombdie' - Sixties slang for a dilapidated and deserted house.

A few years after hearing about this bizarre series of events, I received a telephone call one day at the offices of BBC Radio Merseyside after talking about ghosts in the Everton area whilst on air. An elderly woman, a Mrs Kelly, rang in and said something that really gave me a jolt. She asked me if I had ever heard of the weird ghost in black who had haunted a house on William Henry Street in the late 1950s. The children described this ghost as a tall man in black with a pointed hat, and used to call him the 'Gilly-Gilly Man'. This bears no resemblance to the name 'Hilty', of course - which is what John had heard Jack call the entity, but what was striking was the description of what must surely be the same entity.

Mrs Kelly said the Gilly-Gilly Man was said to live

in the cellar of the empty house on William Henry Street, and he also roamed the city's sewers. Mrs Kelly's mother would often tell her not to talk behind anyone's back, because Gilly-Gilly was listening through plugholes in the bath and also through pipes and keyholes, and he would pass on the bad things he gleaned in this way, to the people spoken about. The mental picture of the ghost eavesdropping in such a way must have frightened children, just as the stories of Spring-Heeled Jack had fifty years before. Who, or what, was the entity that haunted that house on William Henry Street? Was it some evil spirit, or a demon perhaps? Or, was it something from some other dimension or parallel world? At the moment, until I get more information on Hilty, I simply do not know.

Note: just after I had committed this story to the page, something very odd took place. The door to my study opened all by itself until it was wide open, and I saw a long shadow in the hallway but nothing visible was casting that shadow. A moment later the door closed again on its own. I have an uneasy feeling that I might have stirred up Hilty by committing his story to the page.

THE WATERFRONT GHOUL

The River Mersey has been the scene of many maritime mysteries over the years. I have mentioned cases in the past about ships like the *SS President* and the *City of Glasgow*, which left Liverpool in the 19th century and literally vanished without any trace of wreckage, even though they disappeared right in the middle of busy shipping lanes.

There have even been eerie instances of ships vanishing in the middle of the Mersey, within sight of the Liver Buildings.

In September 1943, a large steamship, the *Speke*, set

out from Birkenhead, bound for Preston. The ship was to steam up the coast and make a simple turning into the Kibble, before docking at Preston. But for some bizarre and unaccountable reason, the ship literally vanished from sight near Bootle Docks - in broad daylight. The ship was seen steaming along one moment by lookouts on the tip of the Wirral Peninsula, at Wallasey, then the next instance - she was nowhere to be seen. Scores of dockers up at the Seaforth and Gladstone docks stared in disbelief, because seconds before they had been watching the steamer on her short journey up the river. Now the ship had somehow vanished, as if the sea had suddenly swallowed her up.

The port authorities were naturally baffled at the 217-ton vessel's vanishing act, because not one stick of wreckage was ever found. As it was the middle of the Second World War, it was originally feared that a German U-boat had torpedoed the steamer, but there was no explosion on the river. Because it was wartime, the authorities never gave the weird incident much more thought and concerned themselves, instead, with the Nazi menace.

But curiously, about five months after the ship had disappeared, at the end of January 1944, two elderly night watchmen at Gladstone Docks, witnessed a spine-chilling spectacle, in the early hours of one bitterly cold winter's morning. A full moon shone down on the river, making the waves of the Mersey sparkle with a silvery light. One of the night watchmen was sitting warming himself in front of a rusty old oil drum, filled with burning sticks of wood and a few lumps of coal. His name was Gerry and his mate,

Arthur, was in a hut on the quay side, brewing a pot of tea. As Gerry rubbed his hands together in front of the fire, he yawned, then idly stared out at the moonlit waters of the Mersey. Suddenly, he caught sight of something which made him shiver with fear.

A black, shadowy figure was emerging from the waves, walking out of the Mersey, about 200 yards out from the dockside. Gerry's stomach turned over; he thought the figure was obviously some German frogman, coming ashore from a submarine somewhere in the river. He was probably on a mission to sabotage the ships berthed at the docks. Although Gerry was 70, he leapt to his feet and raced towards the hut as fast as his legs could carry him. Wide-eyed and panting with fear, he stammered out an account of what he had seen to his mate, who panicked and seized the receiver of the old wind-up telephone, mounted on the wall of the hut.

"What are you doin', Arthur?" Gerry asked.

"Calling the police and the Home Guard."

He wound up the phone, then swore as the operator took ages to answer his call. Eventually, a weary girl's voice answered and Arthur asked her to contact the Home Guard urgently. Twenty minutes later, a small, overweight man in uniform, accompanied by a motley assortment of eight men - all over 60 - turned up in an old taxi at the docks. It was the captain of the local Home Guard unit and his men.

The soldiers made a thorough search of all the Gladstone and Hornby Docks, then moved on to search the Seaforth Dock, but none of the watchmen or fire wardens up there reported seeing anyone come ashore. The captain and his men ended up sitting around the night watchman's fire, amicably chatting and cooking baked potatoes. They left at 6am, after the captain had sarcastically hinted that Gerry had been experiencing a so-called, open-eye dream; the product of a tired and overwrought mind. Gerry was furious at the suggestion.

But on the following morning, at 3.30, Gerry again saw the creepy-looking figure emerging from the freezing waters of the Mersey. Arthur was sipping tea while toasting a round of his wife's homemade bread over the fire. He almost dropped the slice into the brazier, as Gerry came up behind him and nudged his arm.

"Arthur! Look! There it is again."

This time, Arthur saw the figure too. He quickly took out a small, brass, folding telescope, pulled it open and trained it on the silhouette.

"Oh! My God what is it?"

"Let's have a look. What can you see?" said Gerry, impatiently, making incessant grabs at the spyglass like an over-excited child.

Arthur looked terrified and he handed the telescope to his friend with a trembling hand. By the time Gerry looked down at the river, he only caught a fleeting glimpse of the figure, disappearing behind the dock wall. Arthur suddenly stood up and looked towards the thing and cried: "It's coming up the steps of the dock wall!"

"No, it's gone," sighed Gerry, with relief, "Thank God!" But, suddenly, there in the moonlight, a mere 150 yards away - the figure reappeared. It limped slowly and menacingly up the stairs towards the night watchmen. Gerry levelled the telescope at the figure and took a closer look at it. A big mistake! The magnified image almost gave him a heart attack. It was a walking corpse; a partly-decomposed male figure, wearing a dark, ragged overcoat and black trousers. His face was greenish-white, puffed up and deeply-wrinkled, as if he had been in the water for some time. His torso looked hollow and something vile dangled from the cavity under his exposed ribcage. "Jesus!" gasped Gerry and recoiled in terror, staggering backwards. The figure speeded up and started to trot towards the frightened night-watchmen with a strange, loping gait. He ran diagonally towards the dock gate, as if he sensed that that was the only way they could escape. Arthur and Gerry fled to the hut and bolted themselves in. They waited and waited, for what seemed like an eternity. Then came the footsteps - heavy, persistent footsteps coming towards the hut. Arthur grabbed the Bakelite handle of the phone in such a nervous state, that it broke off in his hand, making it impossible to telephone for help. To make matters even worse, Gerry accidentally head-butted the oil lantern hanging from the ceiling and it crashed down to the floor and went out. The hut was plunged into total darkness, except for a beam of moonlight, streaming through the small window. Suddenly, the beam was interrupted, as a terribly-disfigured face peered through the window at the terrorised men. The face was crinkled and livid white, tinged with green. Strands of what looked like seaweed, hung from the open jaw like saliva. One of the eyes was hanging from its socket by the loosened optic nerve, and the other eye rolled about sickeningly. As the zombie-like head opened its jaws, repugnant, pale-coloured liquid spurted out with a gurgling noise and splashed against the hut windows. The thing sounded as if it was struggling to say something. It pounded on the window and repeatedly pointed towards the sea's horizon and moaned. Then, for no apparent reason, it slowly turned and moved away from the window. Gerry and Arthur listened intently to the sound of heavy footsteps squelching away from the hut. After about 20 minutes, during which time they had not spoken a single word, Gerry turned towards his friend and whispered: "As soon as I open the door, run to the gate."

But, even as he spoke, the door began to squeak - the handle of the door was turning - the despicable thing was still outside! It started to groan again and knocked heavily on the door. It slithered back to the window and peered in again. This time, the loose eyeball was missing and the grotesque face rammed against the window, almost breaking it. After what seemed like an eternity, the figure finally walked off into the night. All the same, the terrified pair refused to move from that hut until the sun came up.

Shortly after dawn, Gerry cautiously emerged from the hut and immediately slipped on something just outside the door. To his horror, when he looked down, he saw what appeared to be a squashed eyeball, clinging to his shoe. He almost threw up and kicked it away in disgust. The squashed object rolled off the quayside and plopped into the muddy waters of the Mersey.

The night-watchmen told the police all about the horrific-looking figure, but were accused of seeing things after drinking on duty. But Arthur and Gerry stuck rigidly to their strange tale until their deaths in the 1950s.

Just a few years ago, the *Speke* – the ship that had vanished in the Mersey was finally found, intact, on the bed of the river - near Liverpool Bay. Four skeletons of the *Speke's* crew were located within the wreck, encrusted with barnacles. But the body of the fifth crew member was never found and no one has ever found out why it was not in the sunken ship. Unless, perhaps, the fifth crew member was actually the decomposed ghoul which terrorised the nightwatchmen at Bootle Docks, which are a mere stone's throw from the spot where the ship went down.

Strangely enough, in the winter of 1997, two security guards spotted a silhouette emerging from the sea near the lighthouse at the Gladstone Dock, at four o'clock in the morning. The guards immediately alerted the police but the man was never found. Nevertheless, he was seen by the guards regularly over two weeks, always coming from the shore. An Alsatian dog, belonging to one of the guards, still refuses to go near a certain stretch of the Gladstone Dock, where the figure is often seen. Could the sinister entity be the very same waterfront ghoul who terrorised the nightwatchmen during the War?

THE PELLEW STREET HORROR

From 1880 to 1883, Rebecca Solidyke, a widow in her forties, kept an infamous brothel at 44 Pellew Street, which once ran parallel to Copperas Hill. The premises of the Postal Sorting Office now stand on the spot where the house of ill-repute once existed in Victorian times, and in the summer of 1882, something took place in the vicinity of the brothel that has never been explained. Let me take you back in time to the horrors that unfolded that summer. From behind a blackened sandstone wall, pearl plumes of steam blossomed in the balmy air as the locomotive rumbled along the lines into Lime Street Station, bringing someone – or something – from God knows where to the restless city of river breezes and carboniferous smoke. Barefoot children climbed that sandstone wall on Pellew Street to gaze into the chasm far below; at the determined ferns sprouting from the sandstone walls of a sheer drop, and the silver tracks that led to a better life somewhere, gleaming in stark contrast to the gravel and dull stones packed between the wooden sleepers.

On a July day when the blue sky smarted upturned eyes, a stranger appeared on Pellew Street, a street of damned souls, many of them destined for a brief mention in the Coroner's Inquest column of the local newspaper. These were the people the upper classes called loafers; the low life, the great unwashed minions, the riffraff. Why in the world would anyone as well-dressed as the approaching stranger come to Pellew Street? Haggard toothless women were seated on their knife-worn doorsteps; grimy cherubs ran in circles taunting emaciated mongrel dogs with washboard ribcages. A solitary hollow-eyed man in his twenties who had long resigned himself to the midden-dump of wasted youth looked on at the outsider with a blank expression.

The tall broad-shouldered visitor wore a pristine bowler, and beneath its brim was a bush of curly russet hair and a thick uncultivated beard that framed his peculiar pink pig-like face. He carried a bulging canvas sack of the type that returning sailors carry home, and he headed to the dilapidated-looking house next door to the brothel. A key was turned, and the old green warped door opened with some difficulty, but closed firmly behind the foreigner to those parts. The venetian-red front door of the brothel opened to release a fairly satisfied client, and Rebecca Solidyke ventured out onto the doorstep with her pretty 20-year-old daughter Mary. They thought they had heard the front door of the empty house next to the brothel slamming. They returned to their home as ruined folk of the dismal street watched them with contempt.

That evening, as the last shafts of a persimmon sunset lent some beauty to Pellew Street, a Spanish sailor named Mr Byzanti paid a visit to the harlot's house. He was a regular visitor, but in drink he was prone to violent behaviour, and had once given Mrs Solidyke a black eye. On this occasion he was merry but not sodden drunk. He wanted to make love to Mary, but her mother told him he couldn't. A prostitute named Julia took Byzanti into an upstairs room, and the Spaniard smiled at Mary as he went up the stairs. 'Next time,' he told the young woman.

Mrs Solidyke's son Billy came into the house, and Mary quickly ushered him into his room; he'd never come home as late before; even though it was summer. The boy had his little fox terrier Vic with him, and with great difficulty it was carrying a huge rib. Billy said the man who had moved in next door was kind because he had given Vic lots of meat and that rib.

On the following day, Billy and Vic followed the man next door to the butcher's shop on London Road. He bought pork neck ends, pig's trotters, ribs, pigtails, offal, livers, kidneys, brisket, sheep's heads, and customers complained about the stranger buying up everything out the marble slab in the window. The thickset man with the rose pink face and cylindrical pig nose then enquired about sawdust, which surprised the corpulent rosy cheeked butcher and the queue of impatient customers. The man slapped gleaming coins Billy had never seen on the counter and the butcher's assistant carried a sack of sawdust to the house on Pellew Street.

That afternoon, the new resident of Pellew Street slipped out of the house and visited an iron mongers with Billy and Vic, and around 5pm he put a bowl of diced meat on his doorstep which the fox terrier ate in a furious fashion.

Mrs Solidyke thought the man next door was eccentric, and she told her son he was not to go near him or accompany him to town any more. The boy reluctantly obeyed his mother's wishes but Vic would sneak off each day in the late afternoon and wait at the neighbour's doorstep, tilting his head and flicking his ears about in expectation. The door would open slightly and a pink hand would be seen placing the bowl of diced pork or beef on the step.

Vic gradually became rather plump, and while Billy thought it was funny, his mother and sister didn't, so they went next door and Mrs Solidyke hammered on the knocker. The man never answered, so Mary, being the literate one of the house, jotted down a note of complaint and posted it through the neighbour's letterbox, telling him to stop feeding Vic.

One evening, about a week later at 11pm, there was a rat-tat-tat at the brothel door.

Julia answered, and saw the weird-looking neighbour standing on the doorstep. He wore a grey flat cap and a long dark coat. His face was grotesque, and when he smiled, it reminded Julia of the comical painted plaster pig face that adorned a butcher's shop window on

Lime Street.

'Go away,' Julia told him, with a look of disgust.

The neighbour's smile vanished and he gritted his teeth.

'Go on, piss off or I'll call a copper!' the prostitute threatened.

He moved away but Mrs Solidyke came to the door to see why Julia was shouting, and when the latter told her who she was shouting at, Mrs Solidyke called the man next door back.

When she saw his face, she was repulsed yet unaccountably intrigued. She asked him if he wanted to come in and the man said 'Yes,' in a gruff voice.

Miss Solidyke took him into the back parlour, and sat on the edge of a double bed.

He stood by the fireplace for a while, as the head of the brothel questioned him. She wanted to know where he was from. 'The country,' he said, rather enigmatically. What was his name? He never answered, but instead started to take off the long coat. He was naked, except for the boots he wore.

He sat on the bed, next to Mrs Solidyke, and his bulk, landing on the mattress shook her. By the light of a single oil lamp, she could see how his body was as revolting as his face. He had long thick arms and legs, as pink as a carnation, and his chest and abdomen were covered in rolling folds of goose-pimpled fat. He still had his flat cap on, and he suddenly removed it to reveal something that made the prostitute shudder. He had a pair of small rounded ears on each side of his head, but not in the places where normal human ears would be. These ears were on the upper sides of his head, so he looked like some pig-human hybrid.

He suddenly turned and seized Mrs Solidyke, then sucked hard on her delicate white neck. Her face was forced into the cold flesh of his chest, and she found herself being steadily suffocated. She couldn't move because his strong thick arms entrapped her, so she bit into him. She imagined it was like biting into the flesh of a freshly-plucked goose. Her teeth broke his skin and a fat blubbery substance oozed out. There was a dull groan, and he released her. Mrs Solidyke let out a scream and fell off the bed, onto the floor, landing on her backside. She screamed again, and the beast got up and put on the flat cap and long coat. Mrs Solidyke became violently sick as she wiped the white fat substance laced with blood from her lips. As Mary arrived in the hallway she saw the shadowy neighbour opening the front door. By the time the girl had gone to her mother's aid, the client had vanished.

Mary saw her mother's bruised neck, and a pool of vomit on the carpet. Mrs Solidyke gave an incoherent account of what had just taken place and her daughter suggested calling the police. Her mother threw up again and told her to forget the incident. The policemen she knew would never follow up a complaint from a brothel-keeper, and who would believe the bizarre description of the attacker anyway?

Days later, in the afternoon, as Julia was entertaining a customer, a rhythmic tapping sound was heard next door. It was constant, and occasionally became louder. The annoying racket continued throughout the day, and at 5pm, when the Spanish client, Mr Byzanti arrived at the brothel, Mary told the sailor about the assault and the strange physiology of the next-door neighbour. The Spaniard believed he'd have a good chance at making love to the delectable Mary if he went and sorted out the neighbour, and so he went next door and hammered on the knocker. 'Cerdo!' he shouted, which is Spanish for 'pig', and after getting no reply, he began to kick the door in.

At this point, young Billy arrived home and told his mother he couldn't find Vic anywhere. Mrs Solidyke brushed her son aside and went outside to see Mr Byzanti in action.

The sailor from Tarragona managed to kick the door open, and he took an ivory-handled dagger from a special sheath in his boot and stormed the house. A gaggle of enthralled children stood on the doorstep, watching Byzanti walk into the kitchen of the house. Their noses were greeted with an awful aroma; a mixture of rotting eggs and the odour of blood that hung in the air - very reminiscent of the butcher's shop. Bluebottles flew blindly out of the smelly house, striking the faces of the kids.

The 'pig-man' stood in the kitchen, wearing a blood-streaked apron. He held a chopper in his hand. The sawdust on the floor had soaked up quite a quantity of blood. The sailor saw dogs and cats, many without heads, hanging from meat-hooks that had been fixed to the kitchen ceiling. A pool of blood was still widening out from a diced dog on the kitchen table. To the horrified Spaniard's eyes, it looked like the remains of the terrier Vic.

The sailor ran at the abomination in the apron, and it swung the chopper downwards at him, intending to cleave his head open, but instead taking Byzanti's left ear clean off. Just the hole of his auditory canal remained where the ear had been, and blood slicked down his neck into his collar. In shock, the Spaniard lunged at the freak with the dagger, and its blade plunged deep into its chest. The hybrid squealed just like a pig, and blood sprayed everywhere. It turned and fled, and the Spaniard slipped in the bloody sawdust, and landed on the floor in agony, ready to pass out.

There is an uncertain end to this horror story. Some accounts say the porcine hog-featured creature fled bleeding heavily down the warren of alleyways, pursued by a pack of ravenous dogs until it was torn to shreds by the hounds in Bronte Street. Other say the trail of the pig-like man's blood led to the nearby abattoir on Trowbridge Street, where a group of slaughtermen cornered the freak, killed it, chopped it up, and fed the parts to the hungry canines.

Mrs Solidyke told the police about the 'man-beast' next door when they found the remains of the butchered animals, but she was right – the officers of the law did not believe her and looked at her condescendingly as nothing more than a low whore. On a happier note, when the police searched the cellar of the house next door to the brothel, a little dog was found locked in a crate. It was Vic, and once released, he yelped, lumbered to get his little portly frame up the cellar steps, and darted to his master, Billy, who was very pleased to be reunited with the fox terrier. The brothel was closed by the police in the following year, and Mrs Solidyke turned to alcohol and drank herself into an early grave in the autumn of that same year.

Any attempts to explain the taxonomical nature of the beast that moved into Pellew Street always fall flat. Surely some light would have been thrown onto this mystery if the police had discovered the identity of the tenant of the house next door to the brothel, because the man – whatever he was – possessed a key to that house, but in the absence of any concrete information, it's probably useless to speculate on this matter – however, I'll never be able to look at a pig's head in the window of the butchers in the same way again.

CPSIA information can be obtained
at www.ICGtesting.com
Printed in the USA
LVOW13s1028101117
555782LV00012B/296/P